The Ultimate MBA Book

Alan Finn,
Roger Mason,
Stephen Berry and
Eric Davies

T0299563

Alan Finn began his career in the Royal Navy as an engineer in nuclear submarines but now works in B2B marketing and management consultancy for industry, mainly helping technological organizations to grow. His MBA – a specialist MBA in strategic marketing from the University of Hull – opened up many more opportunities and allowed Alan to broaden his career and to develop his own consultancy business.

Roger Mason is a Chartered Certified Accountant and has many years' practical experience as a Financial Director. He now lectures on financial and business topics. In addition, he has edited a financial publication and written many books.

Stephen Berry is a former CFO, an international MBA lecturer in Business Strategy and author of *Strategies of the Serengeti*, which applies the successful strategies of the East African animal residents of the Serengeti to business. The book has been sold in over 100 countries and Stephen's business conference speeches on these strategies have been delivered in 25 countries across four continents. He has also trained many executives in strategic thinking and assisted a wide variety of organizations by facilitating sessions to generate their strategies. Stephen is passionate about making strategy practical, understandable and successful.

Eric Davies BA (Hons), MPhil, DipM has broad-based business experience, including board-level positions in industry and marketing services agencies and setting up a number of new business ventures. He has consulted widely in both the private and public sectors and provided a range of management programmes for the British Institute of Management (now CMI), the British Council and the Institution of Chemical Engineers and contributed to postgraduate programmes at the University of Glamorgan and post-experience programmes at University College Lampeter. In addition, he has contributed articles to a number of journals including *Accountancy, European Journal of Marketing, The Pakistan Management Review, Management Consultancy* and *The Municipal Journal.*

The Ultimate MBA Book

Get the Edge in Business; Master Strategy, Marketing and Finance; Enjoy a Business School Education in a Book

Alan Finn, Roger Mason, Stephen Berry and Eric Davies

First published in Great Britain in 2020 by Teach Yourself, an imprint of John Murray Press, a division of Hodder and Stoughton Ltd. An Hachette UK company.

Copyright © Alan Finn, Roger Mason, Stephen Berry and Eric Davies 2020

The right of Alan Finn, Roger Mason, Stephen Berry and Eric Davies to be identified as the Authors of the Work has been asserted by them in accordance with the Copyright, Designs and Patents Act 1988.

Based on original material from *MBA In A Week; Finance for Non-Financial Managers In A Week; Strategy In A Week; Marketing In A Week*

Database right Hodder & Stoughton (makers)

The *Teach Yourself* name is a registered trademark of Hachette UK.

British Library Cataloguing in Publication Data: a catalogue record for this title is available from the British Library.

Library of Congress Catalog Card Number: on file.

Paperback ISBN: 978 1 473 68951 0

Ebook ISBN: 978 1 473 68949 7

3

The publisher has used its best endeavours to ensure that any website addresses referred to in this book are correct and active at the time of going to press. However, the publisher and the author have no responsibility for the websites and can make no guarantee that a site will remain live or that the content will remain relevant, decent or appropriate.

The publisher has made every effort to mark as such all words which it believes to be trademarks. The publisher should also like to make it clear that the presence of a word in the book, whether marked or unmarked, in no way affects its legal status as a trademark.

Every reasonable effort has been made by the publisher to trace the copyright holders of material in this book. Any errors or omissions should be notified in writing to the publisher, who will endeavour to rectify the situation for any reprints and future editions.

Typeset by Cenveo® Publisher Services.

Printed and bound in Great Britain by Clays Ltd, Elcograf S.p.A.

John Murray Press policy is to use papers that are natural, renewable and recyclable products and made from wood grown in sustainable forests. The logging and manufacturing processes are expected to conform to the environmental regulations of the country of origin.

Carmelite House
50 Victoria Embankment
London EC4Y 0DZ
www.hodder.co.uk

The authorized representative in the EEA is Hachette Ireland,

8 Castlecourt Centre, Dublin 15, D15 XTP3, Ireland (email: info@hbgi.ie)

Contents

Part 1: Your MBA Masterclass

Part 2: Your Finance for Non-Financial Managers Masterclass

Part 3: Your Strategy Masterclass

PART 1
Your MBA Masterclass

Introduction

This part of the book is aimed principally at aspiring and junior managers, most probably working in offices for large corporations, who want to develop their careers, get ahead of the crowd and rise above their peers. They need to learn more broad-based workplace skills across disciplines other than their own but don't have the time or the money to study for a Master of Business Administration (MBA) degree. It may also be useful for those who already have an MBA, earned some years ago, but who want a refresher.

This very practical 'seven-chapter MBA' does not assume prior knowledge and distils the most practical business insights from MBA studies into easy-to-digest bite-sized chunks. Ambitious people on the corporate ladder see achieving an MBA as a way to get ahead and to demonstrate their ambition – in short, to rise head and shoulders above the ranks of the other junior managers in their organizations.

Creating visions for growth and spearheading their implementation gets you noticed by top management looking for vigorous new blood to lead the organizations of the future. But it is difficult to create all-embracing, organization-wide visions for growth if you don't really understand how the other departments – departments other than yours – work together.

A secondary but important benefit that I hope you will take from this part is self-confidence. Leadership is often demonstrated by a personal aura of understated self-confidence, a sure-footed capability to lead. You will find new abilities that will enable you to take forward the part of the overall organization for which you have responsibility, achieving new business improvements and successes along the way.

CHAPTER 1

Global business pressures and change

This area of business and management studies is fundamental to an understanding of management practice today and its likely paths into the future. It is a foundation on which to build a solid understanding of where the business discipline has been and how it is likely to develop, given today's fundamental societal pressures and the forces now acting upon the world and business.

Major pressures

The following list describes just some of the major pressures, in no particular order, and their effects on world business today. The effects of such changes and new pressures have always driven legislation to govern how organizations are run throughout business history.

- **The world's financial economy** – as we recover from the economic downturn that began in 2007/8 and new legislation is imposed on banks and the international banking system
- **Geopolitical changes** – for example, the emergence of China and India as global powers; Russia's renewed ambitions for geographical expansion in Eastern Europe and the spread of Islamic fundamentalism and conflict in the Middle East
- **Communications** – the increasing power and pervasiveness of computing (e.g. the emergence of the 'Internet of Things' (IoT) and 'big data' and their effects on future patterns of employment)
- **Changes to the nature of security, crime, conflict and policing** – for example, the increasing use of robotics and drones in 'remotely controlled warfare'; the emergence of cyber warfare and cyber espionage; and the rising importance of cyber security
- **The evolution of transportation** – of people, emergency and aid services, raw materials and finished goods
- **Environmental change** – and its effects on global demographics (e.g. civil-engineering projects in China such as dams and large canals that lead to the relocation of populations and businesses; and the retreating ice cap in the Arctic, opening up shorter sea routes and allowing more cost-effective mineral extraction in the region).

Let's look at each of these major pressures in turn.

The world's financial economy

Currently, strengthening growth is seen in the West in the USA and in the UK, although continental Europe still has problems with restructuring to free up trade and business practices and the UK is burdened by national and personal debt. The BRIC countries have seen mixed fortunes in recent years: Brazil has an uncertain future politically; Russia is trying to leverage its mineral wealth while exhibiting territorial ambitions; China struggles with popular demands for more democracy, while a new premier in India is trying to create major change. The picture is even more varied in emerging markets such as Indonesia and Mexico as well as in South American and African countries (the so-called 'Next Eleven').

All this change and uncertainty deters investors and slows up world growth. Investors thrive in conditions of confidence and stability and this is in short supply at present. International banks are facing increasingly restrictive demands on their structures and operations, as many countries, particularly the United States and in Europe, try to ensure that the very negative impact banking crises can have on international economies and trade, as in 2007–14, does not happen again. These underlying conditions form the platform from which businesses must try to grow over the next few years.

Business confidence is directly related to international news on the conditions of the world's major economies and thence to the willingness – or otherwise – of businesses to invest in their futures. Without investment, significant business growth is difficult. For businesses to grow and prosper, overall growth in the outputs of economies as a whole is critical. Economic growth is defined as positive change in the gross domestic product (GDP) of a country over a year and the real economic growth of one country relative to another is an important indicator of business opportunity. GDP must be adjusted for inflation effects over time and the resulting value is called 'real growth'.

Real economic growth leads to major improvements in people's living standards, the expansion of existing markets and the opening up of new markets and opportunities. Thus, economic growth, from increases in GDP, leads to an improved environment for business investment, which then leads to those major improvements in people's living standards, general prosperity and well-being.

According to Valentino Piana, writing in an article published by the Economic Web Institute in 2001, investment plays six macroeconomic roles:

1 It contributes to current demand of capital goods and thus increases domestic expenditure.
2 It enlarges the production base (installed capital), increasing production capacity.
3 It modernizes production processes, improving cost effectiveness.
4 It reduces the labour needs per unit of output, thus potentially producing higher productivity and lower employment.
5 It allows for the production of new and improved products, increasing value added in production.
6 It incorporates international world-class innovations and quality standards, bridging the gap between the more advanced countries and others, and helping exports and an active participation to international trade.

Thus, economic growth is critical to business.

Geopolitical changes

The emergence of China and India as global powers, Russia's new appetite for geographical expansion and the spread of Islamic fundamentalism and conflict in the Middle East are just a few examples of current geopolitical changes that are creating instability in the world today. And, as we have seen previously, change and instability directly affect the climate for investment, economic and business growth.

The *Global Risks 2014* report, issued by the World Economic Forum, highlights 'how global risks are not only interconnected but also have systemic impacts':

> *'To manage global risks effectively and build resilience against their impacts, better efforts are needed to understand, measure and foresee the evolution*

of interdependencies between risks,
supplementing traditional risk-management
tools with new concepts designed for
uncertain environments. If global risks
are not effectively addressed, their social,
economic and political fallouts could be far-
reaching, as exemplified by the continuing
impacts of the financial crisis
of 2007–2008.'

The World Economic Forum, *Global Risks 2014*, 9th edition

As an example of these interdependencies, we need only see how recent changes in energy supplies have affected geopolitical change. The dramatic fall of oil prices in 2014 has had major implications for oil-producing nations not only in the Middle East but also for Russia. This effect – together with sanctions imposed internationally on Russia for its activities in Ukraine – may help to constrain any further geopolitical expansionary ambitions by President Putin and bring stability back to the region.

Communications

There have been major changes in businesses' and individuals' communications in the last three decades, changes largely wrought by technology, most notably the increasing power and pervasiveness of computing. The disruptive (as well as creative) effects of computing and the Internet on industries are shown in the following examples:

- global postal systems – owing to the rise of email
- payment systems and banking
- investment, with the increase in crowd-sourcing
- retailing, as consumers' shopping habits change
- entertainment and video rental with the rise of online on-demand providers such as Netflix
- travel, with the arrival of online travel sites and mobile-app-based transportation companies such as Uber

- management and other consultants – making communication and research much easier
- recruitment of people into jobs
- book publishing – self-publishing and the emergence of ebooks
- university teaching – notably, the impact of Massive Open Online Courses (MOOCs).

Technology has also had a broader impact on business and businesspeople:

> *'Business doesn't happen face to face as often as some would like. Instead, today's communication depends on conference calls and email chains that make it challenging to get to know your partners. It's been a common lament among business people dissatisfied with the technology that has become the norm in their daily lives. But with so many workers worldwide now working in virtual teams, many business relationships do depend on technology. And that's not a bad thing – as long they're using the right technologies in the right ways.'*
>
> Natalie Burg, writing in *ForbesBrandVoice* in October 2013

With instant, global information in their pockets, today's businessmen and businesswomen are never out of touch with information systems or their teams or clients, speeding up business processes incrementally.

Changes to the nature of security, crime, conflict and policing

Examples can be seen readily in the increased use of robotics and drones in remotely controlled warfare but also in traffic and crime policing, personal identity theft, the emergence of cyber warfare and espionage and the increasing importance of cyber-security systems. The potential for disruption that these developments represent should not be underestimated:

'New technologies offer the promise of preventing and mitigating insecurity, but can also enable criminal activity. There is nothing predetermined about these multi-dimensional and multi-level threats to security. To understand how and why potential security threats result in real harm, and what interventions are most likely to improve threat prediction and avoid, reduce and manage risks, is an urgent task for the social sciences. Under the New Security Challenges programme, the ESRC [Economic and Social Research Council] has been examining the changing nature of security and risk, for example funding research on understanding the causes and processes of radicalization and violence in contemporary society.'

Economic and Social Research Council (ESRC), *Strategic Plan, 2009–2014*

The need for policies arising from ESRC's research is obvious and fundamental to securing stable business relationships and trade. Without platforms to address security, business cannot advance as it should and energies, activities and investments will be wasted.

The evolution of transportation

The evolution of the on-time delivery of raw materials and finished goods is a fascinating subject and an area in which great efficiencies can be made to cut costs and increase profits. There are changes taking place in transportation systems:

> *'Major constraints on global transport demand in the foreseeable future will include energy costs and scarcity, climate change, congestion, urbanization, scarcity of available funding, the ageing population in developed countries and the need to reduce road traffic deaths and injuries. Innovation – including through the application of new technologies, techniques and policies – must play a role in ensuring that transport contributes to a sustainable future.'*
>
> Report of the International Transport Forum, 2010

But what does all this innovation and change – driven mostly by technology – mean for businesses around the world? Improvements in logistics in a globalizing world have a profound implication for costs – costs of shipping and transport, warehousing of in-bound parts and outbound products – and therefore for profits.

Improving supply chain management

Logistics and supply chain management are major subjects for master's degrees in Business Management. For example, Lancaster University's Business School's Department of Management Science teaches degree courses that have large components focused on the importance and science of data management, one of which is in logistics and supply chain management. This teaches students to use their analytical skills to develop models to improve strategic supply chain management, global sourcing, logistics and 'servitization' – adding value to services as a component.

Raw materials and finished goods reqiure transportation to either factories for assembly into final products or to markets to be sold to final customers. This must be done in a timely manner, at as low a cost as possible, to maximize profits, and data can indicate ways to make great efficiencies in supply chains. New ideas for transportation and shipping, ranging from delivery by flying drones to the use of local secure 'lockups', located in places convenient to final customers, right through to shipping by airships or civilian submarines, are all innovative ways of approaching this problem to drive down overall transportation costs as far as possible.

Environmental change

Global warming and dramatic global weather effects, including warmer winters and floods in Europe and colder winters in the United States, are impacting business models globally at an accelerating rate, sometimes increasing costs and hitting profits – but sometimes creating new opportunities. For example, the retreating polar ice cap in the Arctic will permit shorter sea routes for transportation as well as allow more cost-effective mineral extraction in the northern polar region.

'The new study, GEO-5 for Business, says that the future success of businesses in transport, tourism, finance, food, and other sectors, will hinge on their ability to manage the major risks posed by climate change, depleted natural resources, the loss of biodiversity, and extreme weather conditions. But the study says smart businesses can buck the trend and create competitive advantage, by tapping into future demand for sustainable technologies, services and products, and by reducing their own environmental footprint.'

Bryan Coll in *The Guardian*, June 2013, reporting on a new study by the United Nations Environment Programme

The key is to spot the opportunities and for investors to support them to balance out the risks inherent in our changing environment. Business success, trade and profits are dependent on many variables, and organizations must take a wide variety of factors into account in their business planning activities, including the environment and climate change. Planning for changed energy demand and utility services is just one set of factors for even the smallest of businesses to take into account in the twenty-first century.

MBA recommended reading list

Janice B. Gordon, *Business Evolution: Creating Growth in a Rapidly Changing World* (CreateSpace, 2014)

Janet Morrison, *The Global Business Environment: Meeting the Challenges*, 3rd edition (Palgrave Macmillan, 2013)

World Economic Forum, *Global Risks*, published annually. This can be downloaded from www.weforum.org/reports/

Summary

The pressures, trends and changes described in this chapter have already affected and will continue to change previous conceptions of how business is carried out and regulated. The changes made to business practices in response to these issues will have an impact on regulation and laws that need to be anticipated by smart businesses to reduce their impact on their bottom lines. Trade associations – groups formed by the management of businesses in discrete areas, from banking to manufacturing, from airlines to mineral miners, that are otherwise competitors – are a useful way to address the big issues faced commonly by businesses in their different sectors. Forecasts of trends can be mutually funded, governments can be lobbied and research supported to address the forces for change that they face together, to get some idea of their shape, size and likely impacts. Knowledge shared in this way reduces businesses' risks and develops pressures to adapt and change business laws.

Fact-check (answers at the back)

1. How closely related is daily news on the world economy to general business confidence?
   a) Not at all ☐
   b) Only loosely related ☐
   c) This differs according to geographic areas and economic regions ☐
   d) Daily business news is now dispersed on recipients' preferred social media to great effect ☐

2. How strongly is a positive change in the GDP of one country relative to another an important indicator of business opportunity?
   a) Not a strong indication ☐
   b) Only a very weak signal ☐
   c) This varies totally depending upon countries' different industrial sectors ☐
   d) A very positive signpost ☐

3. Does the emergence of China and India as global powers and an appetite for geographical expansion in Russia have an impact on the stability of the world's economies?
   a) Slightly – only a limited impact ☐
   b) Not at all – global economies are not directly linked to geopolitical tensions ☐
   c) Directly – world stock markets always react negatively to such news ☐
   d) The major effect is local and on countries with strong trade links to those directly affected ☐

4. How might religious fundamentalism arising in the Middle East affect the world's economies?
   a) No impact at all ☐
   b) Short-term effects die quickly but there are increasingly longer-term results ☐
   c) There is only a limited impact when terrorist attacks occur on, for example, European streets ☐
   d) The Middle East supplies a large amount of oil and gas to world energy markets. Any interruption of supplies by terrorist activities has a large impact on the global economy ☐

5. What impact will the emerging 'Internet of Things' (IoT) have on businesses?
   a) In almost every conceivable aspect of our personal, domestic and business lives ☐
   b) Only to integrate domestic needs and activities, such as the automatic adjustment of heating and cooling systems ☐
   c) Mostly only in terms of logistics and supply chains ☐
   d) This will affect only the smart metering of utility supplies ☐

6. How might 'big data' affect businesses?
a) Since big data shows trends in the take-up of new products, it will affect only advertising ❏
b) By highlighting online shopping habits ❏
c) By exposing aspects for improvement in every area of business as trading moves inexorably to online processes ❏
d) By indicating how to make efficiencies in supply chains and logistics ❏

7. What will be the likely impact of technology on personal and business security systems?
a) Mostly in areas such as drones to control traffic and to attack known terrorists in remote areas of the world ❏
b) Internet snooping may uncover threats to security ❏
c) Cyber security has become a major technological business threat today. It can permit disruption to companies' communications and processes, caused by disgruntled or malicious employees, for which no comprehensive defences are yet in place ❏
d) Technology frequently releases users' confidential information and cannot be controlled ❏

8. How will transport be affected by new innovations?
a) Large civilian submarines may become dominant in carrying cargoes securely by sea and gas-filled airships may fill the skies ❏
b) Fuel costs and engine efficiencies will limit road transport systems ❏
c) Inefficiencies in complex international logistics systems will be exposed by big data, the analysis of which will indicate solutions ❏
d) Road transport is very vulnerable to terrorist activities and will decline ❏

9. Global weather systems are changing – how may they affect trade?
a) Not at all – trade is independent of the weather these days ❏
b) Only trade carried out by means of shipping will be affected ❏
c) All trading activities and supporting systems – from communications with stock markets to energy supplies – are affected ❏
d) Forecasting of global weather conditions will be perfected within a decade ❏

10. Business premises waste a lot of energy. How could businesses respond to this issue?

a) They should ignore variations because energy prices fluctuate so widely anyway ❏

b) Environmentally sustainable energy systems – wind, tidal or solar energy systems – are beginning to provide most of our energy so they should budget for lower costs ❏

c) They should plan for changing energy demands and alternative utility services ❏

d) They should audit premises' energy use and plan to reduce it by insulation, reduced heat loss and investment in more efficient heating and cooling plants ❏

CHAPTER 2

Finance, economics and accounting

Finance, economics and accounting are each a different field of study but with similarities and overlaps:

- Finance is the study of how to allocate assets efficiently and is forward-looking, so as to develop an understanding of what an asset may be worth in the future.
- Economics addresses the production, distribution, and consumption of goods and services.
- Accounting communicates an organization's financial information and is really a backward-looking field.

These intertwining fields can be managed to bring value to organizations in volatile and uncertain markets.

Finance and accounting in turbulent times

Today's finance leaders accelerate transformation, bringing overall value to organizations through finance and accounting operations that address volatile and uncertain markets. These new financial leaders need agile finance organizations to support their enterprises, allowing them to cope efficiently and effectively with change.

Since 2007 and the onset of the greatest economic depression in two generations, the world has become much more complex and unpredictable. In the wake of 2011's disastrous earthquake and tsunami in Japan, many international businesses learned that global supply chains, markets and customers have never been more vulnerable to events on the other side of the world. Financial management is central to the successful navigation of global businesses through these uncertain times, as the function that allocates funding for growth and controls expense management.

What is required today is a new generation of chief financial officers (CFOs) to transform the function to support strong, flexible and scalable global operating models, allowing organizations to grasp advantage and growth when surrounded by volatility and uncertainty.

However, that requires a fundamental shift in perspective, a commitment to global growth and a renewed focus on cost controls, the intelligent integration of acquisitions, and professional financial management that can adapt flexibly to fast-changing market conditions.

The influence of IT

The fundamental business disciplines of finance, economics and accounting have evolved since people first began to trade with neighbours – and those further afield – and to take account of the difference between what was bought, hunted, farmed or made, and then subsequently sold – profit! Although counting began with basic support, such as the abacus, it soon evolved into faster counting systems using logarithms, slide rules, calculators and, most latterly, computing. The information technology (IT) discipline started in accounts departments but soon began to permeate every other business discipline.

Today IT is a discrete business department, separate yet helping to underpin the management of all departments and communications, and intimately connected still with counting and understanding the flows of finance that lubricate all businesses.

'Bean-counters'

The scathing term 'bean-counters' is still often used derogatively and broadly to describe all financial, accounting and economic functions, probably to caricature a rather fussy and pedantic accountant responsible for knowing not just the weight of a bag of beans but exactly how many beans were in the bag! The US newspaper *The Fort Wayne News and Sentinel* is often attributed with the first use of the term, in an article in 1919.

Today's finance, economics and accounting functions in businesses are transforming their organizations' abilities to support strong, flexible and scalable global operating models, allowing them to grasp advantage and growth when surrounded by environments that are volatile and uncertain. And yet the very technology – information technology – that has enormously helped financial controls to demonstrate and supervise these flows of money in organizations is often described as one of the principal causes of volatility in economics and finance today. In fact, however, IT controls are used now by stock markets to reduce damaging surges in volatile world markets.

The changing role of the CFO

Ernst and Young (now EY) conducted research and developed a report with very interesting insights into the views of the world held by today's chief financial officers (CFOs).

The report suggests that the role of CFOs is developing rapidly, in terms of:

- the scope of their responsibilities
- the skillsets required for the role
- the development of future CFOs
- the career aspirations of today's CFOs.

'As CFO, I'm in a unique position within the organization, at the absolute center of the universe. The only other executive besides me that has that same presence at the center is the CEO.'

Bruce Besanko, OfficeMax, quoted in 'The DNA of the CFO'

Alongside their traditional role of providing financial insight and analysis, CFOs are becoming increasingly involved in supporting and even developing strategy, guiding key business initiatives. For this reason, the report says, CFOs 'must be versatile individuals with the talent to meet a continually changing set of circumstances'. The CFO remains 'an objective voice on financial performance but contributes to operational decision-making as well. CFOs manage or materially support information technology, investor relations, real estate and strategic M&A — and some are involved in commercial activities'.

Some key findings of the EY report

- 'Most CFOs believe they have viable internal candidates to succeed them in their role, but few organizations have identified a specific candidate or have a formal plan to prepare their next CFO.'
- 'Communications skills are an imperative, as CFOs must convey complex financial results and business performance to external stakeholders while championing specific initiatives internally.'

From the report, it emerges that CFOs' primary concern is with two related issues:

1 having a complete view of the hierarchies of the most important financial data concerning their business
2 their abilities to derive the most insightful strategic kernels of important information from that data and to communicate that information effectively.

In this world of data, finding the 'truth' and communicating it effectively is what keeps CFOs awake at night.

An interesting relationship in many organizations – also revealed by the EY report – is that between the CFO and the top marketing executive. The statement that '[t]oday's CFOs must still attend closely to cash flows, controls, costs and risk [and at] the same time ... continue to seek profitable growth — both in mature markets and in those that hold the promise of rapid growth' indicates quite well where one set of business responsibilities ends and the other begins. The overlap is in finding growth.

Once the areas of potential growth have been found, usually through market research in its various forms, and the marketing function has determined how to reach and satisfy them (see Chapter 4), then the CFO and his/her teams can work to bring them under good financial control. They will then create (along with the marketing department and the function that develops new products or services) forecasts for sales revenues, costs and profits, and thus justifications for investments or divestments, for the future profitable growth of their organizations.

Overlapping responsibilities

All business disciplines make claims about their leadership roles across many other disciplines, and CFOs' responsibilities can be argued to extend to the business areas usually covered by Human Resources (HR), Marketing and even the Legal Department:

'The CFO's role has always been a demanding one, but rapid developments in

regulation, information technology and the economy are defining a new era for the CFO, characterized by a significant expansion in his role and responsibilities. In these circumstances the success of the CFO and his ability to deliver on a broad agenda is contingent on the finance function's ability to establish strong relationships across the enterprise as well as with external stakeholders.'

Karen dela Torre, Vice President, Oracle Corporation

Karen dela Torre argues how the growth of statutory and regulatory reporting has stretched the finance function to the limit, as it seeks to absorb the changes without adding to headcount. As transaction volumes have expanded and business has become ever more complex, the finance function has become almost totally reliant on technology so that the relationship with IT is now crucial to success.

Chief information officers (CIOs), dela Torre points out, now commonly report directly to the CFO. It is worth recalling that, historically, the financial departments in companies often provided the genesis for the development of IT departments – Karen dela Torre describes this as coming full circle, with IT once again falling under the responsibilities of the Finance Department!

It is interesting to examine these areas of overlapping responsibilities in the context of the changing of traditional roles in businesses. The Chartered Quality Institute in the UK has a relevant view:

'Organizations are made up of individuals brought together to enable the organization to achieve its mission. The organization's structure will determine how these individuals are brought together and how

they relate to one another. The success of the organization is dependent on each individual working together to achieve the common goal. If individuals are pulling in different directions, this will have a detrimental impact upon the organization achieving its mission. It is the role of the manager to integrate the activities of individuals, ensuring that they are aware of the institution's priorities and that they are working towards them. Managers achieve this through the authority delegated to them within the organization's hierarchy.'

The Chartered Quality Institute – www.thecqi.org

In other words, the Chief Executive and his or her board, in any organization, will define the extent, borders and overlaps of managers' responsibilities. If they decide that the Finance Department should have a degree of authority and control over areas normally managed by the HR function or by Marketing, for example, so long as these responsibilities are decided, clearly recorded and understood by all, there need be no misunderstanding or confusions about 'who does what'!

Pressures on financial functions

In the future development of the financial functions in organizations, there are several pressures that will force change. These include:

- the internationalization – globalization – of business, which brings with it different currencies and currency movements and differing legal requirements
- changes in banking regulations, forced by the global downturn that started in 2007
- the geopolitical ambitions of leaders of countries such as China, Russia and North Korea, frequently causing problems

to international trade due to the placement of embargoes and trade restrictions
- changes in information technology, which often create great efficiencies in financial operations but can create vulnerabilities to other, sometimes malign, organizations and countries
- changes in the education of future CFOs, mostly owing to MOOCS – Massive Online Open Courses – in which most of the learning is done remotely, at PCs in students' rooms, without challenging face-to-face discussion.

Thus, changes to the structures and operating processes of financial departments are on their way, to accommodate some of the issues described above – and so are changes to the roles of CFOs.

Tools of the trade

Besides a general introduction to why and how financial departments work and are managed, and the future direction of the finance functions, an MBA degree also helps students to become familiar with the tools of the trade, the financial models and structures used commonly to calculate, display and communicate the financial situation of their companies, at any one time, to managers and others. These include:

- the balance sheet
- the profit and loss (P&L) account
- cash flow calculations
- researching accounts using ratio analysis.

Business plans – especially for small companies and start-ups – are often justifications for new strategies and financial investments. As such, a balance sheet, P&L and cash flow projections for the period under critical review are all vital components of the business plan.

'Owner managers today need to be able to understand finance; leaving everything to an accountant is easy, but isn't practical. The basics of finance are worth a bit of effort to learn and understand, as you can glean invaluable business information. [...] Effective control requires effective planning and target setting but it also requires an understanding of financial statements and an ability to interpret the figures.'

Shell LiveWIRE – shell-livewire.org

Ratio analysis

Ratio analysis (RA) is a cornerstone of fundamental, financial and corporate analysis. It is a quantitative analysis of information from a company's financial statements, the line items in the balance sheet, profit and loss account and cash flow statements. The ratios of an item to another item, or combination of items, are calculated and used to evaluate the company's operating and financial performance, for example its efficiency, liquidity, profitability and solvency. Trends in these ratios, studied over time, give important insights into the changing situation and, when compared to those of other companies in the same sector, provide views on comparative performances and valuations.

Understanding how the CFO and the world of financial controls works, the balance sheet, the profit and loss account, cash-flow projections, ratio analysis and their place in business planning, are all critical studies for the business manager and well worth a few hours of extra MBA studies!

MBA recommended reading list

Jason Karaian, *The Chief Financial Officer: What CFOs Do, the Influence They Have and Why It Matters* (Economist Books, 2014)

Roger Mason, *Bookkeeping and Accounting In A Week* (John Murray Learning, 2016)

Hunter Muller, *The Big Shift in IT Leadership: How Great CIOs Leverage the Power of Technology for Strategic Business Growth* (Wiley, 2015)

Summary

Descriptions of drivers of change often emphasize new technology and that is certainly a major force. However, in order to embed the new technology and to harness it to accelerate an organization's progress, managers need wide-ranging skill sets and that is why MBA degrees are taught in business schools to experienced executives midway through their careers. CFOs need to understand and be able to view the organization holistically – to see it in the round – and not only to view their business world through spreadsheets, balance sheets and profit and loss accounts.

Fact-check (answers at the back)

1. How do finance, economics and accounting support world markets?
   a) By bringing stability to volatile markets ❏
   b) By reducing insolvencies ❏
   c) From fostering an understanding of cash flows in international companies ❏
   d) By keeping a tight control of costs in organizations ❏

2. What may cause the greatest risks to world stock markets?
   a) A global company becoming bankrupt ❏
   b) Sudden and catastrophic events causing disruption to global supply chains ❏
   c) Changes in international interest rates ❏
   d) New governments taking control in countries with large world economies ❏

3. What will be the greatest challenge to future CFOs?
   a) To control costs in times of great variations in interest rates ❏
   b) To avoid corruption and the infiltration of fraud and criminal activities ❏
   c) To control salaries and reward structures to maintain motivation but minimize costs ❏
   d) To transform financial functions to support strong, flexible and scalable global operating models in conditions of volatility and uncertainty ❏

4. How might you best describe the present-day accounting function in an organization?
   a) Today's CFOs have a much more central role in broad corporate decision-making ❏
   b) Accounting functions should be kept separate from other parts of the enterprise to preserve their independence and authority ❏
   c) CFOs have an important role in enterprises but one that is subservient to the other disciplines such as marketing or operations ❏
   d) Accounting functions are becoming subservient to HR departments as a way of controlling salaries ❏

5. What are the critical financial statements expected in any business plan?
   a) Budget statements for future capital expenditures ❏
   b) A balance sheet, P&L and cash flow projection for the period under critical review ❏
   c) A view of discounted cash flow statements on key capital investments ❏
   d) A summary of the business's strategy and its likely trajectory ❏

6. How did the IT departments in most businesses begin to take shape?
a) When Microsoft first created Windows software suites ❏
b) Only after IBM initiated business software and sold accounting packages to companies' accounts departments ❏
c) They arose out of accounts departments and thence began to permeate every other business discipline ❏
d) From a need to count profits more accurately ❏

7. What is a root cause of volatility in financial markets?
a) Globalized companies having to trade in many different currencies ❏
b) The integration and maintenance of old legacy IT systems controlling financial operations ❏
c) IT systems and controls used by stock markets to reduce damaging surges ❏
d) Fraud and criminal activities ❏

8. Which of the following are examples of pressures forcing change in the future development of the financial functions in organizations?
a) Changes in banking regulations, forced by the global downturn that started in 2007 ❏
b) New financial governance requirements in the United States ❏
c) The growing international use of Bitcoins ❏
d) Reduction of global interest rates ❏

9. Why is there a now a requirement for new critical relationships across organizations, usually involving CFOs?
a) The CFO's role and responsibilities are expanding ❏
b) There are new international legal requirements ❏
c) There are new international auditing standards ❏
d) The education of future CFOs is being negatively affected by the growth of MOOCs ❏

10. Developments in information technology are leading to changes in the financial functions in organizations. How might this be reflected?
a) In higher IT budgets ❏
b) In opportunities for new revenue streams and novel ways of engaging with customers ❏
c) In the increasing organizational separation of IT departments and financial operations ❏
d) In more subcontracting of the IT function (e.g. 'cloud' computing) ❏

CHAPTER 3

Entrepreneur-ship, ethics and social responsibility

Many MBA students ask for the definitions of, and differences between, ethics and morals. Ethics and morals both make judgements on human behaviours that are either 'right' or 'wrong'. However, ethics is a set of rules given to an individual by another body or organization such as their business (known as 'business ethics'), profession or religion. Morals refer to an individual's own principles regarding right and wrong – their 'moral compass'. Business ethics and social responsibility are very important in entrepreneurial ventures, particularly in decision-making processes.

An ethical frame of mind assists entrepreneurs in making the best decisions for the longer term in fast-moving and complex entrepreneurial environments. A strong sense of social responsibility helps entrepreneurs to make decisions that best enhance benefits and decrease risks for stakeholders and investors in entrepreneurial organizations.

Why be ethical in business?

Business ethics examines ethical principles in business environments and all aspects of business conduct, and relates to how the individuals in businesses and entire business organizations behave with respect to one other and to their external worlds.

Business ethics consists of written and unwritten codes of values, principles and practices that guide the corporate culture – the principles upon which decisions and actions are made in a business. In the business world, business ethics are an agreed, common understanding in companies of the difference between right and wrong practices.

Businesses should be run according to their business and strategic plans, which should always be living documents, a part of daily business life and the touchstone and foundation for all complex decision making. A business's policies should be bound by their ethical principles and frameworks.

Social responsibility, as a subject in today's business world, means doing what is morally right and behaving 'unto others as you would have them behave unto you'. This 'Golden Rule' is integral to ethical principles and behaviours. The International Standards Organization (ISO) gives the following definition of 'social responsibility':

> *'The responsibility of an organization for the impacts of its decisions and activities on society and the environment, through transparent and ethical behaviour that:*
>
> - *contributes to sustainable development, including health and the welfare of society*
> - *takes into account the expectations of stakeholders*
> - *is in compliance with applicable laws and consistent with international norms of behaviour*

● is integrated throughout the organization and practised in its relationships.'

ISO 26000: *Guidance on Social Responsibility*, 2010.

Neglect of business ethics and groupthink

There have been occasions, historically, when some entrepreneurial and dynamic businesses thought that sacrificing ethics and social responsibilities would offer a short cut to increased profitable growth. Such an attitude is fast disappearing. According to the US-based audio-visual and event technology services company Meeting Tomorrow (http://www.meetingtomorrow.com/cms-category/business-ethics-and-social-responsibility), drawing on research from the American Management Association, '56 per cent of surveyed participants ranked ethical behaviour as the most important characteristic of effective leaders'. It goes on to point out:

'Americans have witnessed first-hand the destruction that occurs when corporations do not behave ethically. Businesses who conduct themselves in an ethical manner pass their values, morals, and beliefs down to the employees and customers. The effect can be felt throughout the community, which has a profound impact on local schools, community centers, and other groups. Companies such as Enron, Tyco, Adelphia, and WorldCom are classic examples of what can happen when corporations disregard or neglect the importance of business ethics. A company's ethical behaviour can build or destroy Main Street USA.'

The Enron scandal

The case of Enron in 2001 is the perfect illustration of the effects described above. At the beginning of the new millennium Enron was one of the United States' best-known and most successful companies, employing some 20,000 staff and with revenues of almost $111 billion. At the end of 2001, however, Enron's 'success' was shown to be an illusion, created by a sustained and systematic campaign of corporate fraud and corruption. The resulting scandal threw into question the accounting practices of many US corporations and helped lead to the passing of the Sarbanes–Oxley Act of 2002, which set out stringent new standards and responsibilities for public companies in the United States.

The Enron scandal is an example of a large and entrepreneurial organization neglecting ethics and social responsibility and coming completely unstuck because of that management failure.

Another illustrative example is that of WorldCom, a US company found guilty, in 2002, of accounting irregularities of $11 billion and which subsequently filed for bankruptcy. Analysis of WorldCom's demise suggests that its endemic unethical behaviours were the result of **groupthink**, defined by the US psychologist Irving Janis as:

> *'a mode of thinking that people engage in when they are deeply involved in a cohesive in-group, when the members' strivings for unanimity override their motivation to realistically appraise alternative courses of action.'*

Janis pointed to notable examples of groupthink outside the business sphere – President Kennedy's decision to invade Cuba at the Bay of Pigs and the US decision to escalate the war in Vietnam – but he also showed how corporate groupthink can have deeply destructive effects within business. Feelings of invulnerability, refusal to accept dissent, and self-censorship within the group lead to extremely poor decision making.

The description above of how 'groupthink' within company culture can skew both individuals' moral compasses and whole organizations' business ethics indicates not only how serious but also how insidious this corporate error of management judgement can become.

Whistleblowers

But how should company laws concerning ethics be policed? This can, in part, be addressed by 'whistleblowers'.

'Whistleblowing is when a worker reports suspected wrongdoing at work. Officially, this is called "making a disclosure in the public interest".

A worker can report things that aren't right, are illegal or if anyone at work is neglecting their duties, including:

- *someone's health and safety is in danger*
- *damage to the environment*
- *a criminal offence*
- *the company isn't obeying the law (e.g. not having the right insurance)*
- *covering up wrongdoing.'*

www.gov.uk/whistleblowing

It is important for a business to develop a coherent, objective approach to the issue of whistleblowing, since the actions of a whistleblower can cause disruption in the workplace, inflict serious harm on individuals wrongly accused, and have important financial consequences for a business. A UK survey showed that a little more than half of whistleblowing incidents resulted in external investigations of the companies involved, and more than one-fifth in criminal investigations.

Failure to respond to whistleblowers' concerns, or indeed showing outright hostility, should never have been acceptable, but in today's world are likely to be even more destructive. Merely kicking an incident into the long grass by, for example, dismissing the whistleblower is not an option. Companies who adopt this strategy are increasingly facing legal proceedings – and ultimately large financial penalties as well as poor publicity – as the former employee sues for wrongful dismissal.

The UK government whistleblowing website cited above suggests three ways in which companies can handle whistleblowing effectively and constructively:

1 Employees 'must be informed of the appropriate steps to take in communicating their ethical concerns internally'.
2 Employees 'must believe that their concerns will be taken seriously and will be investigated'.
3 Employees 'must feel confident that they will not suffer personal reprisals for using internal channels to report perceived wrongdoing'.

In this way, companies can provide internal mechanisms that promote critical self-reflection and ethical business development.

Non-executive directors (NEDs)

There is another and parallel means that can be deployed to keep organizations' business cultures on track: the use of non-executive directors (NEDs) on companies' management boards of directors, as a kind of 'internal whistleblowing'. Evidence suggests, however, that the effectiveness of NEDs in this respect can be a mixed bag. While NEDs will certainly have challenged executive decisions and from time to time successfully exposed serious problems, there are also likely to be instances where they have avoided taking action for fear of personal consequences. Moreover, the value of their work where they do challenge corporate behaviours is diminished because it does not become public knowledge and cannot therefore inform public debate.

Thus, while NEDs provide a valuable service in companies today, their positions must be strongly supported by chief executives in order that they can maintain their principled, balanced and independent view of organizations' practices. This service can then provide a valuable supporting bulwark to maintain organizations' practices concerning business ethics and social responsibility.

Corporate governance

Since the corporate scandals of the beginning of the millennium and the financial crisis that began in 2007–8 there has been an upsurge in interest in the corporate governance practices of modern corporations, especially in relation to **accountability**.

The term 'corporate governance' refers to the business activities and processes designed to control and direct the behaviours of corporations to align and balance the interests of their stakeholders. These stakeholders include shareholders, management, customers, suppliers, financiers, government and the broader community served. Corporate governance focuses on the rules and procedures for making decisions in corporate affairs. Managers of organizations may be tempted to make decisions that benefit themselves but may harm others. Corporate governance examines the processes that set corporations' objectives and implement them in social, regulatory and market environments and include observation of the activities, policies and decision making in corporations.

Thus, good corporate governance embeds in organizations mechanisms that monitor and regulate the organizations' adherence to their own guidelines on corporate culture, business ethics and social responsibility:

> *'Effective corporate governance requires balanced boards made up of people with the right skills operating in a transparent and accountable framework. Good practice should be shared across businesses but laying down inflexible rules can result in a tick-box approach, forcing businesses to adopt frameworks that don't work for them and does nothing to improve outcomes.'*
>
> Confederation of British Industry (CBI) – http://news.cbi.org.uk

Case study: Coca-Cola

We will conclude this chapter with a discussion of a company with a highly developed and transparent approach to corporate responsibility and business ethics: Coca-Cola.

> *'We [Coca-Cola] are guided by our established standards of corporate governance and ethics. We review our systems to ensure we achieve international best practices in terms of transparency and accountability. The foundation of our approach to corporate governance is laid out in our Corporate Governance Guidelines and in the charters of our Board of Directors' committees.'*
>
> www.coca-colacompany.com/our-company/ governance-ethics/governance-ethics

Key aspects of Coca-Cola's multi-pronged approach include:

- The management of corporate responsibility through its **Public Policy and Corporate Reputation Council**, a cross-functional group of senior managers from the company and its partners: 'The Council identifies risks and opportunities faced by our business and communities and recommends strategies to address these challenges.'
- A **Code of Business Conduct** that demands of directors, associates and employees 'honesty and integrity in all matters'.
- The overseeing of the Code by an **Ethics and Compliance Committee**, another cross-functional senior management team.
- An **Ethics and Compliance Office** that has 'operational responsibility for education, consultation, monitoring and assessment related to the Code of Business Conduct and compliance issues'.
- **Training courses** for associates and employees worldwide to ensure an ongoing commitment to and understanding of the Code of Business Conduct. In 2010 some 22,000 employees were certified as being in compliance with the Code and Coca-Cola's anti-bribery requirements. On average, employees receive an average of 60 minutes' ethics training every year.

Coca-Cola's complex, global approach shows how seriously organizations today take the subjects of business ethics and corporate and social responsibility. Tackling this issue head on is not for the faint-hearted but the lessons of not doing so, from Enron, WorldCom and others, are still comparatively recent and fresh in the memory.

MBA recommended reading list

Mick Blowfield and Alan Murray, *Corporate Responsibility*, 4th edition (Oxford University Press, 2014)

Andrew Crane and Dirk Matten, *Business Ethics: Managing Corporate Citizenship and Sustainability in the Age of Globalization*, 3rd edition (Oxford University Press, 2010)

Peter Elkind and Bethany MacLean, *The Smartest Guys in the Room: The Amazing Rise and Scandalous Fall of Enron* (Penguin, 2004)

Summary

Business ethics and social responsibility are very important in entrepreneurial ventures and a strong sense of social responsibility helps entrepreneurs to make decisions that best enhance benefits and decrease risks for stakeholders and investors in entrepreneurial organizations. A case study of a company that chose the wrong operational paths – Enron – was examined, as was an example of a company with an exemplary ethical framework – Coca-Cola.

'Whistleblowing' by employees in organizations and the probable benefit of having non-executive directors on company boards were also discussed. Today activist shareholders and investors also make headlines when they try to change corporate behaviours in companies they target.

These activities are all focused on trying to create and maintain patterns and systems of corporate behaviour and the ways in which organizations are run for the better – in the views of stakeholders, employees, the laws under which they should operate and society at large.

Fact-check (answers at the back)

1. Which of the following best describes business ethics?
   a) Rules for business set by governments ❏
   b) Guidelines for responsible managers given by a relevant business body or authority ❏
   c) Business guidelines set by trade associations ❏
   d) Common sense and a knowledge of the law ❏

2. How might you define 'morality' in business?
   a) Legally binding business laws ❏
   b) Operational guidelines for businesses in each business sector ❏
   c) A manager's own business principles regarding the right and the wrong ways in which to operate his or her business – their 'moral compass' ❏
   d) Obeying the law and treating people as you would expect to be treated ❏

3. What does the term 'social responsibility' mean in today's business world?
   a) Being honest and truthful in the use of social media ❏
   b) Looking after the best interests of employees in a business ❏
   c) A subject integral to ethical principles and behaviours in business life ❏
   d) Being as good as your word and keeping your promises to employees ❏

4. How would you best describe the example provided by Enron?
   a) A well-known example of wilful corporate fraud and corruption ❏
   b) A scandal brought about by insider trading ❏
   c) The result of the creation of the Sarbanes–Oxley Act ❏
   d) This is how business has always behaved until caught out ❏

5. What is groupthink?
   a) A kind of mutiny among the directors of a company against the CEO ❏
   b) A strategy to determine a new corporate direction ❏
   c) A group of managers skewing their moral compasses together by a subconscious common agreement ❏
   d) When groups of people who work closely together take decisions in concert ❏

6. What activity, from the early outset in the formation of any company, is vital for the safe future conduct of that company?
   a) Agreement of the CEO's package of rewards ❏
   b) The setting down of written and unwritten codes of values, principles and practices that guide corporate culture ❏
   c) The recruitment of a Chief Ethics Officer ❏
   d) Writing the corporate business plan ❏

7. What is 'whistleblowing'?
a) Where a worker reports suspected wrongdoing at work ❏
b) Where trades union leaders call a strike in the workplace ❏
c) A reliable backup when the fire alarm system fails ❏
d) Telling tales and betraying loyalties ❏

8. Why do companies use non-executive directors (NEDs) on their management board of directors?
a) To check that remuneration of the board of directors is fair ❏
b) Because they are cheaper to employ than executive directors ❏
c) Because NEDs are often able to effectively challenge executive decisions to keep organizations' business cultures on track ❏
d) NEDs are used only on the boards of charities ❏

9. In some situations, NEDs have not been able to challenge executive decisions or expose serious problems. Why might this be so?
a) Because they do not have the authority ❏
b) Because they are not invited to key board meetings ❏
c) Because sometimes they may be fearful of the personal consequences they may suffer ❏
d) Because they fear that the potential repercussions do not balance at their pay grade ❏

10. What is the Code of Business Conduct at the Coca-Cola Company?
a) A committee that sets the agreed formulae for Coca-Cola's drinks in international bottling plants ❏
b) A way to ensure that workers' conditions are managed equably around the world ❏
c) A guide for all the company's associates and directors requiring honesty and integrity in all matters ❏
d) A way of ensuring that product is not pilfered and drunk on the premises ❏

CHAPTER 4

Strategy and marketing

Strategic planning is concerned with the overall direction of the business. It is allied with marketing and involves making decisions about production and operations, finance, human resources and all business issues. Marketing management is key in strategic planning because of the need to understand and manage the connections between the business and the marketplace. At the heart of strategic planning are the questions:

- Where are we now?
- How did we get here?
- Where are we heading?
- Where would we like to be?
- How do we get there?
- What barriers lie ahead?
- How do we overcome them?
- Are we on course?

A natural marriage

Strategic management and marketing are completely intertwined. Yet, for many managers who are untrained in marketing, marketing is a discipline that is synonymous with advertising and promotion. Because of this perception, many businesspeople believe that marketing is an unlikely bedfellow with a 'heavyweight' subject such as the determination of business strategy.

However, marketing is a much broader and more all-encompassing discipline than promotion, which is simply just a very visible component part of the subject of marketing. Marketing and strategy run together because marketing must understand and manage the connections between the business and the marketplace, while strategy must relate the business and its operations to the marketplace and customers. Thus, strategic management and marketing are a natural pairing of business activities with an interlocking fit.

Building and using business models and frameworks is a subject addressed later in this chapter and is an area of business activity that is fundamental to obtaining and maintaining strategic direction.

The close relationship between strategic management and marketing can be seen in the way that strategic decisions are responses to strategic questions about how the organization will compete. For example:

- Who is the target customer for the organization's products and services?
- Where are the customers located and how do they buy the organization's products and services?
- In the eyes of customers and other stakeholders, what makes the organization stand out from its competitors?
- What are the key opportunities and risks for the organization?
- How can the organization grow, both in terms of its base business and new business?
- How can the organization generate more value for investors?

These questions and others like them suggest how a deep understanding of the external environment and a business's markets is critical to the strategic planning process.

Strategies for growth

The determination of business strategy as a subject first appeared in the 1950s and 1960s, in the work of academics such as Peter Drucker, H. Igor Ansoff, Bruce Henderson, Philip Selznick and Alfred Chandler. A major preoccupation of the period was the determination of organizations' SWOTs (Strengths – Weaknesses – Opportunities – Threats).

SWOT analysis

The origins of SWOT analysis are unclear but this planning method, used to determine an organization's (or a project's) strengths, weaknesses, opportunities and threats, had become established by the 1960s.

First, the objective of the organization or project is identified and then the factors that are favourable and unfavourable for the achievement of that objective, both internal (the characteristics of the organization) and external (the characteristics of the environment), are analysed:

Strengths: characteristics of the organization or project that give it an advantage over others	**Weaknesses:** characteristics that place the business or project at a disadvantage relative to others
Opportunities: elements that the project could exploit to its advantage	**Threats:** elements in the environment that could cause trouble for the business or project

The term 'strategic fit' is used to describe the match between the characteristics of the organization and the environment.

In the 1960s there was a heated debate over the risks that companies should take in pursuit of new opportunities (diversification), at the risk of sacrificing their existing competencies. In a classic 1960 article, 'Marketing Myopia', the US economist Theodore Levitt (1935–2006), for example, criticized businesses firms that were too inward-looking, focused on delivering an established product rather than seeking to meet customers' changing needs. When companies fail, he wrote,

> **'it usually means that the product fails to adapt to the constantly changing patterns of consumer needs and tastes, to new and modified marketing institutions and practices, or to product developments in complementary industries.'**
>
> Theodore Levitt, 'Marketing Myopia', *Harvard Business Review* (1960)

The Russian-born applied mathematician Igor Ansoff (1918–2002) – the 'father of strategic management' – argued that more caution was required when companies diversified; Levitt, Ansoff thought, was simply asking companies to take too much risk by investing in new products that might not fit the firm's distinctive competence. Instead, he believed, a company needs to identify whether any new product grows naturally out of its existing ones – that there is a 'common thread' between them. Just because its customers have needs other than those already being met by the company does not mean that it is necessarily in a position to diversify to meet them.

To help companies to identify the relative risks they face as they seek to grow, Ansoff developed the Product/Market Growth Matrix, well known to all MBA students!

The Ansoff Growth Matrix

The Ansoff Growth Matrix is an essential tool in strategic planning to find opportunities for growth:

- by increased penetration of existing markets with current products or services

- by new product or service development
- by entering new markets with current products or services, *or*
- by complete diversification into the relative unknown by entering new markets with new products or services.

	Existing products	New products
Existing markets	Market penetration	Product development
New markets	Market development	Diversification

These strategies for growth are all related to risk. However, the greatest risk (and source of potential opportunity!) lies in diversification – introducing new products or services to new markets.

Besides growth strategies, others also exist, although most businesses focus on strategies to deliver profitable growth, rather than to accept the status quo or decline!

The descriptions of the development of strategic thinking above demonstrate very clearly the intimate, close relationship between the disciplines of strategic development and marketing. It has become accepted that any business strategy that looks only inwards at its own distinctive competencies without taking into account the positions and attitudes of its actual and potential customers can ultimately lead only to failure.

Business modelling

> *'A business model is the means to define why the organization exists and how it creates, delivers, and captures value.'*
>
> Dan Olszewski

An awareness of how business models have evolved over the last five decades or so is vital for any MBA student. Business models are the frameworks of how businesses operate to make sales revenues and profits. Business models are designed when a business is launched but they usually also evolve and improve over time. In *The Business Model Canvas* (2010), Yves Pigneur and Alexander Osterwalder describe how to build and how to improve business models for startups through to mature organizations.

Examples of business models developed by businesses in recent decades are:

The 1960s

- **Oldsmobile** (General Motors) relied upon new product development (e.g. turbocharged engines) and the frequent introduction of new vehicle designs.
- In 1959 **American Airlines** teamed up with IBM to introduce the SABRE (Semi-Automated Business Research Environment), a huge electronic data-processing system that created and managed airline seat reservations and instantly made that data available.

The 1970s

- Fred Smith wrote a paper for an economics class as an undergraduate at Yale University which proposed an overnight delivery service in which one carrier is responsible for a piece of cargo from pick-up through delivery by flying all of its own aircraft and operating its own depots, posting stations and delivery vans. At this time cargo shipment was handled by a chain of companies and Smith's idea was unorthodox – he got a C grade for his paper. Smith, however, went on to found **Federal Express** in the early 1970s. After early financial difficulties and improvements to the business model, Smith's personal wealth today is about $2 billion!

The 1980s

- The first **Blockbuster** store opened in1985 in Texas, founded by David Cook from his background in managing huge databases. Early success was built on customizing a store to its local population's demographics, with films geared specifically to their profiles, popular new releases and lots of catalogue titles. Blockbuster's business model fell victim to Netflix and Redbox in 2010.

- **Home Depot** set up huge stores, with the best possible customer service, helping customers to lay tiles, change valves or use power tools. All customer-facing staff underwent rigorous product training and the stores held clinics to teach customers how to do it themselves. This revolutionized the DIY industry, teaching know-how and bringing the customers the tools to do the job and saving them money.
- In the early 1980s **Intel**'s business was in DRAM memory chips. Strong Japanese competition significantly reduced the DRAM market's profitability by 1983 and the success of the IBM PC motivated CEO Andy Grove to focus on microprocessors and to fundamentally change the company business model. This change of strategy was successful and Intel was set on a ten-year course of profitable growth as the leading hardware supplier to the PC industry in the 1980s and 1990s. Fierce competition in the semiconductor industry has since diminished its position.
- Michael Dell upgraded his IBM-compatible PC in his room in 1983 at the University of Texas. He quickly realized that he could buy components and assemble PCs more cheaply himself instead of upgrading older machines. He began to sell the PCS with the **Dell** name on it directly to customers at a 15-per-cent discount to established brands. He started advertising in trade magazines and grew the order book. Within a year, he dropped out of college to run his business full time and in 1984 his business officially became Dell Computer Corporation.

The 1990s

- **Southwest Airlines'** primary focus has remained short point-to-point flights. By only flying one type of aircraft, it has a heavier flight schedule than its competitors because loading and unloading of its aircraft is completely standardized. Staff and pilots have to learn only one set of skills used repeatedly. Only one type of specialized equipment is required to service and maintain the aeroplane fleet. Many airlines have attempted to emulate Southwest but it has developed a niche. This business model has allowed Southwest to succeed in the airline industry and it will now be difficult for rival airlines to adopt this business model individually to increase productivity.

- The founders of **Netflix** realized that they could send CDs through the US Postal Service without damaging them. The DVD rental-by-mail business put Netflix on the map. In 1997 the video rental market was dominated by Blockbuster and others renting VHS titles. Netflix made a series of smart and lucky decisions to dominate the video rental industry. They first partnered with manufacturers of DVD players to develop consumer interest in this new format, increasing its adoption and gaining visibility for their brand. Then Netflix contacted the film studios to position their service as a market-enhancing proposition. With luck and good fortune, Netflix entered the market just as it became ready for them, and their risks were limited.

- The 'growth first, revenue later' is a risky business model, but a proven one. The high level of risk is one reason why the returns can be so great. Although it is commonly held that **Amazon**'s business model operates in this way, in fact the company does not fit this mould. Founded in 1995 and holding its initial public offering (IPO) in 1997, it is certainly not a firm without revenue or a clear revenue strategy. At the website you can find items you want to buy and they have prices next to them. If you want to buy, you enter your credit card information and buy them. It's the most boring revenue strategy in the world and one of the oldest. It works! This firm remains a darling of Wall Street despite a lack of profitability. But Amazon doesn't turn a profit because it's a darling of Wall Street. Amazon is essentially the beneficiary of large Wall Street trends in its ability to eschew profits, yet it's also bucking the trend among its peer technology giants.

- The real business model for **Starbucks** was real estate. Selling coffee was simply the means to acquire prime commercial real estate. It was the real estate, and not the coffee, that increased shareholder value and made them wealthy. In the 1990s stock analysts understood that Starbucks' model caused the company to increase in value only by opening new stores, although that was never the source of Starbucks' growth. Coffee revenue was simply fed back into Starbucks' real-estate acquisitions, and this is what caused its stock value to explode. Recently, Starbucks began to lose its magic because the world has become overrun with Starbucks. As this business model succeeds, it inherently hits a point of diminishing returns.

The 2000s

- 'One Ford – One Team – One Plan – One Goal.' **Ford**'s 'One Ford' business plan was announced by Ford management in June 2008 as gas prices surged to the highest levels seen on record. The Ford plan, as outlined later that year to the US Senate, identified that the company needed to streamline its operation by unifying its global business. Ford stated that 'six European small vehicles [would be] coming to North America from global B-car and C-car platforms'. B-car models are subcompacts and C-car models are compacts.
- With the relatively recent passing of Steve Jobs, a lingering and much discussed question remains: what will happen to **Apple** without Jobs in charge? How will the company's business model change without Jobs to direct the company into new sectors? How long can Jobs's vision last? The company's business model is volatile. With Tim Cook at the top, new strategies may steer Apple away from Jobs's vision fairly quickly. Cook may do so by changing the company's supply chain, its marketing strategy, its market position, or its pricing strategy. We must watch and wait but the business model is changing...

MBA recommended reading list

Robert S. Kaplan and David P. Norton, *The Balanced Scorecard: Translating Strategy into Action* (Harvard Business Review Press, 1996)

Tom Osenton, *The Death of Demand: Finding Growth in a Saturated Global Economy* (Financial Times Prentice Hall Books, 2004)

Alexander Osterwalder and Yves Pigneur, *The Business Model Generator: A Handbook for Visionaries, Game Changers, and Challengers* (John Wiley & Sons, 2010)

Summary

Marketing management is key in strategic planning for businesses in order to understand, manage and make sense of the connections between their businesses and marketplaces. Strategic planning asks the key questions to position the business. To answer these questions, businesses conduct market research and that research includes intelligence on their competition, their political, social and economic environments and technologies. This information feeds directly into strategic planning, to illuminate the road ahead and all the barriers to their progress towards their objectives.

Testing out ideas for the strategic plan by using business models greatly reduces business risk. Business models prompt the questions to identify risk and to shine a light into any dark and forgotten corners of the business, illuminating issues that may have been previously overlooked, all before starting to trade. Today social media and the Internet offer tools for business managers to investigate with confidence the wants and needs of their actual or targeted customers to determine business models that work well, quickly and effectively.

Fact-check (answers at the back)

1. Why is marketing management key in strategic planning?

a) Because marketing management brings the voice and needs of the customers and the marketplace into the overall management of the business ❑

b) Because marketing management also manages the sales function ❑

c) Because the design and strategies used in advertising and marketing communications must match corporate strategies ❑

d) Because marketing management understands the competition ❑

2. SWOT analysis is still a very popular tool in strategic analysis. However, in what way does SWOT fail to guide us?

a) It over-emphasizes weaknesses over strengths ❑

b) It requires a great deal of very precise information to be useful ❑

c) It does not bring closure to the problem of actually defining a firm's distinctive competence ❑

d) It does not provide direct solutions to the issues raised ❑

3. In his article 'Marketing Myopia' (1960), Theodore Levitt argued what?

a) That customers are notoriously fickle and firms should be wary of investing without thorough customer research ❑

b) That firms seemed to focus too much on delivering a product ❑

c) That supply chain efficiencies were critical for profitable growth ❑

d) That all marketing is subject to myopic vision ❑

4. In new product development theory, H. Igor Ansoff argued that...

a) New products should copy competitors' products as 'me toos' ('I have the same product also') to reduce risk ❑

b) New product development should be left to R&D departments with little involvement from marketing departments being necessary ❑

c) A company should first ask whether a new product had a 'common thread' with its existing products ❑

d) That 'diversification' is too risky a strategy to be undertaken ❑

5. The purpose of business modelling is to...
a) Check that all the elements of the business are in place ❑
b) Define why the organization exists and how it creates, delivers and captures value ❑
c) Demonstrate the business's operations to investors ❑
d) Check the business against competitors' operations ❑

6. In the 1960s American Airlines' business model was...
a) Focused on aeronautical engineering and new aircraft designs ❑
b) A failure, requiring reinvestment ❑
c) Centred on the development of new engines and better fuel consumption ❑
d) Involved a new approach using IT technology to better plan seating reservations ❑

7. Federal Express was created in the 1970s but its business model was...
a) An instant success ❑
b) Judged a failure even by Fred Smith, the entrepreneur who started it up ❑
c) An eventual success, following improvements made to the original business model over time ❑
d) Completely overhauled ❑

8. In the 1990s Netflix's business model was...
a) The complete result of lucky decisions ❑
b) A failure, due to an intervention by Blockbuster ❑
c) Successful, due in part to a technological partnership ❑
d) A failure, due to their relationship with the postal authority ❑

9. Amazon ...
a) Introduced a 'growth first, revenue later' business model that failed badly ❑
b) Is a website-based, sales revenue business model ❑
c) Is unpopular today with Wall Street due to its lack of profits ❑
d) Has no clear revenue strategy ❑

10. In the 2000s Apple's business model...
a) Remains unchanged, following the death of Steve Jobs, its founder ❑
b) Will be soon ditched as the company is due to be taken over by Google ❑
c) Is likely to change especially with with respect to its supply chain ❑
d) Will remain static, as Tim Cook, the new head of Apple, is intolerant of change ❑

CHAPTER 5

Operations management

The term 'operations' is often used for the corporate area in businesses responsible for the production of goods or services. This includes all activities to create and deliver products or services, from procuring suppliers and materials to logistics and supply chain management (SCM). The operations area usually has the greatest number of assets and employees.

Operations as an area is also the foundation for the company's long-term performance because it is usually responsible for product or service quality and is frequently viewed as a source of competitive advantage. Managed well, operations helps to ensure that the organization's strategy is realized.

Making a difference

Together with marketing, operations departments breathe life into corporate strategy, preventing it from remaining just a theoretical exercise by creating and delivering the added value of the business. In 2014 PriceWaterhouseCoopers' (PwC) 17th Annual CEO survey found that broadening operation options for customers is a factor that drives differences in performance and that 71 per cent of US CEOs are planning to remake their fulfilment and service supply chains. The survey found three sources of leverage:

1 Broadening service operation options for customers
2 Engaging service supply chain partners in innovating operational practices
3 Focusing on end-to-end performance in quality and management.

PwC's survey found that a vigorous focus on these activities, in the traditional area of operations management, can drive differences in performance and create increased competitive advantage.

Sourcing a workforce

There is, however, a major problem that hinders the success of operations departments, especially in organizations in the United States and Europe – the recruitment and retention of capable people. Moreover, since, as has already been noted, operations departments usually have the greatest number of employees, this makes recruitment an especially significant issue for organizations, especially smaller ones.

We might even speak of a recruitment crisis in the West, as middle-technology jobs, requiring only a middling level of skill and training, are leaving the United States and Europe for China and other Asian countries:

'I think we should recognize that the period between 1950 and 1980 was an unusual period in Western history, in which there was a massive increase in what you could earn for an ordinary education doing rather ordinary things that didn't really require a lot of skill. It is not sensible for the US and many European countries to send 50 per cent of their children to college, expecting them all to somehow be legislators or managers. That's a hard reality that Europeans and Americans haven't been able to face. They have a lot of unemployment among their own children, and then they import people from the Third World to do the jobs that they won't do.'

Peter Morici, Professor of International Business at Maryland University, quoted by Martin Webber, Business Editor, 24 December 2014

Operations workforces are now being sourced in emerging economies:

'Intel is cutting 1,500 jobs in Costa Rica as it takes steps to cut 5 percent of its workforce by the end of the fiscal year. The job cuts, which will happen over the next two fiscal quarters, are at a site that does chip assembly and testing, said Chuck Mulloy, an Intel spokesman. The assembly and testing operations will be moved to sites in Malaysia, Vietnam and Chengdu, China, where similar functions are already performed.'

Agam Shah, IDG News Service, April 2014

Other pressures, too, are transforming this vital business area:

- big data
- the Internet of Things (IoT)
- new technologies
- globalization.

Big data

In recent years we have experienced, according to Sundar Swaminathan (Senior Director of Industry Strategy and Marketing at Oracle Corporation) writing in 2012, a 'data deluge':

- More than 90 per cent of data in the world today has been created in the last two years, with 80 per cent of it being unstructured, such as images, audio, video, social media, web pages and emails.
- 8 trillion gigabytes of new data were created in 2011.
- Data is expanding at a rate that doubles every two years.
- By 2020 the digital universe will be 40 trillion gigabytes.
- Most US companies have at least 100 terabytes stored.

Businesses are collecting this flood of data via a variety of sources, often in near-real time:

- Electronic On Board Recorders (EOBRs) in trucks
- sensors and radio-frequency identification (RF ID) tags in trailers
- RF readers in distribution centres
- handheld devices (smartphones and tablet PCs)
- business-to-business data exchanges.

To help them process and analyse this data, organizations are introducing new software tools to manage otherwise known as 'big data'.

'[The term "big data"] evolved in 2013–14 and describes the volumes of structured, semi-structured and unstructured

data – often derived from online purchasing information – that can be mined for commercial information. Data analysis has a major impact today on the efficiencies of operations and in logistics and supply chain management, significantly lowering costs and creating major efficiencies in terms of the time and resources required in manufacturing and supply systems. Companies need a strategy to handle the data deluge to acquire, organize and analyze this information. This data can equip executives and operations personnel with whole new insights into their customers, operations, and partner networks, helping them make better strategic and real-time decisions that offer real competitive advantage.'

Sundar Swaminathan, Oracle's *Profit* magazine

So technology is now centre-stage in logistics, supply chain management and operations management, just as it has permeated every other area of business – and, again, this has resulted in difficulties in recruitment of technically capable staff.

The Internet of Things (IoT)

The Internet of Things as a concept is now beginning to get a lot of attention as a reality – and it will have quite dramatic effects on stock control and supply chain management.

'The Industrial Internet of Things will transform companies and countries, opening up a new era of economic growth and

competitiveness. We see a future where the intersection of people, data and intelligent machines will have far-reaching impacts on the productivity, efficiency and operations of industries around the world.'

Accenture, www.accenture.com

The IoT has come into being as a result of several factors – the ubiquity today of the Internet, low-cost sensors in all fields, from medical diagnostics to location detection, and fast and reliable data transfer rates.

The IoT is becoming a huge connected network, linking computers and the Internet with intelligent sensors and devices in our homes, workplaces and in every part of our lives. This increasingly sophisticated network of systems will bring more convenience, security and efficiencies into our lives, allowing us to do more with less.. These 'smart' embedded devices will permit the automation of many applications that are manually controlled today:

- simple applications for smart thermostat systems and laundry washer-driers using WiFi for remote monitoring
- advanced applications like smart grids, including heart-monitoring implants and 'wearable' health-monitoring devices
- biochips for animals
- cars equipped with sensors for many new applications (people, street 'furniture', other cars)
- sensors and controls for security, police, fire and search-and-rescue operations.

Far more automation will simplify our lives and make them safer.

IoT will have a significant impact on operations management and will be key element of smarter manufacturing. While manufacturing companies have incorporated sensors and computerized automation into manufacturing systems for a long time now, these have often been disconnected from IT and operational systems. IoT overcomes this gap, enabling items in the physical world, and sensors within or attached to these items, to communicate with the Internet via wireless and wired network connections.

The Internet of Things:

- gathers and transmits data from inanimate objects (e.g. industrial equipment, medical devices)
- gathers and transmits data from living objects (e.g. people, animals and even plants)
- shares this data with software systems and with people, from factory floor workers to plant managers.

New technologies

New technology, more generally, is revolutionizing manufacturing operations, not only as a means of providing administrative support at lower costs, but directly, as a means of making products. Perhaps the most significant of these new technologies is 3D printing, which is now becoming mainstream.

3D printing

3D printing, or 'additive manufacturing', slowly builds up layers of materials to 'print' solid objects according to a digital blueprint or set of instructions in its memory. A new business has even begun to scan people and create perfect miniature statues of them! Building complex products by adding tiny layer by tiny layer of material, rather than cutting out a shape by machining parts by removing metal, these printers can produce detailed and intricate products that are difficult or expensive to create by other means.

It remains to be seen whether 3D printing will constitute a new 'industrial revolution', as some like to claim, but its impacts certainly look set to be profound.

'The invention or the implementation of the assembly line changed the way manufacturing works and 3D printing is going to change the way manufacturing works in the future. When the web took off, it gave us the tool for everybody ... to become a publisher... Well, with 3D printing, we're all able to be manufacturers.'

Doug Angus-Lee, Rapid Prototype Account Manager,
Javelin Technologies, Oakville, Ontario

The list of materials that can be ingested and outputted by 3D printers is growing, some might say into sci-fi territory. The capabilities of 3D printing hardware are evolving rapidly, too. They can build larger components and achieve greater precision and finer resolution at higher speeds and lower costs. Together, these advances have brought the technology to a tipping point – it appears ready to emerge from its niche status and become a viable alternative to conventional manufacturing processes in an increasing number of applications.

Should this happen, the technology would transform manufacturing flexibility – for example, by allowing companies to slash development time, eliminate tooling costs, and simplify production runs – while making it possible to create complex shapes and structures that weren't feasible before. Moreover, additive manufacturing would help companies improve the productivity of materials by eliminating the waste that accrues in traditional (subtractive) manufacturing and would thus spur the formation of a beneficial circular economy.

'The promise of a 3-D printing-based supply chain is simple: additive manufacturing will democratize the manufacturing process.'

Ed Morris, director of NAMII

Globalization

The term 'globalization' in economic or business terms can be applied to three principal phenomena:

1 The integration of national economies as the flow of goods and capital across borders increases
2 The fragmentation of businesses' operations internationally, as they locate each stage of production in the country where it can be done at the least cost. (As we have seen, typically, less skilled activities are sent abroad while more skill-intensive activities are kept at home.)
3 The transmitting of ideas for new products and new ways of making products around the globe.

These have had – and will continue to have – a major impact on organizations' strategies and operations, especially in the liberal economies of the West. In the case of the UK, which has one of the most open economies in the world, these impacts include:

- high levels of foreign direct investment – both inwards and outwards
- rising levels of import penetration
- a speeding-up of the process by which the comparative advantage of an industry alters over time – largely because of the speedier diffusion of new technology
- structural change in industries (e.g. long-term reduction in output and employment in industries such as textiles and other manufacturing sectors)
- a reduction in the UK government's ability to levy business taxes freely – because globalized corporations can move production to countries offering the lowest tax base.

Thus for the UK, as throughout the West, these impacts require both businesses and government to:

- improve the skills and flexibility of the workforce, as human capital becomes ever more crucial as a factor determining long-term economic growth
- invest in high-value goods and services (e.g. in high- and medium-high technology manufacturing and in knowledge-intensive service sectors).

MBA recommended reading list

Jay Heizer and Barry Render, *Operations Management: Sustainability and Supply Chain Management*, 11th edition (Pearson, 2013)

Nigel Slack, Alistair Brandon-Jones and Robert Johnston, *Operations Management*, 7th edition (Pearson, 2013)

Summary

The term 'operations' is often used for the corporate area in businesses responsible for the production of goods or services. This includes all activities to create and deliver products or services, from procuring suppliers and materials to logistics and supply chain management.

There are many changes taking place in international business that are impacting operations management. One powerful force for change is in new technology, which is directly revolutionizing manufacturing operations, not only as a means of providing administrative support at lower costs but directly, as a means of making products. The Internet, too, is yielding vast amounts of data that can be analysed in 'big data' systems for commercial advantage from greater efficiencies.

As globalization and competitive pressures on organizations increase, new product development (NPD) becomes important as a source of competitive advantage.

Fact-check (answers at the back)

1. What does the term 'operations' relate to?
   a) The sales teams' activities in organizations ❑
   b) The corporate area in businesses responsible for the production of goods or services ❑
   c) The ways in which an organization's export strategy is carried out in different countries ❑
   d) It's just another name for 'business activities' ❑

2. Which departments in organizations typically have the greatest concentration of resources, people and assets?
   a) Sales departments ❑
   b) Accounts departments ❑
   c) Human resources departments ❑
   d) Operations departments ❑

3. Why are operations departments frequently viewed as particular sources of competitive advantage?
   a) Because they are low cost ❑
   b) Because they produce the organization's products or services ❑
   c) Because they control the quality of the finished products or services ❑
   d) Because their overtime payments may be cut to allow lower prices ❑

4. What is a significant problem facing operations departments?
   a) Recruitment and retention of skilled people ❑
   b) Obtaining raw materials at the necessary cost to drive profits ❑
   c) Trades union activities that cause disruption in production ❑
   d) Controlling production staff's wages and overtime payments ❑

5. What is 'big data'?
   a) Numerical data using more than three decimal places ❑
   b) Numerical data that exceeds the processing power of an organization's IT department ❑
   c) The flood of near real-time data that businesses are collecting through a variety of sources ❑
   d) More data than a conventional PC can hold ❑

6. In what major way is 'big data' affecting operations and logistics in organizations?
a) By equipping executives and operations personnel with whole new insights into their customers, operations and partner networks, particularly for greater efficiencies in logistics and supply chain management ❏
b) By providing justification for more powerful IT systems ❏
c) By assisting the accounts departments to improve costing systems ❏
d) By increasing the need for training in data analysis techniques ❏

7. Where and how will the most dramatic effects of the Internet of Things (IoT) be felt in operations departments?
a) On the speed of the Internet in organizations ❏
b) On stock control and supply chain management systems in organizations ❏
c) On the cost of downloading data from the Internet ❏
d) By the maintenance staff to keep data recording equipment running ❏

8. What does the term 'additive manufacturing' mean?
a) Making more products than had been asked for by forecasting systems ❏
b) Adding the production flows of different manufacturing processes together ❏
c) Another term for '3D printing' ❏
d) Adding more manufacturing lines to an operations department ❏

9. How may the globalization of production affect operations departments in organizations?
a) By lowering the wages of production workers to the lowest levels around the world ❏
b) By raising the incentive to produce in regions with relatively low-cost access to foreign markets ❏
c) By spreading management practices from the West to other, poorer countries ❏
d) By planning production volumes to match shipping capabilities ❏

10. By what is the power of operations, manufacturing, logistics and supply chain management in operations departments today mostly driven? ❏
a) A better-educated workforce ❏
b) Greater fluency in foreign languages under the pressure of globalization ❏
c) The forces of 'technology plus globalization' ❏
d) The costs of staff wages and overtime payments ❏

CHAPTER 6

Organizational behaviour and human resources management

The importance of organizational behaviour and HR departments and their impacts on communications and efficiencies in the management of businesses receive a lot of attention in MBA degrees and in business schools today.

People, processes and work link organizational behaviour (OB) and HR management (HRM), emphasizing intercultural and cross-cultural perspectives for organizational development, talent management, personal development and leadership. Emotional intelligence (EI) is emphasized increasingly in HR departments and executive boardrooms as a useful skill to increase people's abilities to recognize behaviours, moods and impulses, and to manage them effectively in any situation.

The ability to understand people's emotions and how they may be controlled encourages better management and more effective communications in workplaces.

From Theory X to Theory Y ... and beyond

In 1911 the US mechanical engineer Frederick W. Taylor (1856–1915) published his groundbreaking study *Principles of Scientific Management*, in which he addressed the issue of how to motivate workers to produce more. Taylor argued that workers were primarily motivated by money and accordingly developed a differential piece-rate system for the workplace: those workers who did not meet the expected output received a lesser rate of pay, while those who achieved or exceeded the expected output earned the higher rate. This approach has subsequently become known as **Theory X**, and has been much criticized on account of its rather reductive approach to both motivation and human nature.

Strikingly absent from Taylor's understanding of motivation was the role of group behaviour. This was addressed directly by a new generation of theorists (writing from the 1920s until as late as the 1960s), **human relationists**, who argued that, in addition to money, workers sought respect, fair treatment and attention; they wanted to be wanted.

The Hawthorne Experiments

In the 1920s workplace efficiency researchers observed how lighting affected workers assembling electronic components at Western Electric's Hawthorne plant near Chicago. Results indicated that lighting did not affect production consistently – increasing light increased production, but reducing light also increased production! Workers, it seemed, weren't responding to the change in lighting but to the fact that they were being observed by the researchers – later dubbed the 'Hawthorne Effect'. Management was taking an interest in them and that was enough to increase productivity!

Their studies revealed that a worker's motivation was shaped not only by his or her personality and needs but also by the group to which he or she belonged. While one clique of workers might have developed an ethic of hard work and a sense of responsibility, another might encourage 'clock-watching' and doing only so much work as was required and no more.

The next generation of theorists focused on the role of the manager in improving efficiency and output. Previously, management had been about control; now it was about facilitation by meeting workers' needs. People work to make a living, of course, but they also work to fulfil certain needs, including:

- to contribute to organizational objectives
- to attain a feeling of accomplishment
- to use their creativity in the work environment.

To maximize motivation, managers need to keep the full variety of needs in mind when dealing with workers. This approach has since been termed **Theory Y**, as it so sharply contrasts with Taylor's.

Understanding the particular needs of a particular employee (rather than applying a wholesale theory to a whole team or workforce) is key here.

Self-direction, self-control and effective, two-way communication are all key values in the Theory Y approach.

Most recently of all, theorists have emphasized an all-round, or **'systemic'**, approach to motivation, looking at five main strands or components:

1 The individual – the person in focus
2 The formal organization – in which the person is unquestionably a part
3 The informal organization – the social dimensions to which the individual adheres
4 The fusion process, in which the first three modify and shape one another
5 The physical environment – the place in which the organizational behaviour is exhibited and enacted.

All these work together to determine organizational behaviour. This systemic approach is rooted in the behavioural sciences: psychology (the study of individual behaviour), sociology (the study of social behaviour) and anthropology (the study of the cultural development of human beings).

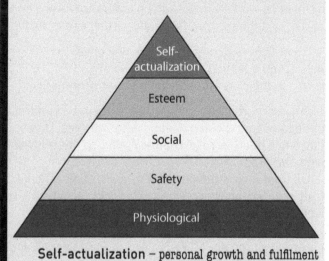

Maslow's hierarchy of needs

The classic tool for understanding employees' varying needs is still Abraham Maslow's 'hierarchy of needs', first outlined in 1943 but given its fullest expression in his book *Motivation and Personality* (1954).

Self-actualization – personal growth and fulfilment

Esteem – achievement, status, responsibility, reputation

Social – belonging and affection needs, family, relationships, groups

Safety – protection, stability, order, security

Physiological – biological and basic life needs, air, food, water, warmth

Organizational behaviour (OB)

Behavioural scientists try to work out why people behave the way they do, both as individuals and in groups. They also investigate the factors that shape personality, including genetic, situational, environmental, cultural and social factors, and analyse personality types, and the relationship between personality traits and the success of a business. Does an authoritarian manager have the effect of getting things done in the face of a crisis or does he or she undermine workers' self-esteem? Generally, experts conclude that a good balance of personality types is useful for an organization but that the more negative aspects of each must be carefully handled. Self-awareness is crucial.

Assessment tools

Personal and personality assessment tools include the Myers-Briggs Type Indicator (MBTI) and the DISC system. DISC is easier to understand and apply than MBTI, less clinical and more memorable for those being assessed.

Researchers have also developed a number of concepts that show how workplace interpersonal relationships can become warped and have a negative impact on business. These include:

- **Stereotyping** – the process of categorizing people based on partial or limited information
- **Halo effect** – the use of known personal traits as the basis for an overall evaluation
- **Projection** – an individual's attribution of his or her own undesirable traits or characteristics to others
- **Groupthink** (see Chapter 3).

Many researchers have suggested ways in which organizations can recast or restructure workplace relationships in order to stimulate maximum job satisfaction and hence productivity. Studies have sought to identify those company cultures that lead to better communication, increased engagement, a reduction in stress, and a better quality of life among employees.

Quality circles – in which teams drawn from every area of a company identify and resolve work-related problems – and **participative management schemes** – in which employees are encouraged to offer, comment on and implement new ideas in the workplace – are two widespread practical models that have arisen from such research.

What is a group?

Perhaps the most basic issue scholars have addressed in the area of group behaviour is the definition of 'group'. They have agreed that there is no one definition. Therefore, they have looked more at why people join groups, types of groups, and group activities and goals. Studies have focused on group norms, individuals' behaviour within groups and how it changes, their roles within groups, and what groups can accomplish that individuals can not. Many researchers believe that a group is more than the sum of the individual members, even though its goals, interactions and performance are determined primarily by the individuals within it.

Theory Z

The US organizational behaviour scientist William Ouchi (1943–) recommends that companies look to Japanese management concepts to enrich management practices. This he dubbed 'Theory Z'. Ouchi believes that using Theory Z reduces employee turnover, increases work commitment, improves morale and job satisfaction and greatly increases productivity. He proposes that organizations should:

- develop strong company philosophies and culture
- set up staff development programmes and long-term employment policies to encourage loyalty
- have policies for consensus in decision-making
- encourage employees to be 'generalists' (but with some specializations)
- show a sincere concern for the happiness and well-being of workers
- have informal management controls in place but alongside formalized assessment measures
- recognize individuals' responsibilities but within the context of a team.

Of course, not all such ideas will be appropriate for every organization. If there is one thing that all researchers have recognized, it is that every company is different, with its own 'personality' and needs.

Key issues in organizational behaviour

Teamwork and collaboration

Many organizations include 'teamwork' and 'collaboration' prominently among their stated values, but what is it that makes people work together well, and, conversely, what can cause collaboration to break down? As we might expect, there is no catch-all answer, but communication styles seem to be crucial.

In modern business, email has become perhaps the primary tool for efficient, speedy and cheap communications. However, there is growing evidence that email, like other 'mechanical' forms of communication, undermines effective collaboration by fostering feelings of mistrust and remoteness. By contrast, face-to-face discussion – although possibly time-consuming – appears to improve teamwork.

Good leadership is vital in fostering effective teamwork.

Leadership vs management

Organizational behaviour scientists have drawn attention to the important and useful distinction between leadership and management:

- **Management** is the process of accomplishing tasks
- **Leadership** is the process of getting things done by influencing other people.

A good manager is not necessarily a good leader, and vice versa.

There are common characteristics shared by leaders – intelligence, dependability and responsibility among them – but otherwise it is hard to pin down exactly what qualities are needed and whether these can be learned or acquired.

Communication

Good, clear and timely communications are critical to the efficient running of any business. The following 'soft skills' are crucial:

- an ability to **listen attentively** to the other party – customers, employees, managers, peers
- an ability to **orchestrate discussion**
- an ability to **negotiate** with the goal of achieving a win/win outcome.

It is important that the links between effective communications in businesses and types of organizational behaviour are recognized.

> *'One lesson from OB is informal communications can be even more important than formal organizational communications. Employees often obtain more information from their direct managers – and even from their co-workers informally through the grapevine — than they do from formal organizational announcements.'*
>
> Brian Kreissl, blog on 'HR Policies and Practice' in the
> *Canadian HR Reporter*, 2011

Power and conflict

According to organizational behaviour scientists, there are five basic types of power that managers and leaders use to influence subordinates. The table shows the advantages and disadvantages of each:

Power type	Definition	Advantage	Disadvantage
Reward	The extent to which managers may use rewards to influence others	Produces quick and easy wins	May tempt unethical behaviour to meet targets

Power type	Definition	Advantage	Disadvantage
Coercive	The opposite of reward power, used by managers to punish subordinates	Leads to short-term and quick obedience (e.g. in the armed forces)	In the longterm, if wielded unintelligently, produces dysfunctional behaviour
Legitimate	Power and authority derived from the manager's position in the organization	Power that is owned by right and easy to deploy	Workers may not feel a sense of commitment or are unwilling to co-operate
Referent	Derives from employees' respect for a manager and wish to emulate that manager	Can be a simple spin-off from good leadership	Difficult to apply in cross-cultural situations and relies on trust
Expert	Derives from respect for an individual's high level of knowledge or highly specialized skills	The superior may not rank higher, formally, than the other people	Expertise diminishes as knowledge is shared

Inexperienced managers often use political tactics to exert influence over others, using stratagems such as:

- blaming others for their own mistakes
- forming 'power coalitions' and 'power bases'
- flattering colleagues who appear to be useful as allies
- using overly threatening behaviour
- developing alliances in subordinates for support.

Unfortunately, such tactics often lead to conflict, another area that is much studied by organizational behaviour scientists.

In any workplace, conflict – both at the individual and group level – is inevitable. The problem is how to deal with such conflict effectively and efficiently, and even to harness it constructively. Solutions might include fostering:

- **mutual problem solving** – this involves subordinates and peers, so as to build trust in teams
- **compromise** – this is not always a good idea but flexibility will overcome barriers

- **avoidance** – if issues and conflicts can be avoided, then do so (though some issues need to be faced down!)
- **displaying honesty and integrity** – this will pay off in the longer-term.

All too often, however – researchers have discovered – conflict resolutions are only temporary and they have sought ways to make them more permanent in order to build or to reinforce positions of authority – often mistakenly!

Managing change

Change management is another major area of OB research, and has become crucial as organizations struggle to adapt and evolve in the face of social and demographic trends, new technologies, economic cycles and regulation, among other things. Key questions include:

- How does change affect people in an organization?
- How can change be managed to maximize its success and minimize unintended disruptions?
- Do we agree on the need for change?

OB scientists distinguish between first-order change – change that is incremental and ongoing – and second-order change – change that is radical and episodic. Both can be disruptive if not handled carefully, but second-order change requires a very safe and skilful pair of hands indeed.

Downsizing

Downsizing is perhaps one of the most potentially disruptive second-order changes a company can undertake and it demands skilful and sensitive change management if it is to be successful. Downsizing affects not only those workers who are laid off but, crucially for the organization, those who remain, who may easily become demoralized, disengaged and mistrustful if they perceive that managers have acted in a high-handed or unfair way. Handled well, however, the remaining workforce can 'rally to the cause', working harder and more collaboratively and in other ways that will ultimately benefit the organization.

Emotional intelligence

Good communications in the workplace are affected by levels of emotional intelligence (EI) demonstrated by staff at all levels in a business. The part played by EI in effective communications and better management practices is increasingly being recognized today. The following quote is indicative in this respect:

'A bright future belongs to those organizations where positive, adaptive, purposeful and empathetic relationships define the quality of care of those they serve. Liberty Lutheran, Ambler, PA [a not-for-profit company that runs hospices], considers staff its most important resource. We continually source and develop dynamic business tools that support our commitment to providing world-class internal customer service to realize a competitive benefit. A well-cared-for staff will not only stay, but will fully engage in the process of nurturing meaningful professional relationships amongst one another and especially, our residents and family members.

We've worked to create a culture defined by open communication, trust and accountability...'

Christopher Ridenhour, for Liberty Lutheran, 'Bringing Emotional Intelligence to Staff Training', *Leading Age Magazine*, March/April 2014

The concept of emotional intelligence is hardly new, but it was only in the 1990s that it became the subject of serious academic research. Two of its pioneering theorists, US psychologists John D. Mayer and Peter Salovey, defined it as 'the subset of social intelligence that involves the ability to monitor one's own and others' feelings and emotions, to discriminate among them and to use this information to guide one's thinking and actions'. Another key theorist was Daniel Goleman, whose seminal work *Emotional Intelligence: Why It Can Matter More Than IQ* (1995) continues to dominate this field today.

EI allows difficult and sensitive situations in the workplace to be resolved more readily and satisfactorily for the longer term.

> **'The willingness to admit your weaknesses and your vulnerabilities is actually very powerful. You can gain strength by admitting your faults to yourself and your peers. When you admit it, you make it a part of what we share as information about ourselves. It makes it okay for me to bring it up, which is crucial for working through conflict. You can even joke about it to ease tension. "You're doing that thing again."'**
>
> Daniel Goleman, 'Finding Strength in Admitting Your Weakness', March 2015

MBA recommended reading list

Travis Bradberry, *Emotional Intelligence 2.0* (TalentSmart, 2009)

Jill Dann, *Emotional Intelligence In A Week* (John Murray Learning, 2016)

Daniel Goleman, *Emotional Intelligence: Why It Can Matter More Than IQ* (Bloomsbury, 1996)

Daniel Goleman, *Working with Emotional Intelligence* (Bloomsbury, 1999)

Laurie J. Mullins, *Management and Organisational Behaviour* (FT Publishing International, 2013)

Summary

Organizational behavioural studies in areas such as individual behaviours, group behaviours, organizational structures and organizational processes help to describe and predict how workers will behave in organized environments. They investigate motivation and job satisfaction in organizations in order to understand the relationship between motivation, reward and improved productivity in the workplace.

Change and conflict management and emotional intelligence are critical subjects in today's Human Resources departments, and indeed in every part and at every level of organizations. Emotional intelligence, for example, assists the management of people by encouraging managers' abilities to recognize behaviours, moods and impulses and to manage people effectively in any situation.

The ability to understand people's emotions and how they may be controlled encourages better management and more effective communications in workplaces.

Fact-check (answers at the back)

1. What is 'organizational behaviour'?
   a) The study of how to control teams of workers ❏
   b) The encouragement of better manners in working groups ❏
   c) An academic discipline that describes and predicts workers' behaviours in organized group environments ❏
   d) The study of how to get the most from working in groups ❏

2. What are the formal links between studies in 'organizational behaviour' and the discipline of HR management?
   a) Legally – by laws ❏
   b) People, processes and work ❏
   c) Trades unions' rules ❏
   d) Because understanding behaviours encourages better working practices ❏

3. In which decade did emotional intelligence (EI) finally gain prominence and recognition in management studies?
   a) In the 1930s ❏
   b) In the 1950s ❏
   c) In the 1970s ❏
   d) In the 1990s ❏

4. What was the breakthrough idea of F. W. Taylor concerning workers' motivation and productivity?
   a) The creation of team leaders ❏
   b) The introduction of trades unions' shop stewards ❏
   c) To use systems of planning and rewards to increase workers' levels of motivation and productivity ❏
   d) The suggestion that only more money works effectively as a workplace reward ❏

5. What or who are 'human relationists'?
   a) People whose ideas on workers' levels of motivation include giving workers more personal and individual attention ❏
   b) Scientists who try to find relational links between workers ❏
   c) HR staff who specialize in tracking down family relationships in organizations ❏
   d) People who recommend employing relatives in businesses ❏

6. What were the 'Hawthorne Experiments'?
a) Experiments in horticulture in the workplace ❏
b) Experiments designed to show how workers' performances are affected by changes to working environments ❏
c) Attempts to create productivity efficiencies for their own sake ❏
d) Psychological experiments designed to achieve improvements to working efficiencies ❏

7. What are 'quality circles'?
a) Groups of workers taking tea breaks in their working areas ❏
b) Circles of workers formed by managers to speak to them in their workplaces ❏
c) Team-based approaches to identifying and resolving work-related problems ❏
d) Games to encourage fitness and to relieve boredom in the workplace ❏

8. What is the 'halo effect'?
a) An award for good operations management ❏
b) An award for the best workers ❏
c) A form of cognitive bias in which an impression of a someone or thing is skewed by their appearance or the environment around them to give a false impression ❏
d) How someone with an extrovert personality can rise in management circles ❏

9. How do behavioural scientists differentiate between managers and leaders?
a) Managers discipline workers but leaders only reward them ❏
b) Managers complete tasks through people but leaders inspire and influence people to achieve ❏
c) Leaders are not usually visible to workers but managers are constantly seen in the workplace ❏
d) Leaders are paid more than managers ❏

10. Why should emotional intelligence be fostered in the workplace?
a) To gain information about workers' private lives ❏
b) To allow individuals to monitor their own and others' feelings and emotions to better guide their decisions, activities and communications ❏
c) To prevent or reduce the likelihood of emotions getting out of control in the workplace ❏
d) To help workers become more intelligent ❏

CHAPTER 7

Research
and change
management

By a combination of sensitively applied quantitative and qualitative research conducted with an organization's employees, management, suppliers, customers – both past and present – and all key stakeholders, a clear understanding of where the business is today can be obtained as a solid foundation from which to determine the change-management process for the future.

Research programmes form critical elements of change-management processes for people and for organizations. Research is the vital first step to understand how people are behaving today, how they feel about their work and its objectives – and then how they might react to changes in working directions and methods.

Rooted in that research, change management – a vital component of all MBA programmes – tries to realign people and organizations to perform more effectively by working in new ways.

Using research

Both quantitative and qualitative research are commonly used in management consulting to provide an initial, reliable picture of an organization's situation. By using one or, preferably, both of these research methods, a consultant can then begin to form opinions about the best ways to effect change, to achieve a much-improved future position for that organization.

Quantitative research

Quantitative research relies primarily on numerical data as the main subject of analysis. Its most typical tool is the **questionnaire survey**, which uses a series of closed questions to gather large quantities of data from a wide number of people, the results of which can then be analysed by computer. Questionnaires can be handed out and then collected face to face, sent by post or, as is becoming increasingly common, posted online.

Generally speaking, however, the more personal the contact between the researcher and the potential respondent, the higher the response rate. Thus, online surveys have a response rate of less than 20 per cent, while for face-to-face surveys this figure is usually a great deal higher.

Primarily, quantitative research is used because it is statistically more valid and thus more reliable and objective and often reduces and restructures a complex problem to a more limited number of variables. Under controlled circumstances, it can be used to test theories and hypotheses and establish cause and effect, thus providing important information for business decisions. However, it is less detailed than qualitative research data and a desired, particular response from the participant may be missed.

Qualitative research

Typically, qualitative research provides much more in-depth information about people's reactions, feelings, perceptions and decision-making processes. It relies on words rather than numerical data. The classical instrument of qualitative research is the **focus group**, although the **one-to-one interview** is also common. The results of qualitative research, based on a relatively small group, are used to represent the whole demographic being researched.

Because qualitative research is extremely labour-intensive, it tends to be small scale. Focus groups require highly trained conveners, and responses and interviews need to be transcribed and the results analysed by researchers, ideally different from those who conducted the focus group or interview. Nonetheless, the ultimate result of qualitative research is incomparably richer and more meaningful.

Qualitative research is used typically in circumstances in which valuable data for the design of a new product or service is required, including subjective information on behaviour patterns and users' needs. It can provide subjective information on emotions and personality characteristics that quantitative studies cannot achieve and a variety of information essential to design a product or service to fit into users' lives.

This table summarizes the advantages and disadvantages of each method:

Research method	Advantages	Disadvantages
Quantitative	• Statistical data from large samples • More reliable • Yields important information for business decisions	• Less detailed than qualitative research data • A desired, particular response may be missed
Qualitative	• Provides subjective information on behaviour patterns and users' needs • Gathers essential information to design a new product or service to fit into users' lives	• Does not have a valid statistical base • Results may be skewed by interviewer's bias • The constituents in the sample must be chosen very carefully

Change management

The subject of change management is much used in management consulting. In simple terms, it means understanding:

- where an organization is today
- where it wants to be in the future
- how to move it most effectively to where it should be by changing organizational procedures and behaviours and also those of individuals.

In 1996 the Harvard professor John Kotter published the best-selling *Leading Change* – a seminal study of change management.

John Kotter

Dr John P. Kotter is widely regarded as the foremost writer, speaker and authority on the subjects of leadership and change management – how the best organizations achieve successful change. As Harvard Business School's Konosuke Matsushita Professor of Leadership, Emeritus, Kotter's intellectual dominance of successful change management and leadership are well proven. He created and co-founded Kotter International, helping Global 5000 company leaders to lead change in complex and large-scale businesses.

Since then, hundreds of articles and books have been published on the subject and most have agreed on what constitutes the building blocks of a successful programme. There must be:

1 a **compelling story** – employees must see the point of the change and agree with it
2 **role modelling** – employees must also see the CEO and managers adopting the new desired behaviour
3 **reinforcing mechanisms** – systems, processes and incentives must align with the new behaviour
4 **capability building** – employees must acquire the skills needed to make the desired changes.

For all that change management plays a central role in business, and for all that it has become a subject of study in almost every leading MBA course, it is still all too often poorly conducted. In *Leading Change*, back in 1996, Dr Kotter pointed out that only 30 per cent of change programmes succeeded; more than a decade later, in 2008, a McKinsey survey of 3,199 executives around the world found that the success rate was just the same – one in three. Clearly, much more work needs to be done.

One diagnosis of this problem is that, while the four principles outlined above are clearly common sense, the managers who implement them all too often fail to take into account the realities of human nature, which is not always rational. Individuals' behaviours are deeply entrenched and changing them – *permanently* – is challenging.

> *'Leaders must understand and apply the knowledge of behavioural psychology to manage organizational change successfully. In the past, efforts at organizational change have systematically failed because they have neglected the reality that change doesn't happen without individual people changing their thinking, beliefs, and behaviour. In the article by Emily Lawson and Colin Price they argue that change management success, in large organizations, depends on groups and individuals changing the way they function... In effect, management must alter the mind-sets of their employees – no easy task.'*
>
> Ray Williams, 'Why Change Management Fails in Organizations'

There is also evidence to suggest that managers all too often assume that employees are motivated only by money (see Chapter 6) and use this to underpin their change management programmes.

David Rock, a leadership consultant and author of *Quiet Leadership: Six Steps to Transforming Leadership at Work*, and Jeffrey Schwartz, a research scientist at UCLA, apply neuroscience concepts to leadership and have coined the term 'neuroleadership':

> *'The traditional command-and-control style of management doesn't lead to permanent changes in behavior. Ordering people to change and them telling them how to do it fires the prefrontal cortex's hair trigger connection to the amygdala. The more you try to convince people that you're right and they're wrong, the more they push back. The brain will try to defend itself from threats.'*
>
> David Rock and Jeffrey Shwartz, 'The Neuroscience of Leadership',
> in *Strategy + Business* (2006)

Case study: Accenture's 'journey management'

Although really focused on large change programmes involving information technology, Accenture, one of the world's leading organizations providing management consulting, technology and outsourcing services, has a concept of 'journey management', developed in 2013, which has wide and general implications for all forms of organizational change. For Accenture, a typical 'journey of change' should be managed in five phases:

1 Assess the current environment and drivers for change – a detailed and fact-based assessment of the current state leads to a deeper understanding of why change needs to be undertaken.
2 Articulate a compelling description of the future state and vision of the organization – leaders responsible for managing a change journey should agree on what the future state of the organization will be – with tangible business outcomes.
3 Assess the gap between current and desired future state – assessments of the functions affected by the change journey, effectiveness of existing talent strategies, relevance of current leadership development programmes, the culture of the organization and more.
4 Create a journey road map to plan and prioritize activities – detail multiple initiatives within the change portfolio and integration points, and prioritize them according to impact and ability of the organization to absorb the changes.
5 Proactively monitor the journey and change portfolio to keep the organization on track – move beyond traditional programme management so that multiple strands of work can be coordinated effectively.

It is worth emphasizing here that Accenture's journey begins with a careful, in-depth assessment of 'why change needs to be undertaken' and takes us back to the research methodology with which we began this chapter – that the application of good research techniques reduces the likelihood of failure in change management projects right from the outset.

Flexibility

Flexibility is critical in the implementation of research results because there is always the temptation to delay putting recommendations into practice until there is very clear evidence that it will be successful. The champion of the research project will usually bear the responsibility for any failures! So pragmatism and flexibility in the interpretation and implementation of results are often critical to success.

MBA recommended reading list

Mike Bourne and Pippa Bourne, *Change Management In A Week* (John Murray Learning, 2016)

Esther Cameron and Mike Green, *Making Sense of Change Management: A Complete Guide to the Models, Tools and Techniques of Organizational Change* (Kogan Page, 2015)

John P. Kotter, *Leading Change*, new edition (Harvard Business Review Press, 2012)

Michael D. Myers, *Qualitative Research in Business and Management*, 2nd edition (SAGE Publications, 2013)

Richard Smith et al. (eds), *The Effective Change Manager's Handbook: Essential Guidance to the Change Management Body of Knowledge* (Kogan Page, 2014)

Summary

By the careful and thoughtful application of suitable research techniques, managers can achieve a clear understanding of where their business is today as a solid foundation for a new future. The changes required can be defined for the organization's management in the consultants' report but the actual changes required, over time, take a lot of management attention and constant effort to keep the implementation of those changes on track. Qualitative and quantitative research techniques may show the way but the hardest tasks often lie in the determined implementation of the changes, while allowing for a degree of flexibility as unexpected roadblocks occur.

Fact-check (answers at the back)

1. What is quantitative research?
   a) Research conducted in quantum physics ❏
   b) Research conducted with a numerically large sample base ❏
   c) Research conducted in small quantities ❏
   d) Research by quantity surveyors ❏

2. What is qualitative research?
   a) Finding out how suitable job applicants are ❏
   b) Small individual or group discussions to discover how people react to certain, often complex, situations and subjects ❏
   c) Trying to understand how quality control systems work best ❏
   d) Marketing research into what drives quality in brands ❏

3. What are focus groups?
   a) Study groups used to help short-sighted people to read better ❏
   b) Workplace groups set up to advise management on problems on which to focus ❏
   c) A research method commonly used in qualitative research ❏
   d) Groups of people with a common interest or background ❏

4. Why does qualitative research tend to be small scale?
   a) Because it uses only a few people in its implementation ❏
   b) Because the use of too many people obscures the results ❏
   c) Because it is hugely labour-intensive ❏
   d) Because it is conducted using discussions in controllable groups ❏

5. What does the term 'triangulation' mean in research terms?
   a) Using just three groups of people in the research programme ❏
   b) Bringing a number of research methods to bear upon a question ❏
   c) A simple research technique that uses just three main questions ❏
   d) Checking the research results at least three times ❏

6. What is change management?
   a) An employee recruitment technique ❏
   b) A strategy to deliberately confuse competitors by suddenly changing business direction ❏
   c) Managing a longer-term change for an organization to a new defined future ❏
   d) Recruiting a new management team to replace those currently in place ❏

7. Change management is best achieved by which of the following?
a) Authoritarian management ❏
b) Understanding where an organization is today, where it wants to be, and how to move it most effectively to where it should be in the future ❏
c) Issuing new procedures in writing to all employees ❏
d) Inviting the trades unions in the workplace to create change ❏

8. John Kotter's seminal work on change programmes found that...
a) 85 per cent of change management programmes succeed ❏
b) 30 per cent of change programmes fail ❏
c) Change programmes never succeed for very long ❏
d) 30 per cent of change programmes succeed ❏

9. The principal successful motivation in changing employees' behaviours has been shown to be...
a) Financial rewards ❏
b) Paid vacations ❏
c) A diversity of factors including a personal interest in their jobs and a good working environment ❏
d) Threats to workers' employment contracts ❏

10. How is organizational change effected?
a) By changing organizational procedures and behaviours and also those of individuals ❏
b) Only with the support of the trades unions ❏
c) Only over a very long period of time ❏
d) By the use of firm managerial authority ❏

7 × 7

1 Seven key ideas

- Limited liability – this concept, intended to protect either creditors or investors, is crucial to much company law.
- Chief financial officers today grasp advantage and lead growth in conditions of increasing volatility and uncertainty in the global economy by implementing research and strategic planning.
- Ethics and morals in business life help make the best decisions for the longer term in fast-moving and complex entrepreneurial environments.
- Strategic planning, allied with marketing, is concerned with the overall direction of the business, making decisions about production and operations, finance, human resources and all business issues.
- Increased competitive advantage can be gained by giving customers more options and power in commercial engagements, as Internet trading has proved.
- Emotional intelligence (EI) encourages better management and more effective communications in workplaces.
- Professionally applied change-management processes move organizations quickly and effectively towards better futures.

2 Seven resources

- Keep daily tabs on the forces acting on the world and business at the BBC website: www.bbc.co.uk/news/business
- Maintain an up-to-date understanding of global economies and their pressures and challenges by subscribing to *The Economist*: www.economist.com/

- A good guide to how and why businesses should follow ethical principles is 'Business Ethics and Social Responsibility' from the Free Management Library: managementhelp.org/businessethics/index.htm

- A world-leading resource on marketing management and strategic planning is the Chartered Management Institute's research page: http://www.managers.org.uk/insights/research

- A key resource on the critical relationships between customers, marketing and operations management is provided by the Institute of Operations Management at: https://ciltuk.org.uk/About-Us/Professional-Sectors-Forums/Sectors/Operations-Management

- The Chartered Institute of Personnel and Development carries out research for effective communications: www.cipd.co.uk/research/

- Quantitative and qualitative research techniques are explored further by the Department of Sociology at the University of Warwick (UK): www2.warwick.ac.uk/fac/soc/sociology/staff/academicstaff/hughes/researchprocess/

3 Seven great companies

- Amazon is a paradox: a company known for making virtually no profits despite strong revenues and a sizeable market share. CEO Jeff Bezos is now betting on a new technological trend – the Internet of Things – as the next big thing as Amazon continues to ride global pressures, shifts and trends.

- Ernst & Young Global Limited (EY) is the world's 'most globally integrated professional services organization'. Its motto, 'When business works better, the world works better', should be on the desk of every CEO.

- Coca-Cola provides a good example of a global organization's approach to corporate responsibility and business ethics: www.coca-colacompany.com/our-company/governance-ethics/governance-ethics

- Dyson, a great engineering and strategic company, has set a leading example in championing engineering education systems in the UK.
- Apple's new product development process always starts with design and continues into its 'Apple New Product Process' that ensures the right product emerges at the right time.
- Intel's 'Materials Communications Strategy' delivers communications that are timely, accurate and effective.
- British Airways (BA) was failing customers and shareholders but introduced a change-management process for the future and is today a well-managed and successful company.

4 Seven inspiring people

- Lee Kwan Yew (1923–2015), the founding father of independent Singapore, inspired even China's leaders to manage their citizens in new ways in times of dramatic social and political change
- Tim Cook (1960–), Apple's CEO, has put his own imprint on the company, with his own set of values and priorities, showing inspiring leadership.
- Mahatma Gandhi (1869–38), the inspiring leader who fought for the independence of India, believed that life could not be compartmentalized and that all actions are interrelated. A good lesson for business.
- H. Igor Ansoff (1918–2002), 'the father of strategic management', was a Russian-American applied mathematician and business manager, perhaps best known by marketing and MBA students for his 'Product–Market Growth Matrix'.
- Carolyn McCall (1961–) joined EasyJet as CEO in 2010 and led the company to record performances and was awarded an OBE for inspirational services to women in business.

- Michelle Obama (1964–) is an inspirational communicator and uses emotional intelligence to appear confident, likeable and authentic.
- The UK's Royal Mail is a must-cover case study for MBA business students. CEO Moya Greene (1954–) was named as Financial Times Person of the Year in 2014 and is an inspirational leader managing change in a large organization.

5 Seven great quotes on change

- 'Business is like a man rowing a boat upstream. He has no choice; he must go ahead or he will go back.' Lewis E. Pierson
- 'Only the wisest and stupidest of men never change.' Confucius
- 'There is nothing more difficult to take in hand, more perilous to conduct, or more uncertain in its success, than to take the lead in the introduction of a new order of things.' Niccolò Machiavelli, *The Prince* (1532)
- 'The rate of change is not going to slow down anytime soon. If anything, competition in most industries will probably speed up even more in the next few decades.' John P. Kotter in *Leading Change* (1996)
- 'We would rather be ruined than changed,
  We would rather die in our dread
  Than climb the cross of the moment
  And let our illusions die.'

  W.H. Auden, *The Age of Anxiety: A Baroque Eclogue* (1947)

- 'Everybody has accepted by now that change is unavoidable. But that still implies that change is like death and taxes – it should be postponed as long as possible and no change would be vastly preferable. But in a period of upheaval, such as the one we are living in, change is the norm.' Peter Drucker in *Management Challenges for the 21st Century* (1999)
- 'It's not the progress I mind, it's the change I don't like.' Mark Twain

6 Seven top executive MBA courses in 2015 (according to *The Economist*)

- IE Business School, Spain
- University of Oxford, Saïd Business School, UK
- Northwestern University, Kellogg School of Management, USA
- UCLA/NUS Business School, USA/Singapore
- Northwestern (Kellogg) / York (Schulich), USA/Canada
- Northwestern (Kellogg) / WHU (Beisheim), USA/Germany
- Thunderbird School of Global Management, USA

7 Seven trends for tomorrow

- New investment trends such as crowd-funding are bringing new innovations to markets faster...
- The emergence of China and India as global powers will reshape the world and everyone's lives...
- Augmented Virtual Reality and the 'Internet of Things' will affect future employment...
- Cyber security and crime-related technology are limiting the exchange of knowledge...
- New materials will create great changes in transportation and energy use...
- Global greenhouse gas emissions may have peaked (Energy World, April 2015) – can we relax?
- Disadvantaged young men in the rich world are falling behind in jobs, social lives and relationships...

PART 2

Your Finance for Non-Financial Managers Masterclass

Introduction

Depending on how far you are willing to stretch the definition, there are well over two million non-financial managers in the UK, with considerably more in other countries. Many of them would like to know more about finance, and the knowledge would help them do their jobs and progress in their careers.

A basic understanding of finance is very relevant to our personal lives. It is also important to virtually all managers and supervisors, both junior and senior. This has always been so and its significance has considerably increased in recent years.

Some managers have been financially trained but many more wish to increase their level of understanding. Doing so will enable them to become more effective and improve their scope for development and promotion.

CHAPTER 8

An introduction to the Profit Statement

Nearly all private sector businesses are conducted in the hope of making a profit, though of course not all succeed in doing so. Profits and losses, which perhaps should be called surpluses and deficits, are also important to large parts of the public sector and to such bodies as charities and membership organizations. There is of course much more to it, but many managers would say that the point of bookkeeping and accounting is to find out the amount of the profit or loss.

The Profit Statement is important and an introduction to it is a very good way of starting this part of the book. More advanced published accounts are explained in Chapter 10, but first we will study an internal document produced for managers.

We will work through:

- a simple example
- a trading company
- a manufacturing company
- some further concepts
- preparing a full example.

A simple example

The heading 'Profit Statement' may be optimistic because it implies that a profit has been made. In some cases it would be more appropriate to call it a 'Loss Statement'.

Profit Statement is the name often given to an internal document setting out the trading activity and results. It is sometimes called the Profit and Loss Account or Income Statement and these are the titles used in the more formal published accounts.

Understanding the principles of the Profit Statement is the first step towards using it to improve future performance. This is covered later in this part but as a first step we will consider a simple example.

Julia Brown writes a book. Her agreement does not provide for royalties, just a fee of £5,000 payable on delivery of the manuscript to the publisher. The costs of the enterprise are small and she pays them in cash as she goes. After receipt of the £5,000 her Profit Statement may well look like the following:

	£	£
Income		5,000
Less Costs:		
Typing costs	600	
Stationery	100	
Travel	200	
Postage	30	
Telephone	40	
Miscellaneous	120	
		1,090
Net Profit before Tax		3,910

The profit (or loss) is the difference between money received and all the money paid out. Julia Brown may need the Profit Statement for her bank and for Her Majesty's Revenue and Customs (HMRC). She may use the information herself. For example, if she has spent 391 hours working on the book her time has been rewarded at the rate of £10 per hour.

A trading company

Numerous very small businesses do prepare simple Profit Statements in the manner of the previous example. However, there is another step when things are bought and sold.

It is essential that the costs shown in the Profit Statement relate only to goods sold during the period. All Profit Statements cover a defined period with a specified starting date and a specified closing date. For published accounts this period is often a year but for internal documents it can be whatever period is considered most useful.

Many businesses produce quarterly Profit Statements, but it may be desirable to produce them monthly or even weekly. Some intensively managed retailers, such as Tesco and Asda, produce key profit information on a daily basis. They withdraw items and change displays according to the results shown.

A distorted result will be given if costs include articles purchased (and paid for) but still in stock at the end of the period. This is overcome by counting stock at the beginning and end of the period. The cost of sales is calculated by adding purchases to the opening stock, then subtracting the closing stock.

If there has been any theft or other form of stock shrinkage, the cost of sales will be increased accordingly.

Sometimes the calculation as far as gross profit is shown in a separate trading account. However, the following simple example shows everything in one Profit Statement.

A Borough Council leisure centre operates a bar and prepares monthly Profit Statements. Sales in the month of July were £30,000 and purchases in the same month were £20,000.

Stock of food and drink at 30 June was £10,000 and at 31 July it was £9,000. Wages were £4,000, insurance was £1,500, and the total of all other overheads was £3,000.

The Profit Statement for July was as follows:

	£	£
Sales		30,000
Stock at 30 June	10,000	
Purchases	20,000	
	30,000	
Less stock at 31 July	9,000	
		21,000
Gross Profit		9,000
Less Overheads:		
Wages	4,000	
Insurance	1,500	
All other	3,000	
		8,500
Net Profit		500

A manufacturing company

It is only a small step to set out the Profit Statement of a manufacturing company. It is essential that the cost of manufacturing must exactly relate to the goods sold. The cost of these goods, no more and no less, must be brought into the Profit Statement.

Probably, stocktakes will be necessary at the beginning and end of the period. However, according to circumstances, this may not be necessary. If internal controls are good a calculated stock figure may sometimes be used, though the results are never quite so accurate or dependable. It is most likely to be done when the results are produced very quickly.

The following example shows the principles. Sometimes the manufacturing costs are shown in a separate manufacturing account but in this straightforward example they are included in the Profit Statement.

Chiltern Manufacturing Company Ltd manufactures and sells household goods. Sales in the year to 31 December 2017 were

£750,000. Purchases of raw materials and components in the year were £300,000. Stock at 31 December 2016 was £280,000 and at 31 December 2017 it was £320,000.

Wages of production staff were £200,000, power costs were £60,000 and other production costs were £80,000. Salaries of salesmen, administration staff and management totalled £70,000 and other overheads totalled £85,000.

The Profit Statement for the year to 31 December 2017 is as follows:

	£	£
Sales		750,000
Stock at 31.12.16	280,000	
Purchases	300,000	
	580,000	
Less stock at 31.12.17	320,000	
	260,000	
Production wages	200,000	
Power costs	60,000	
Other production costs	80,000	
Cost of Manufacturing		600,000
		150,000
Less Overheads:		
Salaries	70,000	
Other overheads	85,000	
		155,000
Net Loss before Tax		(5,000)

(Note that the brackets indicate a minus figure.)

Key points so far

● There are definite starting and finishing dates.
● Total Sales appears at the top.
● Profit or Loss appears at the bottom.
● Only expenditure on goods actually sold is included.

Some further concepts

All the examples so far have been extremely simple but unfortunately real life is often more complicated. It is necessary to be familiar with certain further principles that are likely to be incorporated into many Profit Statements.

Accruals (costs not yet entered)

Examples so far have assumed that all costs are paid out as they are incurred, but this is unrealistic. Invoices are submitted after the event and some will not have been entered into the books when they are closed off.

This problem is overcome by adding in an allowance for these costs. The uninvoiced costs are called accruals.

Let us take as an example a company whose electricity bill is around £18,000 per quarter. Let us further assume that accounts are made up to 31 December and that the last electricity bill was up to 30 November. The accountant will accrue £6,000 for electricity used but not billed.

If electricity invoices in the period total £60,000 the added £6,000 will result in £66,000 being shown in the Profit Statement.

Prepayments (costs entered in advance)

A prepayment is the exact opposite of an accrual. Costs may have been entered into the books for items where the benefit has not yet been received. An example is an invoice for production materials delivered after stocktaking.

Consider an insurance premium of £12,000 paid on 1 December for 12 months' cover in advance. If the Profit Statement is made up to 31 December the costs will have been overstated by $\frac{11}{12}$ x £12,000 = £11,000. The accountant will reduce the costs accordingly. These reductions are called prepayments.

Bad debt reserves and sales ledger reserves

Many businesses sell on credit, and at the end of the period of the Profit Statement money will be owed by customers.

Unfortunately not all of this money will necessarily be received. Among the possible reasons are:

- bad debts
- an agreement that customers may deduct a settlement discount if payment is made by a certain date
- the customers may claim that there were shortages, or that they received faulty goods; perhaps goods were supplied on a sale-or-return basis.

The prudent accountant will make reserves to cover these eventualities, either a bad debt reserve or sales ledger reserve. Sales (and profit) will be reduced by an appropriate amount.

Time will tell whether the reserves have been fixed at a level that was too high, too low, or just right. If the reserves were too cautious there will be an extra profit to bring into a later Profit Statement. If the reserves were not cautious enough there will be a further cost (and loss) to bring into a later Profit Statement.

Depreciation

Fixed assets are those that will have a useful and productive life longer than the period of the Profit Statement. Examples are factory machinery, computers, motor vehicles and so on.

It would obviously be wrong to charge all the costs of fixed assets to the Profit Statement in the year of purchase. The problem is overcome by charging only a proportion in each year of the expected useful life of the asset.

There are different methods of doing this calculation but the simplest, and most common, is the straight-line method. For example, let us consider an item of equipment costing £300,000 with an expected useful life of five years. The Profit Statement for each year would be charged with £60,000.

This is one of many examples of how profit accounting may differ from the equivalent position in cash. It is quite possible to be profitable and still run out of cash. This will be examined later.

Prudence and the matching of costs to income

Earlier it was explained that costs must be fairly matched to sales. This is so that the costs of the goods actually sold, and only those costs, are brought into the Profit Statement. This is very important, and sometimes very difficult to achieve.

Consider a major building project lasting four years and for which the contractor will be paid £60,000,000. Costs over the four years are expected to be £55,000,000 and the anticipated profit is £5,000,000. Almost certainly the contractor will receive various stage payments over the four years.

This poses a multitude of accounting problems and there is more than one accounting treatment. The aim must be to bring in both revenue and costs strictly as they are earned and incurred. Accounting standards provide firm rules for the published accounts.

The full £60,000,000 will not be credited until the work is complete. In fact there will probably be a retention and it will be necessary to make a reserve for retention work. The final cost and profit may not be known for some years.

Conventions of prudent accounting should ensure that profits are only recognized when they have clearly been earned. Losses on the other hand should be recognized as soon as they can be realistically foreseen. Failure to act on this convention has led to scandals and nasty surprises for investors, the collapse of Enron being just one example.

Before leaving this section, tick off the following boxes to confirm that you understand the principles.

- Accruals are costs incurred, but not yet in the books. ❏
- Prepayments are costs in the books, but not yet incurred. ❏
- Profit is reduced by expected bad debts. ❏
- Depreciation is a book entry to reduce the value of fixed assets. ❏
- Profit accounting may differ from cash accounting. ❏
- Profit Statements should be prudent. ❏
- Costs must be matched to income. ❏

Preparing a full example

Here is a slightly more advanced example incorporating the points covered so far.

J. T. Perkins and Son Ltd manufactures and sells pottery. Sales in the year to 31 December 2017 were £800,000. At 31 December 2017 the company expects to issue a credit note for £10,000 for faulty goods that have been delivered. It also believes that £30,000 owing to it will turn out to be a total bad debt. No such expectations existed at 31 December 2016.

Invoices received for parts and raw materials delivered during the year totalled £240,000, but a £20,000 invoice is awaited for a delivery received on 22 December.

Stock at 31 December 2016 was £308,000. Stock at 31 December 2017 was £302,000.

Manufacturing wages were £150,000 and other manufacturing costs were £60,000. Plant and machinery used for manufacturing originally cost £900,000 and is being depreciated at the rate of 10 per cent per year.

Overheads paid have been:

Salaries	*£80,000*
Rent	*£70,000*
Insurance	*£60,000*
Other	*£50,000*

Insurance includes a premium of £7,000 for a year in advance paid on 31 December 2017.

J. T. Perkins and Son Ltd

Profit Statement for the year to 31 December 2017

	£	£
Sales		790,000
Stock at 31.12.16	308,000	
Add purchases	260,000	
	568,000	
Less stock at 31.12.17	302,000	
	266,000	
Wages	150,000	
Depreciation of plant and machinery	90,000	
Other manufacturing costs	60,000	
Cost of Sales		566,000
Gross Profit		224,000
Less Overheads:		
Salaries	80,000	
Rent	70,000	
Insurance	53,000	
Other	50,000	
Reserve for bad debts	30,000	
		283,000
Net Loss before Tax		(59,000)

Summary

In this chapter we have been introduced to the basic principles of the following:

- Simple Profit Statements
- Trading companies
- Manufacturing companies
- Accruals and prepayments
- Bad debt reserves and sales ledger reserves
- Depreciation
- Prudence and the matching of costs to income
- An example illustrating most of the principles

Next, we will take a look at Balance Sheets.

Fact-check (answers at the back)

1. To what is the term 'Profit Statement' given?
   a) A published Profit and Loss Account ☐
   b) An internal document setting out the trading activity and results ☐
   c) A statement for the tax authorities ☐
   d) A statement for the shareholders ☐

2. In a Profit Statement, where is the figure for income usually placed?
   a) At the top ☐
   b) At the bottom ☐
   c) On the left ☐
   d) On the right ☐

3. In the Profit Statement of a trading company, to what must the figure for Cost of Sales relate?
   a) Goods stored in the period ☐
   b) Goods purchased in the period ☐
   c) Goods paid for in the period ☐
   d) Goods sold in the period ☐

4. If goods for sale are stolen, how will the Cost of Sales in the Profit Statement be affected?
   a) It will increase ☐
   b) It will decrease ☐
   c) It will not be affected ☐
   d) It will be estimated ☐

5. Which stock figures appear in the Profit Statement of a manufacturing company?
   a) None ☐
   b) Figures for the beginning and end of the period ☐
   c) The figure for the beginning of the period ☐
   d) The figure for the end of the period ☐

6. The telephone bill is usually about £3,000 per quarter. The last invoice received was for the quarter to 31 May. What should be the accrual for the three months to 30 June?
   a) £3,000 ☐
   b) Nothing ☐
   c) £1,000 ☐
   d) £2,000 ☐

7. On 29 December rent of £6,000 was paid in advance for the quarter to the following 31 March. What should be the prepayment for the three months to 31 December?
   a) Nothing ☐
   b) £6,000 ☐
   c) £1,000 ☐
   d) £3,000 ☐

8. The Profit Statement for the month of December included a bad debt reserve of £10,000 in respect of money owed by Smith Ltd. On 17 January Smith Ltd paid in full. What is the effect on the Profit Statement for January?
   a) There is no effect ❏
   b) A contribution to profit of £5,000 ❏
   c) A contribution to profit of £20,000 ❏
   d) A contribution to profit of £10,000 ❏

9. A company buys a car for £40,000 and using the straight-line method depreciates it over four years. What is the depreciation charge in the Profit Statement in the second year?
   a) £40,000 ❏
   b) Nothing ❏
   c) £10,000 ❏
   d) The square root of £40,000 ❏

10. Which of the following should be reflected in the Profit Statement?
   a) Prudence ❏
   b) Optimism ❏
   c) Pessimism ❏
   d) Happiness ❏

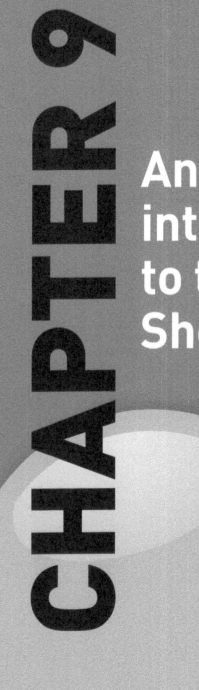

CHAPTER 9

An introduction to the Balance Sheet

The main constituents of a set of accounts are the Profit and Loss Account and the Balance Sheet, which in the published accounts may be called the Statement of Financial Position. The Balance Sheet is extremely important and fulfils a completely different function from the Profit Statement. If someone wants answers to questions such as 'What are the assets?' or 'Is the company safe?' it is a very good place to start.

The Balance Sheet gives details of the assets and liabilities of the business, and this detailed information is often very valuable to the users of accounts. It also reveals the 'net worth' of the business, though perhaps it would be more accurate to say that it does so according to sometimes controversial accounting rules. When a business is sold it is rare for the sum realized to be the same as the 'net worth' according to the Balance Sheet.

In this chapter we will study the Balance Sheet and cover:

● what the Balance Sheet is
● two accounting rules
● a simple example
● some further concepts
● questions to test your knowledge.

What is the Balance Sheet?

The clue is in the name. The Balance Sheet is a listing of all the balances in the accounting system, and what is more it must balance. The debit balances must equal the credit balances or, put another way, the assets must equal the liabilities. If they do not, a mistake has been made.

A freeze-frame picture

Unlike the Profit Statement, the Balance Sheet does not cover a trading period. It is a snapshot of the financial position at a precise moment and the date is always given as part of the heading. It is usually produced to coincide with the last day of the trading period.

To complete the photographic analogy, the Balance Sheet is like a freeze-frame picture of the finances of an enterprise. If the picture were to be taken a day earlier or a day later, different financial details would be revealed.

Format of the Balance Sheet

A long time ago it was the custom to set out the figures side by side. The assets (debit balances) went on the right-hand side and the liabilities (credit balances) went on the left-hand side. The two columns, of course, added up to the same figure.

You will not see a Balance Sheet displayed in this way because Balance Sheets are now shown in a vertical format. The whole thing adds down to the net worth of the business, which is shown at the bottom. There are still two figures which must be the same and which prove that the Balance Sheet balances.

Grouping of figures

Of course not every individual balance is listed in the Balance Sheet. If they were, the Balance Sheet of Marks and Spencer PLC would cover hundreds of pages. For example, a company may have six different bank accounts, all overdrawn by £100,000. The total of all these overdrafts would be shown as just one figure of £600,000.

Two accounting rules

In order to improve your understanding of Balance Sheets you must be familiar with the following two fundamental accounting rules.
- For every debit there must be a credit.
- Balance Sheet assets are debit balances and Balance Sheet liabilities are credit balances.

Debit and credit balances

If a moment of levity could be excused, the first rule of double-entry bookkeeping is said to be that debit is nearest the window and credit is nearest the door and I was certainly told this on my first morning as a trainee. It is of course only true if you sit with your left shoulder nearest the glass and in any case computers have probably made the joke obsolete. The real first rule of double-entry bookkeeping is that for every debit there must be a credit. Accountancy students are traditionally told this on their very first day. This means that an accounting entry always involves one account being debited and another account being credited. Scientists sometimes help themselves to remember this by thinking of the law of physics: 'every action has an equal and opposite reaction'.

For example, let us consider what happens when a £20,000 car is purchased. The Motor Vehicles account (which is an asset) is debited with £20,000. The bank account is credited with £20,000. At this stage you might be confused by which entries are debits and which are credits. This is explained in the next section.

Assets and liabilities

Assets in the Balance Sheet are the debit balances in the bookkeeping system. Liabilities in the Balance Sheet are credit balances in the bookkeeping system. This is probably exactly the opposite of what you would expect.

In the Profit Statement, sales and income are the credit balances: costs are the debit balances. The net total of all the balances is the profit or loss.

This one figure goes into the Balance Sheet as a single item. A profit is a credit which is listed with the liabilities. This, too, is probably exactly the opposite of what you would expect.

The explanation is that the profit belongs to someone outside the business. If the Balance Sheet is for a company, the profit belongs to the shareholders. It may one day be paid to them in the form of a dividend or by return of capital on the winding up of the company.

A simple example

John Brown commences business as a gardener on 1 July 2017, using the name Cotswold Gardeners. On his first day he pays £6,000 capital into the business. He buys a motor van for £5,000 and a motor mower for £500. They are immediately second-hand so he depreciates them by 20 per cent.

By the end of the gardening season on 31 October he has invoiced his customers £7,000 and been paid in full. His costs have been £2,000, of which he has paid £1,700 and still owes £300.

During the four months he has taken £4,000 out of the business for his living expenses.

Look at the following Balance Sheet and, with a pencil, make sure that you understand how each of the figures is calculated. The figure for profit is after deducting £1,100 depreciation. You should particularly notice that:

- The Balance Sheet is headed and dated, and it balances.
- The creditor of £300 is money owing by the business. It is an accrual, which is one of the things that we studied in the previous chapter.
- The business is separate from John Brown's personal affairs. This is why the payment of £4,000 living expenses to John Brown takes money out of the business and affects the Balance Sheet.

John Brown Trading as Cotswold Gardeners
Balance Sheet at 31 October 2017

	£	£
Fixed Assets		
Motor vehicle	4,000	
Motor mower	400	
		4,400
Current Assets		
Bank account	1,800	
Less Current Liabilities		
Creditor	300	
		1,500
		5,900
Capital employed		
Capital paid in at 1/7/17	6,000	
Add profit since 1/7/17	3,900	
	9,900	
Less drawings since 1/7/17	4,000	
		5,900

Some further concepts

Balance Sheets that will be audited and published are laid out according to certain rules and we will look at these in Chapter 10. In this chapter, we are concerned with Balance Sheets prepared just for management use. It will be very helpful if you are completely familiar with the following concepts.

Fixed assets and depreciation

Fixed assets are grouped together in the Balance Sheet and one total is given for the net value of all of them. Examples of fixed assets are:

- freehold property
- plant and machinery
- computers
- motor vehicles.

They are assets that will have a value to the business over a long period, usually understood to be any time longer than a year.

They do usually lose their value, either with the passage of time (e.g. a lease), with use (e.g. a piece of machinery that wears out) or due to obsolescence (e.g. computers). Therefore, as we saw in Chapter 8, they are written off over a number of years. Depreciation is a book entry and no cash is involved. The entry is:

● debit depreciation (thus reducing profit)
● credit the asset (thus reducing the value of the asset).

Current assets

Different types of current asset are listed separately in the Balance Sheet with one total being shown for the sum of them all. They are assets with a value available entirely in the short term, usually understood to be a period less than a year.

This is either because they are what the business sells, or because they are money or can quickly be turned into money. Examples of current assets are:

● stock
● money owing by customers (debtors)
● money in the bank
● short-term investments.

Current liabilities

These, too, are listed separately in the Balance Sheet with one total given for the sum of them all. They are liabilities which the business could be called upon to pay off in the short term, usually within a year. Examples are a bank overdraft and money owing to suppliers (creditors).

Definitions of debtors and creditors

● A debtor is a person owing money to the business (e.g. a customer for goods delivered).
● A creditor is a person to whom the business owes money (e.g. an unpaid electricity bill).

Working capital

This is the difference between current assets and current liabilities. In the simple example given earlier it is £1,500.

It is extremely important, as we will see later. A business without sufficient working capital cannot pay its debts as they fall due. In this situation it might have to stop trading, even if it is profitable.

Possible alternatives might include raising more capital, taking out a long-term loan, or selling some fixed assets.

Prudent reserves

When something happens that causes an asset to lose value, it is written off. For example, if some stock is stolen, the value of stock in the Balance Sheet is reduced.

The same thing must happen if a prudent view is that an asset has lost some of its value. This happens, for example, if some of the stock is obsolete and unlikely to sell for full value. Normally the Balance Sheet will just show the reduced value, which will be explained with notes.

The creation of a stock reserve reduces the profit. If it is subsequently found that the reserve was not necessary, the asset is restored to its full value and the profit is correspondingly increased in a later period.

It is often necessary to create a bad debt reserve to cover money that may not be collectable from customers.

Test your knowledge of Balance Sheets

A Balance Sheet for Patel Brothers is given below. For the sake of brevity, taxation and the explanatory notes have been omitted.

Now test your knowledge of Balance Sheets by answering the following questions. The answers are given at the end of this chapter, immediately before the end-of-chapter Fact-check.

1 Is the capital employed of £448,000 an asset or a liability?
2 Suggest two possible additional types of current asset.
3 What is the working capital?

4 What would the working capital be if stock valued at £10,000 was sold for £18,000 (payable after 30 days) and if an extra piece of machinery was purchased for £30,000?

5 Assume that a customer had paid a debt of £3,000 written off as bad at 31 October 2017.

  a What would the profit for the year have been?

  b What would Trade Debtors at 31 October 2017 be?

Patel Brothers
Balance Sheet at 31 October 2017

	£	£
Fixed Assets		
Freehold premises	200,000	
Fixtures and fittings	30,000	
Plant and machinery	50,000	
		280,000
Current Assets		
Stock	130,000	
Trade debtors	190,000	
Other debtors	16,000	
	336,000	
Less Current Liabilities		
Trade creditors	70,000	
Bank overdraft	48,000	
	118,000	
		218,000
Bank Loan repayable on 31/12/20		(50,000)
		448,000
Capital employed		
Capital at 31/10/16	350,000	
Add profit for year	300,000	
	650,000	
Less drawings for year	202,000	
		448,000

Summary

In this chapter we have been introduced to the basic principles of the following:

- What is the Balance Sheet?
- Format of the Balance Sheet
- Elementary rules of double-entry bookkeeping
- An example of a simple Balance Sheet
- Fixed assets and depreciation
- Current assets and current liabilities
- Debtors and creditors
- Working capital
- Prudent reserves

Finally, we have examined another Balance Sheet and tested our understanding of it.

Next, we will try to understand published accounts.

Test your knowledge of Balance Sheets – Answers

1. Liability
2. Short-term investments, bank accounts, cash
3. £218,000
4. £196,000
5.
    a) £303,000
    b) £190,000 (no change)

Fact-check (answers at the back)

1. Which words complete the following: 'The total of the debit balances must equal'?
   a) the total of the assets ❏
   b) the total of the liabilities ❏
   c) the total of the credit balances ❏
   d) the income ❏

2. The figures in the Balance Sheet reflect the position at which point in the trading period?
   a) The beginning ❏
   b) The end ❏
   c) The average ❏
   d) One week before the end ❏

3. What is not shown in a Balance Sheet?
   a) Net worth of the business ❏
   b) Fixed assets ❏
   c) Current liabilities ❏
   d) Salaries ❏

4. What are Balance Sheet liabilities? ❏
   a) Certain credit balances ❏
   b) Certain debit balances ❏
   c) Loss for the period ❏
   d) Overheads ❏

5. Where in the Balance Sheet is a bank overdraft shown?
   a) Fixed assets ❏
   b) Current assets ❏
   c) Current liabilities ❏
   d) Capital employed ❏

6. Plant and machinery cost £400,000 and depreciation to date has been £100,000. What will be shown in the Balance Sheet?
   a) £300,000 in the fixed assets ❏
   b) £300,000 in the current assets ❏
   c) £400,000 in the fixed assets ❏
   d) £100,000 in the current liabilities ❏

7. What is the period during which an asset can reasonably be expected to be turned into cash in order for it to be classed as a current asset?
   a) One month ❏
   b) Six months ❏
   c) One year ❏
   d) Two years ❏

8. What is a creditor?
   a) A director ❏
   b) A person or business to whom the business owes money ❏
   c) A person or business who owes money to the business ❏
   d) An employee who behaves in a creditable way ❏

9. What is working capital?
   a) The difference between all the assets and all the liabilities ❏
   b) All the assets ❏
   c) The employees ❏
   d) The difference between current assets and current liabilities ❏

10. What is the effect of a stock reserve?

a) It reduces the profit ❏
b) It increases the profit ❏
c) It increases the current liabilities ❏
d) It reduces the fixed assets ❏

CHAPTER 10

Understanding published accounts

In this chapter, we will be studying published accounts and it will be helpful if you obtain a set of accounts. The accounts will be particularly useful if they are for a company well known to you, such as your employer. Advice on how to get hold of published accounts is given in the first section of this chapter.

A study of published accounts cannot help but be interesting and useful. One of the reasons is that it will help you understand your investments and help you decide whether to buy or sell. You may think that you do not have investments but you very probably do, perhaps through the medium of a pension fund or a share-based ISA. Another possible reason is to help judge the security of your employer or prospective employer. Published accounts, of course, have many other uses and, short of fraud, much information must be disclosed and cannot be hidden.

This chapter's programme is perhaps the most demanding. It looks at:

- availability of published accounts
- what is included
- the Profit and Loss Account and Balance Sheet
- the remainder of the Annual Report and Accounts.

Availability of published accounts

Accounts are published for one or both of the following reasons:

- because it is required by law
- as a public relations exercise.

All but a tiny number of registered UK companies are required by law to produce accounts annually, although, subject to strict limits the period can be changed. In many cases an audit is required. A private company must file accounts at Companies House within nine months of the balance sheet date and a public company must do so within six months of the balance sheet date. An extension of the filing period may be allowed in rare and exceptional cases. The law and accounting standards stipulate the minimum content and standard of the accounts.

Certain bodies other than companies are also required to produce accounts. Examples are building societies, charities and local authorities. Our work in this chapter deals exclusively with the accounts of companies.

Companies House

The address for companies registered in England and Wales is *Companies House, Crown Way, Cardiff CF14 3UZ*. There is an office in Edinburgh for companies registered in Scotland and an office in Belfast for companies registered in Northern Ireland. The telephone number for all three offices is *0303 1234 500* and the website for all three offices is www.gov.uk/government/organisations/companies-house. There are over 3,750,000 companies on the active register and the accounts of all but a handful of them may be inspected.

How to obtain published accounts

A listed public company will probably be willing to make accounts available. A request should be made to the Company Secretary's department.

Alternatively, you can get the accounts of any company, even the corner shop, by applying to Companies House. You can also get a copy of the company's annual return, articles and other documents. You will need to give the company's exact registered name or its registered number, preferably both. You can telephone and have the document posted to you or do it through the website. There is a charge of £3 per document if it is posted. You can pay with a credit or debit card. It may be useful and particularly interesting if you look at the accounts of your employer or another company that you know well.

Late filing

Unfortunately, a small minority of companies file their accounts late or even not at all. This is an offence for which the directors can be punished and the company incur a penalty, but it does happen. It is often companies with problems that file late.

What is included

The content of the Annual Report and Accounts is governed by the law and accounting standards, though directors do still have some discretion. Listed companies are required to use international accounting standards, whereas other companies can use international accounting standards or UK accounting standards. However, once international standards have been used a company can only go back to UK standards in exceptional circumstances. Which set of accounting standards is used makes a difference, both to the presentation and to the figures.

If you are looking at the Report and Accounts of a listed company, you will see the following:

- Independent Auditors' Report
- Balance Sheet (it might be called Statement of Financial Position)
- Statement of Comprehensive Income (it might be called Income Statement); this corresponds with the Profit and Loss Account
- Statement of Changes in Equity
- Statement of Cash Flows
- notes to the financial statements
- Chairman's Statement

- Directors' Report
- Business Review
- Directors' Remuneration Report.

If the company is using UK standards, the financial information will comprise:

- Balance Sheet
- Profit and Loss Account
- Statement of Total Recognized Gains and Losses
- probably a Cash Flow Statement
- notes to the financial statements.

Reports will be filed with this financial information.

Space here is limited and there is so much detail that there is really no substitute for diving in and having a look at the Report and Accounts of your chosen company. Try not to get bogged down and I wish you the best of luck. Assuming that you are not looking at the Report and Accounts of a small or medium-sized company and assuming that the company uses UK accounting standards, can you locate the following?

- the pre-tax profit (Profit and Loss Account)
- details of the fixed assets (Balance Sheet and supporting notes)
- the amount of any exports (the notes)
- is it an unqualified audit report? (the Audit Report)
- details of any political or charitable donation (the Directors' Report)
- was there a cash outflow in the period? (the Cash Flow Statement)
- details of the share capital (Balance Sheet and supporting notes)
- the amount of the capital employed (the Balance Sheet).

Profit and Loss Account and Balance Sheet

These are the core of the accounts and we have already looked at some of the principles in the first two chapters. The Profit and Loss Account will give the figures for the previous period as well as the current period. Figures in the Balance Sheet will be given as at the previous Balance Sheet date as well as for the present one.

Now we will have a look at what will be shown in the published Profit and Loss Account and Balance Sheet of a company and once again UK accounting standards are assumed. Some of the information may be given in notes with a suitable cross-reference.

Profit and Loss Account

Most people consider that the key figure is the one for Profit before Tax. You may think that taxation is fair, or at any rate inevitable, and that Profit before Tax is the best measure of the company's success. The bottom part of the Profit and Loss Account will look rather like this. Fictitious figures have been inserted.

Profit before Tax	£10,000,000
Less Tax on Profit	£3,200,000
Profit for the Year	£6,800,000
Less Dividends Paid and Proposed	£4,000,000
Retained Profit for the Year	£2,800,000
Retained Profit brought forward	£7,000,000
Retained Profit carried forward	£9,800,000

In this example Her Majesty's Government is taking £3,200,000 of the profit and £4,000,000 is being distributed to shareholders. The company started the current period with undistributed profits of £7,000,000 and it is prudently adding £2,800,000 to this figure. Undistributed profits are now £9,800,000 and this figure will appear in the Balance Sheet.

The Profit and Loss Account will give the turnover, which is the total invoiced sales in the period. This is very important and it is useful to work out the relationship between the profit and the turnover.

Balance Sheet

Fixed assets are normally the first item appearing in the Balance Sheet. Usually you will see just one figure for the net amount of the fixed assets and a cross-reference to a note. This note will:

- break down the assets by type
- give cumulative expenditure for each type
- give cumulative depreciation for each type
- give net asset value for each type
- state the depreciation policy for each type.

The fixed assets are usually one of the most interesting sections of the accounts. This is because it is rare for the assets to be worth exactly the figure shown.

Depreciation, according to accounting rules, rarely reflects the real-life situation, especially in times of inflation. One wonders what would be the book value of St Paul's Cathedral if the Church of England had followed depreciation rules at the time of Sir Christopher Wren.

In practice, companies sometimes revalue property assets though not usually other assets. Asset strippers specialize in buying undervalued companies then selling the fixed assets for more than book value. This is one of the reasons why the details, which will be in the notes, are so important.

Current assets and current liabilities
First the current assets will be listed by type and a total of the current assets will be given. Then the current liabilities will be listed by type and the total of the current liabilities will be given.

The difference between the two figures will be stated and this is the *net current assets* or the *working capital*. A problem is usually indicated if the current assets are smaller than the current liabilities or only slightly larger.

The assets and liabilities will be cross-referenced to notes giving appropriate details such as the following:

- a breakdown of stocks into finished goods and work in progress
- a split of debtors between trade debtors (customers) and other debtors
- details of the different types of creditor.

Capital and reserves
In Chapter 9 we examined the net worth of an organization shown at the bottom of its Balance Sheet. This section is about the net worth of the company.

If the company were to be solvent and wound up, ignoring the costs of the winding up and in the unlikely event of all the assets and liabilities realizing exact book value, the total given in this section is the amount that would be distributed to shareholders.

A note will give details of the different types of share capital if there are more than one. It will also give the figures for the different types of reserves, and the retained figure in the Profit and Loss Account.

The remainder of the Annual Report and Accounts

Notes to the Accounts

There are always notes to the Profit and Loss Account and Balance Sheet. Their purpose is to give further details, and they are in the form of notes to prevent the accounts getting horribly detailed and complicated. Many of the notes give a breakdown of such figures as stock and debtors.

The notes also state the accounting policies and conventions used in the preparation of the accounts. These are extremely important because these policies can greatly affect the figures. An example of such a policy would be to value stocks at the lower of cost and net realizable value. Any change to this policy could greatly affect the profit figure.

The Directors' Report

The directors are required by law to provide certain information. This includes, for example, the amount of directors' remuneration and details of any political or charitable contributions. This information is disclosed in the Directors' Report.

Cash Flow Statement

There are sometimes disputes about the figures in the Profit and Loss Account and Balance Sheet. This is one reason why cash is so important. Cash is much more a matter of fact rather than of opinion. It is either there or it is not there.

Where the cash came from (banks, shareholders, customers) is also a matter of fact. So too is where the cash went to (dividends, wages, suppliers, etc.). The Cash Flow Statement gives all this information.

The Auditor's Report

The law requires company accounts to be audited by a person or firm holding one of the approved qualifications.

Subject to certain conditions and exceptions, no audit is required for a non-charitable company if it qualifies (on a group basis) as a small company. It must meet two out of three conditions in the current and preceding financial period. One of the conditions is that turnover must not exceed £10,200,000. The auditors will state whether in their opinion the accounts give a true and fair view. They do not certify the accuracy of the figures, a point which is often misunderstood.

If the auditors have reservations, they will give reasons for their concern.

Serious qualifications are rare, partly because it is in the interests of directors that they be avoided. Technical, and less serious, qualifications are more common. It is a matter of judgement how seriously each one is regarded.

Consolidated Accounts

A large group may have a hundred or more companies. It would obviously give an incomplete picture if each of these companies gave information just about its own activities. This is especially true when companies in a group trade with each other.

This is why the holding company must include consolidated accounts as well as its own figures. The effect of inter-group trading is eliminated and the Consolidated Balance Sheet gives the group's position in relation to the outside world. This does not, however, remove the obligation for every group company to prepare and file its own accounts. Such accounts must include the name, in the opinion of the directors, of the ultimate holding company.

Summary

In this chapter we have:

- examined the obligation to publish accounts and seen where copies can be obtained
- seen what is included in the Annual Report and Accounts
- tested our knowledge
- conducted an outline study of the Annual Report and Accounts.

Now, we will go on to look at accounting ratios and investment decisions.

Fact-check (answers at the back)

1. Where is the Companies House for companies registered in Scotland located?
   a) London ❏
   b) Cardiff ❏
   c) Edinburgh ❏
   d) Glasgow ❏

2. Which bodies do not have to make published accounts generally available?
   a) Building societies ❏
   b) Registered charities ❏
   c) Local authorities ❏
   d) General partnerships ❏

3. How much does Companies House charge for sending a copy of a company's accounts by post?
   a) £3 ❏
   b) £4 ❏
   c) £5 ❏
   d) £20 ❏

4. To what extent must listed companies use international accounting standards?
   a) Always ❏
   b) Usually ❏
   c) Always unless special permission is obtained ❏
   d) Never ❏

5. What is the turnover limit (subject to conditions) for the filing of abbreviated accounts for small companies at Companies House?
   a) £1,000,000 ❏
   b) £5,000,000 ❏
   c) £10,200,000 ❏
   d) £7,500,000 ❏

6. Which document explains the change in the amount of cash?
   a) The Balance Sheet ❏
   b) The Statement of Cash Flows ❏
   c) The Directors' Report ❏
   d) The Independent Auditors' Report ❏

7. Which document gives details of any charitable donations?
   a) The Profit and Loss Account ❏
   b) The Directors' Report ❏
   c) The Balance Sheet ❏
   d) The Cash Flow Statement ❏

8. What does the auditor do?
   a) Give an opinion ❏
   b) Certify the figures ❏
   c) Prepare the accounts ❏
   d) Comment on whether the directors are being fairly paid ❏

9. How many companies in the UK send accounts to Companies House?
   a) More than 50,000 ❏
   b) More than 1,000,000 ❏
   c) More than 2,000,000 ❏
   d) More than 2,500,000 ❏

10. Must a Business Review be provided in the Report and Accounts of a listed company?
    a) Yes, always ❏
    b) Usually ❏
    c) Sometimes ❏
    d) No ❏

CHAPTER 11

Accounting ratios and investment decisions

So far we have studied accounts and what they mean. Now we will devote a chapter to the active use of financial information. First we will take a look at ratios in the accounts, and then move on to investment decisions. This chapter is far from the easiest but, provided that you have mastered the basics, it should be one of the most interesting and rewarding.

The programme for this chapter covers:

- accounting ratios
- four key questions
- testing our understanding of accounting ratios
- investment decisions.

Accounting ratios

There are many useful ratios that can be taken from accounts. The following are among the most important but there are many others. It is a good idea to have a set of accounts with you as you work through this section. Pick out relevant figures, work out the ratios, and try to draw conclusions.

Profit to turnover

For example:

Annual turnover	**£10,000,000**
Annual profit before tax	**£1,000,000**
Profit to turnover	**10%**

This uses Profit before Tax but it may be more useful to use Profit after Tax. Perhaps you want to define profit as excluding the charge for bank interest. You should select the definition most relevant to your circumstances.
The ratio may be expressed in different ways (e.g. 1 to 10 instead of 10%).

Return on capital employed

For example:

Capital employed	**£5,000,000**
Annual profit after tax	**£1,000,000**
Return on capital employed	**20%**

Again, the profit may be expressed before or after tax.
Capital employed is the net amount invested in the business by the owners and is taken from the Balance Sheet. Many people consider this the most important ratio of all. It is useful to compare the result with a return that can be obtained outside the business. If a building society is paying a higher rate, perhaps the business should be closed down and the money put in the building society.
Note that there are two ways of improving the return. In the example, the return on capital employed would be 25 per cent

if the profit was increased to £1,250,000. It would also be 25 per cent if the capital employed was reduced to £4,000,000.

Stock turn

For example:

Annual turnover	**£10,000,000**
Annual cost of sales (60%)	**£6,000,000**
Stock value	**£1,500,000**
Stock turn	**4**

As the name implies, this measures the number of times that total stock is used (turned over) in the course of a year. The higher the stock turn the more efficiently the business is being run, though adequate safety margins must of course be maintained.

It is important that the terms are completely understood and that there are no abnormal factors. Normally the definition of stock includes all finished goods, work in progress and raw materials.

The stock value will usually be taken from the closing Balance Sheet but you need to consider if it is a typical figure. If the business is seasonal, such as a manufacturer of fireworks, it may not be. A better result may be obtained if the average of several stock figures throughout the year can be used.

Number of days' credit granted

For example:

Annual turnover including VAT	**£10,000,000**
Trade debtors	**£1,500,000**
Number of days' credit	**55**

The calculation is $\dfrac{1,500,000}{10,000,000} \times 365 = 55$ days

Obviously the lower the number of days the more efficiently the business is being run. The figure for trade debtors normally comes from the closing Balance Sheet and care should be taken that it is a figure typical of the whole year.

If £1,500,000 of the £10,000,000 turnover came in the final month, the number of days' credit is really 31 instead of 55. Care should also be taken that the VAT-inclusive debtors figure is compared with the VAT-inclusive turnover figure. VAT is normally excluded from the Profit and Loss Account.

Number of days' credit taken

The principle of the calculation is exactly the same. In this case the figure for closing trade creditors is compared with that for the annual purchases.

Gearing

The purpose of this ratio is to compare the finance provided by the banks and other borrowing with the finance invested by shareholders. It is a ratio much used by banks, who may not like to see a ratio of 1 to 1 (or some other such proportion) exceeded.The ratio is sometimes expressed as a proportion, as in 1 to 1. Sometimes it is expressed as a percentage: 1 to 1 is 50 per cent because borrowing is 50 per cent of the total. Gearing is said to be high when borrowing is high in relation to shareholders' funds. This can be dangerous but shareholders' returns will be high if the company does well. This is what is meant by being highly geared.

For example:

Loans	**£6,000,000**
Shareholders' funds	**£3,000,000**
Gearing	**200%**

Dividend per share

This is the total dividends for the year divided by the number of shares in issue. Any preference shares are normally disregarded.

For example:

Total dividends	**£2,000,000**
Number of issued shares	**10,000,000**
Dividend per share	**20p**

Price/earnings ratio

This is one of the most helpful of the investment ratios and it can be used to compare different companies. The higher the number the more expensive the shares will be. It is often useful to do the calculation based on anticipated future earnings rather than declared historical earnings, although of course you can never be certain what future earnings will be.

The calculation is the current quoted price per share divided by earnings per share.

For example:

Profit after tax	£5,000,000
Number of issued shares	10,000,000
Earnings per share	50p
Current share price	£7.50
Price/earnings ratio	15

For all the ratios, if you have access to frequently produced management accounts the ratios will be more useful.

Before leaving accounting ratios please take warning from a true story. Some years ago one of the accountancy bodies asked examination candidates to work with ratios and draw conclusions from a Balance Sheet given in the examination paper.

Many of the students said that the company was desperately short of working capital and predicted imminent trouble. They were badly mistaken because the Balance Sheet had been taken from the latest published accounts of Marks and Spencer PLC. The students had not spotted the possibilities that the sales were for cash, the purchases were on credit and the business was very well managed.

Four key questions

There are many traps in using financial information and interpreting accounting ratios. You are advised to approach the job with caution and always to keep in mind four key questions.

Am I comparing like with like?

Financial analysts pay great attention to the notes in accounts and to the stated accounting policies. One of the reasons for this is that changes in accounting policies can affect the figures and hence the comparisons.

Consider a company that writes off research and development costs as overheads as soon as they are incurred. Then suppose that it changes policy and decides to capitalize the research and development, holding it in the Balance Sheet as having a long-term value. A case can be made for either treatment but the change makes it difficult to compare ratios for different years.

Is there an explanation?

Do not forget that there may be a special reason for an odd-looking ratio.

For example, greetings card manufacturers commonly deliver Christmas cards in August with an arrangement that payment is due on 1 January. The 30 June Balance Sheet may show that customers are taking an average of 55 days' credit. The 31 December Balance Sheet may show that customers are taking an average of 120 days' credit.

This does not mean that the position has deteriorated dreadfully and the company is in trouble. The change in the period of credit is an accepted feature of the trade and happens every year. It is of course important, particularly as extra working capital has to be found at the end of each year.

What am I comparing it with?

A ratio by itself has only limited value. It needs to be compared with something. Useful comparisons may be with the company budget, last year's ratio, or competitors' ratios.

Do I believe the figures?

You may be working with audited and published figures. On the other hand, you may only have unchecked data rushed from the accountant's desk. This sort of information may be more valuable because it is up to date. But beware of errors. Even if you are not a financial expert, if it feels wrong, perhaps it is wrong.

Test your understanding of accounting ratios

The Balance Sheet of Bristol Adhesives Ltd follows. The following information is available for the year to 31 October 2017.

Turnover was	*£6,600,000*
Profit before tax was	*£66,000*
The bank overdraft limit is	*£800,000*
Cost of sales was	*50%*

1 What was the ratio of Profit to Turnover?
2 What was the Return on Capital Employed?
3 What was the Stock Turn?
4 What was the number of days' credit granted? (Ignore possible VAT implications.)
5
   a What is the working capital?
   b Does this give cause for concern?

Answers are given at the end of the chapter, just before the Fact-check.

Bristol Adhesives Ltd
Balance Sheet at 31 October 2017

	£	£
Fixed Assets		2,000,000
Current Assets		
Stock	1,800,000	
Trade debtors	700,000	
Other debtors	300,000	
	2,800,000	
Less Current Liabilities		
Trade creditors	1,400,000	
Bank overdraft	800,000	
Other creditors	400,000	
	2,600,000	
Net Current Assets		200,000
		2,200,000
Capital and Reserves		
Called-up share capital		1,500,000
Profit and Loss Account		700,000
		2,200,000

Investment decisions

Some investment decisions are easy to make. Perhaps
a government safety regulation makes an item of capital
expenditure compulsory. Or perhaps an essential piece of
machinery breaks down and just has to be replaced.

Many other investment decisions are not nearly so clear cut
and hinge on whether the proposed expenditure will generate
sufficient future cash savings to justify itself. There are many
very sophisticated techniques for aiding this decision, but now
we will look at three techniques that are commonly used.

Payback

This has the merit of being extremely simple to calculate and understand. It is a simple measure of the period of time taken for the savings made to equal the capital expenditure. For example:

A new machine will cost £100,000. It will save £40,000 running expenses in the first year and £30,000 per year after that.

The payback period would be three years because this is the time taken for the saving on costs to equal the original expenditure. Hopefully this only took you a few seconds to work out and it is very useful information to have.

The disadvantage of the payback technique is that no account is given to the value of holding money. The £30,000 saved in year 3 is given equal value to £30,000 of the £100,000 paid out on day 1. In fact, inflation and loss of interest mean that, in reality, it is less valuable.

Return on investment

This takes the average of the money saved over the life of the asset and expresses it as a percentage of the original sum invested. For example:

A new machine will cost £100,000 and have a life of eight years. It will save £40,000 running expenses in the first year, and £30,000 in each of the remaining seven years.

The return on investment is $\dfrac{250,000 \times 100}{100,000 \times 8} = 31.25\%$ p.a.

Return on investment, like payback, takes no account of the time factor. A pound in eight years' time is given equal value to a pound today.

Discounted cash flow

This technique takes account of the fact that money paid or received in the future is not as valuable as money paid or received now. For this reason it is considered superior to payback and to return on investment. However, it is not as simple to calculate and understand.

There are variations to the discounted cash-flow technique but the principles are illustrated by the following example.

The purchase of two competing pieces of machinery is under consideration. Machine A costs £100,000 and will save £60,000 in year 1 and £55,000 in year 2. Machine B costs £90,000 and will save £55,000 in both year 1 and year 2. The savings are taken to occur at the end of each year and the company believes that the money saved will earn 10 per cent p.a. in bank interest.

The calculations are:

	Machine A	Machine B
Expenditure now	£100,000	£90,000
Less year 1 savings (discounted)	£54,600	£50,050
	£45,400	£39,950
Less year 2 savings (discounted)	£45,650	£45,650
Savings at Net Present Value	£250	£5,700

The example has of course been unrealistically simplified. However, it shows that after bringing the future values back to Net Present Value, Machine B is the better purchase.

Summary

In this chapter, we have looked at how financial information is actively used and specifically at:

- useful accounting ratios
- four possible reasons for caution
- our understanding of accounting ratios
- financial techniques aiding investment decisions.

Next, we shall go on to increase our understanding of cash and the management of working capital.

Test your understanding of accounting ratios – Answers

1. 66,000/6,600,000 = 1%
2. 66,000/2,200,000 = 3%
3. 3,300,000/1,800,000 = 1.8
4. 700,000/6,600,000 x 365 = 39 days
5.
    a) £200,000
    b) Yes (cause for further enquiry anyway)

Fact-check (answers at the back)

The following information is taken from a Profit and Loss Account, Balance Sheet and other sources. Please use it to answer the first seven questions.

Turnover for year (excluding VAT)	£100,000,000
Turnover for year (including VAT)	£120,000,000
Profit after tax for year	£6,000,000
Capital employed (shareholders' funds)	£40,000,000
Loans	£50,000,000
Cost of sales for year	£50,000,000
Stock	£10,000,000
Trade debtors	£20,000,000
Dividends paid and proposed	£4,000,000
Number of shares in issue	10,000,000
Current share price	£6.00

1. What is the ratio for profit to turnover (excluding VAT)?
   a) 10% ❏
   b) 5% ❏
   c) 6% ❏
   d) 20% ❏

2. What is the return on capital employed?
   a) 10% ❏
   b) 12% ❏
   c) 15% ❏
   d) 20% ❏

3. What is the stock turn?
   a) 4 ❏
   b) 5 ❏
   c) 6 ❏
   d) 7 ❏

4. What are the number of days' credit taken by customers?
   a) 55 days ❏
   b) 60 days ❏
   c) 61 days ❏
   d) 64 days ❏

5. What is the gearing?
   a) 50% ❏
   b) 80% ❏
   c) 100% ❏
   d) 125% ❏

6. What is the dividend per share?
   a) 20p ❏
   b) 40p ❏
   c) 60p ❏
   d) 80p ❏

7. What is the price/earnings ratio?
   a) 10.0 ❏
   b) 10.5 ❏
   c) 11.0 ❏
   d) 11.5 ❏

8. A new machine will cost £500,000 and will save £200,000 running expenses for each of five years. What is the payback period?
   a) 24 months ❏
   b) 30 months ❏
   c) 36 months ❏
   d) 60 months ❏

9. A new computer system will cost £80,000 and have a life of four years and it will then be scrapped. It will save £50,000 per year. What is the return on investment?
   a) 60.0% ❏
   b) 62.5% ❏
   c) 65.0% ❏
   d) 67.5% ❏

10. Which of the following (in the opinion of many people) makes discounted cash flow superior to return on investment? The other three statements are not true.
   a) It is easier to calculate ❏
   b) It is a legal requirement ❏
   c) It is recommended by the European Union ❏
   d) It takes account of the changing value of money ❏

CHAPTER 12

Cash and the management of working capital

It is a bad mistake to underestimate the importance of cash and it is another bad mistake to confuse cash and profit. They can be very different and the reasons are explained in this chapter. It is sometimes said that 'Cash is King'. The origins of the saying are not beyond doubt but the words are often attributed to Jim Slater. He was the financier of Slater Walker fame who, in his words, became a minus millionaire, but went on to recover much of his fortune.

In this chapter we look at the importance and management of cash. We also look at the management of working capital and the place of cash within it.

The programme for this chapter covers:

- the distinctions between profit and cash
- what is cash?
- the Cash-Flow Forecast
- the management of working capital.

The distinctions between profit and cash

Cash is completely different from profit, a fact that is not always properly appreciated. It is possible, and indeed quite common, for a business to be profitable but short of cash. Among the differences are the following:

- Money may be collected from customers more slowly (or more quickly) than money is paid to suppliers.
- Capital expenditure (unless financed by hire purchase or similar means) has an immediate impact on cash. The effect on profit, by means of depreciation, is spread over a number of years.
- Taxation, dividends and other payments to owners are an appropriation of profit. Cash is taken out of the business, which may be more or less than the profit.
- An expanding business will have to spend money on materials, items for sale, wages, etc. before it completes the extra sales and gets paid. Purchases and expenses come first. Sales and profit come later.

It is worth illustrating the problems of an expanding business with a hypothetical but realistic example.

Company A manufactures pens. It has a regular monthly turnover of £20,000. The cost of the pens is £10,000 (50%). Other monthly costs are £8,000 and its monthly profit is £2,000.

At 31 December, Company A has £3,000 in the bank and is owed £40,000 by customers to whom it allows two months' credit.

It owes £15,000 to suppliers who are paid within 30 days. Monthly costs of £3,000 are payable in cash.

The company secures an additional order for £60,000. The extra pens will take two months to make and will be delivered on 28 February. The customer will then have 60 days to pay.

The cost of the additional pens will be £30,000 (50%) and there will be extra expenses of £14,000 in the two months. The new order will contribute a very satisfactory £16,000 extra profit.

By 30 April, Company A will have made £24,000 profit. This is the regular £2,000 a month plus the £16,000 from the additional order.

Now let us assume that the new customer pays on 1 May, just one day late. Despite the extra profit, on 30 April the £3,000 bank balance will have turned into a £33,000 overdraft. The calculation is as follows:

Balance at 31 December	£3,000
Add receipts in four months	£80,000
	£83,000
Less payments to creditors in four months	£90,000
	(£7,000)
Less cash expenses in four months	£26,000
Overdraft at 30 April	(£33,000)

What is cash?

Cash includes the notes and coins in the petty cash box. It also includes money in bank current accounts, and money in various short-term investment accounts that can quickly be turned into available cash.

It is common for a Balance Sheet to show only a tiny amount for cash. This is because the business has an overdraft and only such things as the petty cash are included.

Practical management usage of the term cash includes a negative figure for an overdraft. A Cash-Flow Forecast can often result in a series of forecast overdrafts.

The Cash-Flow Forecast

It is extremely important that cash receipts and payments are effectively planned and anticipated. This has not been done in nearly all businesses that fail. A good manager will plan that sufficient resources are available but that not too many resources are tied up.

This can be done in isolation but it is better done as part of the overall budgeting process. Budgets are examined in Chapter 14.

The preparation of a detailed Cash-Flow Forecast will yield many benefits. Calculating and writing down the figures may suggest ideas as to how they can be improved. For example, the figures for cash payments from trade debtors will be based on an estimate of the average number of days' credit that will be taken. This will pose the question of whether or not payments can be speeded up.

When the Cash-Flow Forecast is finished it will be necessary to consider if the results are acceptable. Even if resources are available the results might not be satisfactory, and improvements will have to be worked out.

If sufficient resources are not available, either changes must be made or extra resources arranged. Perhaps an additional bank overdraft can be negotiated. Either way, a well-planned document will help managers to take action in good time.

The principles of a Cash-Flow Forecast are best illustrated with an example and a good one is given in the following table.

Variations in the layout are possible but a constant feature should be the running cash or overdraft balance.

Do not overlook contingencies and do not overlook the possibility of a peak figure within a period. For example, Ace Toys Ltd are forecast to have £17,000 on 31 March and £5,000 on 30 April. Both forecasts could be exactly right but the company might still need a £15,000 overdraft on 15 April.

Ace Toys Ltd – Cash-Flow Forecast for half year

	January £000	February £000	March £000	April £000	May £000	June £000
Receipts						
UK customers	50	55	55	55	60	80
Export customers	20	20	20	20	25	20
All other	5	5	8	2	12	6
	75	80	83	77	97	106
Payments						
Purchase ledger suppliers	30	33	29	40	44	38
Wages (net)	14	13	13	17	13	13
PAYE and National Insurance	4	4	4	4	5	4
Corporation tax	–	–	30	–	–	–
Capital expenditure	7	4	25	20	2	2
All other	8	9	9	8	6	11
	63	63	110	89	70	68
Excess of Receipts over Payments	12	17	[27]	[12]	27	38
Add Opening Bank Balance	15	27	44	17	5	32
Closing Bank Balance	27	44	17	5	32	70

It will help fix the principles in your mind if you now prepare your own personal Cash-Flow Forecast. Set it out in accordance with the format illustrated below.

The figures will be smaller but the principles are identical. Most people have never done this and the results may well be revealing. The opening bank balance in month 1 should be the latest figure on your personal bank statement.

	Month 1	Month 2	Month 3
	£	£	£
Receipts			
Salary			
Interest			
Dividends			
Other (specify)			
Payments			
Mortgage or rent			
Telephone			
Gas and electricity			
Food			
Car expenses			
Other (specify)			
Excess of Receipts over Payments			
Add Opening Bank Balance			
Closing Bank Balance			

The management of working capital

Is it important?

The effective management of working capital can be critical to the survival of the business and it is hard to think of anything more important than that. Many businesses that fail are profitable at the time of their failure, and failure often comes as a surprise to the managers. The reason for the failure is a shortage of working capital.

Furthermore, effective management of working capital is likely to improve profitability significantly. Turn back to Chapter 11's section on return on capital employed. You will remember that the percentage return increases as capital employed is reduced. Effective management of working capital can reduce the capital employed. It increases profits as well as enabling managers to sleep soundly without worries.

The four largest elements affecting working capital are usually debtors, stock, creditors and cash. Success in managing the first three affect cash, which can be reinvested in the business or distributed. We will consider the first three elements in turn.

Debtors

British business is plagued by slow payment of invoices and it is a problem in many other countries, too. Most businesses, and the government, would like to see an improvement. A statutory right to interest has been in place for a number of years but nothing seems to make much difference. An improvement can significantly affect working capital.

It is a great problem for managers, who sometimes are frightened of upsetting customers and feel that there is little that they can do. This is completely the wrong attitude.

Customer relations must always be considered, but a great deal can be done. Some practical steps for credit control are summarized below:

● Have the right attitude; ask early and ask often
● Make sure that payment terms are agreed in advance
● Do not underestimate the strength of your position
● Give credit control realistic status and priority
● Have well-thought out credit policies
● Concentrate on the biggest and most worrying debts first
● Be efficient; send out invoices and statements promptly
● Deal with queries quickly and efficiently
● Make full use of the telephone, your best aid
● Use legal action if necessary.

This may sound obvious, but it usually works. To sum up: be efficient, ask and be tough if necessary.

Stock

The aim should be to keep stock as low as is realistically feasible, and to achieve as high a rate of stock turnover as is realistically feasible. In practice, it is usually necessary to compromise between the wish to have stock as low as possible, and the need to keep production and sales going with a reasonable margin of safety.

Exactly how the compromise is struck will vary from case to case. Purchasing and production control are highly skilled functions and great effort may be expended on getting it right.

You may be familiar with the phrase 'just in time deliveries'. This is the technique of arranging deliveries of supplies frequently and in small quantities. In fact, just in time to keep production going. It is particularly successful in Japan where, for example, car manufacturers keep some parts for production measured only in hours.

It is not easy to achieve and suppliers would probably like to make large deliveries at irregular intervals. It may pay to approach the problem with an attitude of partnership with key suppliers, and to reward them with fair prices and continuity of business.

Finished goods should be sold, delivered and invoiced as quickly as possible.

Creditors

It is not ethical advice, but there is an obvious advantage in paying suppliers slowly. This is why slow payment is such a problem and, as has already been stated, the control of debtors is so important. Slow payment is often imposed by large and strong companies on small and weak suppliers.

Slow payment does not affect the net balance of working capital, but it does mean that both cash and creditors are higher than would otherwise be the case. Apart from moral considerations, there are some definite disadvantages in a policy of slow payment:

180

- Suppliers will try to compensate with higher prices or lower service.
- Best long-term results are often obtained by fostering mutual loyalty with key suppliers; it pays to consider their interests.
- If payments are already slow, there will be less scope for taking longer to pay in response to a crisis.

For these reasons it is probably not wise to adopt a consistent policy of slow payment, at least with important suppliers. It is better to be hard but fair, and to ensure that this fair play is rewarded with keen prices, good service and perhaps prompt payment discounts.

There may be scope for timing deliveries to take advantage of payment terms. For example if the terms are 'net monthly account', a 30 June delivery will be due for payment on 31 July. A 1 July delivery will be due for payment on 31 August.

Summary

In this chapter we have:

- studied the distinctions between profit and cash
- examined an example illustrating the differences
- learned what is meant by the term 'cash'
- looked at Cash-Flow Forecasts
- studied the importance of working capital and looked closely at debtors, stock and creditors.

Next, we will continue by taking a look at costing.

Fact-check (answers at the back)

1. 'A business may be profitable but short of cash'. How prevalent is this?
   a) It is relatively common ❏
   b) It is relatively uncommon ❏
   c) It is very uncommon ❏
   d) The statement in the question is self-evidently absurd ❏

2. Money is collected from customers more slowly than in the past. What effect will this have on cash in the business?
   a) There will be no effect ❏
   b) It will reduce the cash in the business ❏
   c) It will increase the cash in the business ❏
   d) It will greatly increase the cash in the business ❏

3. How important (in many people's opinion) is it that the Cash-Flow Forecast is regularly prepared?
   a) It is a waste of time ❏
   b) It might be interesting ❏
   c) It could be useful ❏
   d) It is important ❏

4. Which of the following is not included in the definition of cash?
   a) Notes and coin in the petty cash box ❏
   b) Money in bank current accounts ❏
   c) Money owing by customers and due to be paid within three days ❏
   d) Bank overdrafts ❏

5. Which of the following statements is not true?
   a) The cash requirement in the middle of a month may be higher than the cash requirement at the beginning and end of the month ❏
   b) Capital expenditure is a cash outflow ❏
   c) The running cash or overdraft balance should always be a feature of the Cash-Flow Forecast ❏
   d) Cash is the same as retained profit ❏

6. Which of the following will not help keep working capital at a satisfactory level?
   a) Persuading customers to pay quickly ❏
   b) Reducing dividends paid by the company ❏
   c) Changing the policy on depreciating fixed assets ❏
   d) Turning over stock more quickly ❏

7. Payment terms are 'net monthly account'. When is an invoice dated 6 September due for payment?
   a) 6 September ❏
   b) 30 September ❏
   c) 6 October ❏
   d) 31 October ❏

8. Slower payment by customers has which two of the following consequences?
a) Debtors are increased ❑
b) Creditors are increased ❑
c) Cash is increased ❑
d) Cash is reduced ❑

9. What are the two ways to increase the return on capital employed?
a) Increase the profit ❑
b) Increase the fixed assets ❑
c) Reduce the capital employed ❑
d) Negotiate better terms with the bank ❑

10. Who is famous for coining the phrase 'Cash is King'?
a) Gordon Brown ❑
b) Robert Maxwell ❑
c) Jim Slater ❑
d) Richard Branson ❑

CHAPTER 13

Costing

It is probably true to say that most non-financial managers instinctively know that costing is important. Unfortunately it is probably also true to say that most non-financial managers do not know very much about it. This is a pity because it affects so many business decisions. To take just one example, the fact that the fixed costs of running a cruise ship do not vary (or realistically only vary slightly) according to the number of passengers is the reason that large last-minute price reductions are often available. Think of that when you book your holiday.

A basic understanding of the principles of costing is important in business management. The aim is to master these key basic costing principles:

- the value of costing
- the uses of costing
- absorption costing
- break-even charts
- marginal costing and standard costing.

The value of costing

The value of costing can be illustrated with a simple example. Consider a company with three products. Its financial accounts show sales of £1,000,000, total costs of £700,000 and a profit of £300,000. The managers think that this is very good and that no significant changes are necessary. However, the costing details disclose the following:

	Product 1 £000	Product 2 £000	Product 3 £000	Total £000
Sales	600	300	100	1,000
Fixed costs	70	60	50	180
Variable costs	280	160	80	520
Total costs	350	220	130	700
Profit contribution	250	80	(30)	300

This shows that Product 1, as well as having the biggest proportion of sales, is contributing proportionately the most profit. Despite the overall good profit, Product 3 is making a negative contribution.

The obvious reaction might be to discontinue Product 3, but this may well be a mistake: £50,000 of fixed costs would have to be allocated to the other two products and the total profit would be reduced to £280,000.

Product 3 should probably only be discontinued if the fixed costs can be cut, or if the other two products can be expanded to absorb the £50,000 fixed costs.

It is increasingly common for cost accounts to be integrated with financial accounts. If cost accounts are kept separately, they go further than financial accounts. Cost accounts break down costs to individual products and cost centres. Financial accounts are more concerned with historical information.

Much, but not all, of the information comes from the financial accounts. It is important that if cost accounts are kept separately they are reconciled with the financial accounts.

Cost accounts are much more valuable if the information can be made speedily available. Sometimes it is necessary to compromise between speed and accuracy.

The uses of costing

It costs time and money to produce costing information and it is only worth doing if the information is put to good use. The following are some of these uses.

To control costs

Possession of detailed information about costs is of obvious value in the controlling of those costs.

To promote responsibility

Management theorists agree that power and responsibility should go together, although often they do not do so. Timely and accurate costing information will help top management hold all levels of management responsible for the budgets that they control.

Care should be taken that managers are not held responsible for costs that are not within their control. As many readers will know from bitter experience, this does sometimes happen.

To aid business decisions

The case given earlier might be such a decision.

Management must decide what to do about the unprofitable product.

To aid decisions on pricing

We live in competitive times and the old 'cost plus' contracts are now virtually never encountered. What the market will bear is usually the main factor in setting prices. Nevertheless, detailed knowledge concerning costs is an important factor in determining prices. Only in exceptional circumstances will managers agree to price goods at below cost, and they will seek to make an acceptable margin over cost.

Accurate costing is vital when tenders are submitted for major contracts and errors can have significant consequences. It is a long time ago but massive costing errors on the Millennium Dome at Greenwich were a spectacular example of what can go wrong.

Absorption costing

This takes account of all costs and allocates them to individual products or cost centres. Some costs relate directly to a product and this is quite straightforward in principle, although very detailed record-keeping may be necessary. Other costs do not relate to just one product and these must be allocated according to a fair formula. These indirect costs must be *absorbed* by each product.

There is not a single correct method of allocating overhead costs to individual products and it is sometimes right to allocate different costs in different ways. The aim should be to achieve fairness in each individual case.

Among the costs that can be entirely allocated to individual products are direct wages and associated employment costs, materials and bought-in components.

Among the costs that cannot be entirely allocated to individual products are indirect wages (cleaners, maintenance staff, etc.), wages of staff such as salesmen and accountants, and general overheads such as rent and business rates.

Great care must be taken in deciding the best way to allocate the non-direct costs. There are many different ways and the following two are common examples.

Production hours

The overhead costs are apportioned according to the direct production hours charged to each product or cost centre. For example, consider a company with just two products, A having 5,000 hours charged and B having 10,000 hours charged. If the overhead is £60,000, Product A will absorb £20,000 and Product B will absorb £40,000.

Machine hours

The principle is the same but the overhead is allocated according to the number of hours that the machinery has been running.

This is best illustrated with an example. You should try to write down the cost statement before checking the solution.

Fruit Products Ltd manufactures three types of jam. Its overhead costs in January are £18,000 and it allocates them in the proportion of direct labour costs. The following details are available for January:

	Strawberry	Raspberry	Apricot	Total
Jars manufactured	26,000	60,000	87,000	173,000
Direct labour	£2,000	£4,000	£6,000	£12,000
Ingredients	£6,000	£11,000	£17,000	£34,000
Other direct costs	£2,000	£3,000	£6,000	£11,000

The resulting cost statement is shown below:

Fruit Products Ltd – January Cost Statement

	Strawberry	Raspberry	Apricot	Total
Jars produced	26,000	60,000	87,000	173,000
	£	£	£	£
Costs				
Direct labour	2,000	4,000	6,000	12,000
Ingredients	6,000	11,000	17,000	34,000
Other direct costs	2,000	3,000	6,000	11,000
Total Direct Costs	10,000	18,000	29,000	57,000
Overhead allocation	3,000	6,000	9,000	18,000
Total Cost	13,000	24,000	38,000	75,000
Cost per jar	50.0p	40.0p	43.7p	43.4p

You will notice that in the example, direct labour is smaller than the overhead cost that is being allocated. If the overheads had been allocated in a different way, perhaps on floor area utilized, then the result would almost certainly not have been the same.

The trend in modern manufacturing is for direct costs, and particularly direct labour costs, to reduce as a proportion of the total costs. This increases the importance of choosing the fairest method of apportionment.

Break-even charts

In nearly all businesses there is a close correlation between the level of turnover and the profit or loss. The managers should know that if invoiced sales reach a certain figure the business will break even. If invoiced sales are above that figure the business will be in profit.

The break-even point depends on the relationship between the fixed and the variable costs. It is often shown in the form of the following chart:

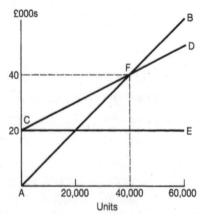

A break-even chart

In the example, fixed costs (shown by line C–E) are £20,000. Variable costs are 50 pence per unit and the total costs (shown by line C–D) are the result of adding these to the fixed costs.

The revenue (shown by line A–B) is the result of sales at £1 per unit.

The break-even point is 40,000 units sold at £1 each. This is equal to the total cost of £40,000 (£20,000 fixed and £20,000 variable). It is at point F where the lines cross. Profit or loss can also be read from the chart.

In practice, the relationships are rarely quite so straightforward, as some of the costs may be semi-variable.

Marginal costing and standard costing

Marginal costing

Marginal costing is a useful way of emphasizing the marginal costs of production and services. This information is of great help in making pricing decisions.

If the selling price is less than the variable cost (direct cost), the loss will increase as more units are sold. Managers will only want to do this in very exceptional circumstances, such as a supermarket selling baked beans as a loss leader.

If the selling price is greater than the variable cost, then the margin will absorb part of the fixed cost. After a certain point profits will be made. Marginal costing explains why some goods and services are sold very cheaply. It explains, for example, why airline tickets are sometimes available at extremely low prices for last-minute purchasers.

Once an airline is committed to making a flight, an extremely high part of the cost of that flight can properly be regarded as a fixed cost. The pilot's salary will be the same whether the plane is empty or full. The variable cost is only the complimentary meals and a few other items. It therefore makes sense to make last-minute sales of unsold seats at low prices. As long as the selling price is greater than the variable cost, a contribution is made.

Standard costing

Standard costing involves the setting of targets, or standards, for the different factors affecting costs. Variances from the standard are then studied in detail.

For example:

Standard timber usage per unit of production	4.00 metres
Standard timber price	£2.00 per metre
Actual production	3,500 posts
Actual timber usage	14,140 metres
Actual cost of timber used	£27,714

Material Price Variance is   £566 favourable (2%)
(£28,280 less £27,714)

Material Usage Variance is   £280 adverse (1%)
([14,140 metres less 14,000 metres] x £2)

The material price variance happens because the standard cost of the 14,140 metres used was £28,280 (at £2 per metre). The actual cost was £27,714, a favourable variance of £566. On the other hand, 140 metres of timber too much was used, resulting in an adverse material usage variance.

Summary

Costing is a big subject and there is only space to set out some of the basic principles. However, in this chapter we should have:

- formed an understanding of the concept of costing
- formed an understanding of the uses and value of costing
- studied the principles of absorption costing
- examined break-even charts
- answered the basic question 'What is marginal costing?'
- answered the basic question 'What is standard costing?'

Next, we will finish our examination of finance with a look at budgets.

Fact-check (answers at the back)

1. Which of the following is not one of the possible uses of costing information?
   a) To control costs ❏
   b) To ensure that the trial balance balances ❏
   c) To aid business decisions ❏
   d) To aid decisions on pricing ❏

2. What should happen if the cost accounts are kept separately from the financial accounts? There could be at least a tenuous case for all of the following but one of them is particularly important.
   a) They should be kept in the same building ❏
   b) They should be reconciled with the financial accounts ❏
   c) They should be kept by senior managers ❏
   d) They should be locked up ❏

3. Should managers (in the view of the writer and many others) be held responsible for costs that are not within their control?
   a) Always ❏
   b) Usually ❏
   c) Not usually ❏
   d) Of course not ❏

4. Which of the following is a feature of absorption costing?
   a) All costs are allocated to individual products or cost centres ❏
   b) It is very interesting (or sometimes even absorbing) ❏
   c) Fixed costs are disregarded ❏
   d) Variable costs are disregarded ❏

5. Which of the following can be entirely allocated to individual products?
   a) Indirect wages ❏
   b) Rent ❏
   c) Direct wages ❏
   d) The salary of the managing director ❏

6. Which of the following is not a valid way of allocating non-direct costs?
   a) According to the wishes of the government ❏
   b) Pro-rata to production hours ❏
   c) Pro-rata to machine hours ❏
   d) Pro-rata to direct labour costs ❏

7. A business sells watches for £10 each. Fixed costs are £10,000 and indirect costs are £5 per watch. Referring to a break-even chart, if you can prepare one, how many watches must be sold before break-even point is reached?
   a) 1,500 ❏
   b) 2,000 ❏
   c) 2,500 ❏
   d) 3,000 ❏

8. Using the information in question 7 above, how many watches must be sold to achieve break-even if the costs are unchanged but the selling price is reduced to £8?
   a) 2,500 ❏
   b) 3,000 ❏
   c) 3,334 ❏
   d) 3,667 ❏

9. Which of the following would be true in the event of the variable cost being greater than the selling price?
   a) The more units sold the more the loss would increase ❏
   b) Variable costs would have to be reallocated ❏
   c) The more units sold the more the loss would reduce ❏
   d) The directors would have to resign (just joking) ❏

10. Standard material cost per unit of production £5
    Actual production 3,000 units
    Actual material cost £15,500
    What is the material usage variance?
    a) £1,000 unfavourable ❏
    b) £500 unfavourable ❏
    c) £500 favourable ❏
    d) £1,000 favourable ❏

CHAPTER 14

Budgets

Budgeting is probably the element of finance that has most impact on the time of non-financial managers and for this reason most of them have at least some knowledge of the subject. Of course, some non-financial managers resent this time commitment and see budgeting as an unproductive chore. It can be, but this should not be the case if it is handled well and budget relationships are understood.

In this chapter we will look at:

- budgeting in different types of organization
- the profit budget
- the sales budget
- revenue expenditure budgets
- the capital expenditure budget
- cash and the Balance Sheet
- after the budget has been approved.

Budgeting in different types of organization

In very large organizations, hundreds of managers may be involved in the budgeting process, and the complete budget will probably be a very thick document. This would be true of, say, a National Health Service Trust and in the private sector of companies such as Shell.

This involvement takes a lot of management time but, if the budgeting is done well, it is likely to be time well spent. This is because the budget will probably be a realistic one, and because after approval the managers should feel committed to it.

When the budget has been approved, individual managers are responsible for their section of it. The responsibility is like a pyramid. At the base of the pyramid are the most junior managers, supervising a comparatively small section, perhaps involving expenditure only. These junior managers should, however, have some knowledge of the overall budget and objectives.

In the middle may be more senior managers and divisional directors, each with a wider area of responsibility for achieving the complete budget objectives. If everyone else meets their targets they will have an easy job.

Budgets should be designed to meet the needs of a particular organization and its managers. For example, a large school could well have an expenditure budget of about £4,000,000. There will be little income and the budgeting emphasis will be on capital expenditure and revenue expenditure. The main aims will be informed choice and value for money.

The rest of this chapter's work is devoted to the budget of a large company because this best illustrates the main principles. However, a smaller organization should budget using the same methods. There will be fewer managers involved, and less paper, but the same procedures should be followed.

In Chapter 8 we considered Julia Brown's book, and in Chapter 9 we considered John Brown's gardening business. Even their budgets follow the same principles. John Brown's van and motor mower constitute his capital expenditure budget. In their case the budgets will probably be on just one or two pieces of paper.

The profit budget

There are usually several budgets and they all impact on each other. The profit budget is arguably the most important and this is considered first.

There are two basic approaches to budgeting in a large organization, both having advantages and disadvantages:

- The so-called 'bottom up' method. Proposals are taken from the lower management levels. These are collated into an overall budget that may or may not be acceptable. If it is not, then top management calls for revisions.
- The so-called 'top down' method. Top management issues budget targets. Lower levels of management must then submit proposals that achieve these targets.

In practice, there is often less difference between the two methods than might be supposed. It is important that at some stage there is a full and frank exchange of views. Everyone should be encouraged to put forward any constructive point of view, and everyone should commit themselves to listening with an open mind. Needless to say, top management will, and should, have the final decisions.

It is a common mistake for managers to be too insular and to overlook what changes competitors are making.

All the budgets are important but in a commercial organization the overall profit budget is likely to be considered the most important. A summarized six-month profit budget for a large organization is given below.

Kingston Staplers Ltd – Profit Budget for half year

	January £000	February £000	March £000	April £000	May £000	June £000	Total half year £000
Sales							
UK	1,500	1,400	1,450	1,700	1,600	1,800	9,450
Export	200	220	180	190	400	340	1,530
	1,700	1,620	1,630	1,890	2,000	2,140	10,980
Less cost of sales	1,020	970	990	1,150	1,230	1,320	6,680
Gross Profit	680	650	640	740	770	820	4,300
Overheads							
Sales Department	200	220	230	210	210	220	1,290
Finance Department	190	200	180	190	220	210	1,190
Administration Department	230	240	250	250	250	260	1,480
Total overheads	620	660	660	650	680	690	3,960
Net Profit/(Loss)	60	(10)	(20)	90	90	130	340

Please particularly note the following points:

- Most budgets are for a year but this is not a requirement. They can be for six months or for any other useful period.
- This budget gives monthly figures, which is the most common division, but again this is not fixed. The divisions can be weekly, quarterly, or some other period.
- The figures are summarized in thousands of pounds.
- This is suitable for a summary budget of a large organization. The budgets leading up to these summarized figures will be more detailed. January's budget for postage might, for example, be £2,850.
- As we will see, various subsidiary budgets and calculations feed figures through to this summary budget.

The sales budget

This should be in sufficient detail for management to know the sources of revenue. The figures will be broken down into different products and different sales regions. Each regional sales manager will have responsibility for a part of the sales budget. A section of the sales budget might look like the following:

Scottish Region Sales Budget

	Jan £	Feb £	March £
Product A	16,000	12,000	17,000
Product B	13,000	13,000	13,000
Product C	40,000	45,000	50,000
	69,000	70,000	80,000

Before the sales budget is done it would be normal for top management to issue budget assumptions concerning prices, competition, and other key matters.

The sales budget will be for orders taken. There will usually be a timing difference before orders become invoiced sales.

Revenue expenditure budgets

Still using the example of Kingston Staplers Ltd, the cost of sales will consist of direct wages, items bought for resale, raw materials and so on. The Sales, Finance, and Administration Departments will make up the overhead budget. In practice, this overhead budget is likely to be divided into three, with a different manager responsible for each section.

As with all the other budgets, each manager should submit a detailed budget for the section for which he or she is responsible.

As with the sales budget, top management should give initial guidance on expected performance and policy assumptions. For example, a manager might be told to assume a company-wide average pay rise of 5 per cent on 1 April.

The capital expenditure budget

This is extremely significant in some companies, less so in others. It will list all the planned capital expenditure showing the date when the expenditure will be made, and the date that the expenditure will be completed and the asset introduced to the business. Major contracts may be payable in instalments and the timing is important to the cash budget.

A sum for miscellaneous items is usually necessary. For example, major projects might be listed separately and then £15,000 per month added for all projects individually less than £5,000.

Within the capital expenditure budget, timing is very important. Expenditure affects cash and interest straight away. Depreciation usually starts only on completion.

Cash and the Balance Sheet

When the profit budgets are complete, it is important that a cash budget is prepared. This is a Cash-Flow Forecast, which was examined in detail in Chapter 12. You might like to spend a few minutes referring back to this.

In practice, the profit budget and cash budget are linked and a chicken and egg problem has to be resolved. The profit budget cannot be completed until the interest figure is available. This in turn depends on the cash budget. The cash budget depends partly on the profit budget.

Dilemmas like this are quite common in budgeting. It is usual to put in an estimated figure for interest and then adjust everything later if necessary. This can be very time-consuming, and budgeting is much simpler if it is computerized. Several hours' work can be reduced to minutes and management is much freer to test budgets with useful 'what if' questions.

You will recall that one of Chapter 9's accounting rules stated that every debit has a credit. It follows that every figure in the budgets has a forecastable consequence in a future Balance Sheet. It is normal to conclude the budgets by preparing a month-by-month forecast Balance Sheet and bankers are likely to ask for this. It may be that some aspect of the Balance Sheet is unacceptable and a partial re-budget is necessary.

In practice, top management is likely to review and alter some aspects of the budgets several times.

After the budget has been approved

After the budget has been approved comes . . . quite possibly nothing at all. This is a pity but it does not mean that the budgeting exercise has been a complete waste of time. The participants will have thought logically about the organization, its finances and its future. Some of the detail will remain in their minds and influence their future actions.

Nevertheless, the budgets will be much more valuable if they are used in an active way. Regular performance reports should be issued by the accountants. These should be in the same format as the budgets, and should give comparable budget and actual figures. Variances should also be given.

All levels of management should regularly review these figures and explain the variances. Significant variances will pose the question of whether corrective action needs to be taken.

Finally, budgets do not necessarily have to be done just once a year. They may be updated, reviewed, or even scrapped and redone as circumstances dictate.

Summary

Finance affects the jobs of virtually all non-financial managers and by studying the last seven chapters you should have significantly increased your knowledge of the subject. Many elements of finance have been examined and much ground has been covered.

The following summarizes the subjects studied:

Profit Statements (Chapter 8)
- A simple example
- A trading company and a manufacturing company
- Further concepts
- A full example

Balance Sheets (Chapter 9)
- What is a Balance Sheet?
- Accounting rules and a simple example
- Further concepts
- Test your knowledge

Published accounts (Chapter 10)
- Availability of published accounts
- Profit and Loss Account and Balance Sheet
- Other items included in published accounts

Fact-check (answers at the back)

1. In a very large company individual junior managers each have responsibility for a relatively small cost centre. Which phrase best describes their cost centres' place in the overall company budget?
   a) In the centre of the circle ❏
   b) At the edge of the rectangle ❏
   c) At the base of the pyramid ❏
   d) Pulsating in the pentagon ❏

2. A large company has a full set of budgets. Which of the following statements should be true?
   a) They should all be independent of each other ❏
   b) Some should impact on each other ❏
   c) The capital expenditure budget should not affect the other budgets ❏
   d) They should all impact on each other ❏

3. Which of the following is a feature of the so-called 'top down' method of budgeting?
   a) Top management issues budget targets ❏
   b) Lower management issues budget proposals without prior guidance ❏
   c) There are frequent meetings
   d) Only revenue budgets are required ❏

4. Must budgets cover a period of a year?
   a) No – and they usually cover a period of six months ❏
   b) No – but they often do ❏
   c) No – and they never do ❏
   d) Yes ❏

5. In a big company, in what way is it normal for the sales budget to be broken down?
   a) By region ❏
   b) By period ❏
   c) By product ❏
   d) By all of the above ❏

6. When does capital expenditure usually start to affect cash and interest?
   a) When the orders are placed ❏
   b) When the capital items are brought into use ❏
   c) When payment is made ❏
   d) When depreciation starts ❏

7. How important is the cash budget likely to be?
   a) Important ❏
   b) Not very important ❏
   c) Not at all important ❏
   d) A complete waste of time ❏

8. Can the capital expenditure budget be altered without the balance sheet budget being affected?
   a) Yes ❏
   b) Sometimes ❏
   c) Not usually ❏
   d) No ❏

9. What should happen after the budgets have been approved?

a) Nothing ❏

b) They should be kept available for inspection when required ❏

c) Top managers should look at them from time to time ❏

d) All levels of management should regularly review actual and budget figures and explain the variances ❏

10. What are the advantages in involving all levels of management in budget preparation?

a) The budget is more likely to be realistic ❏

b) Managers are more likely to feel committed to it ❏

c) It may be good for morale ❏

d) All of the above ❏

7 × 7

1 Seven things to do today

- If your business sells goods, make sure you are holding the right amount of stock. Too much and working capital is being tied up unnecessarily; too little and you risk losing sales.
- Make sure you know the cash position and plan accordingly.
- Check which customers have not paid on time and chase them for the money.
- Check the business's progress against the budgets and take any necessary action.
- Keep an eye on the accounting ratios.
- If you do not understand any of the financial figures, ask to have them explained to you. Your colleagues will probably respect you for asking.
- Make sure you understand the differences between profit and cash. They are almost never the same.

2 Seven things to do soon

- The seven things to do today are still good ideas. So do them all again.
- Make friends with your customers, your suppliers and your bank manager.
- Try not to get bogged down in meetings. Make them effective and try to have fewer of them.
- Try to get much of your business borrowing in the form of long-term loans, rather than in overdrafts repayable on demand.
- Check that your anti-virus software is up to date.
- Check that your suppliers are still giving you a good deal. There may be better alternatives.

- Think about the saying (relating to a profit and loss account) that if you take care of the top line the bottom line will look after itself. Then discard it, because it is not true.

3 Seven key ideas

- Remember that the principles of finance are the same whether you work in a mighty corporation or a small business. The difference is in the size of the figures.
- Do not underestimate yourself. You are the expert in what you do.
- It is easy and common to drown in financial detail. Keep your eye on what is important and do not make that mistake.
- Take credit control seriously. If you are being paid late, you are being cheated.
- Prevention is better than cure.
- The information in the accounts is always out of date.
- Be sceptical about expert advice. Experts will probably give you good advice, but do not overlook the possibility that they may be mistaken. For centuries experts said that the world was flat, but Christopher Columbus proved them wrong.

4 Seven trends for tomorrow

- The population of many Western countries is ageing. This will create both opportunities and problems for businesses.
- More and more people are seeking a satisfactory work–life balance. This has important implications (both problems and opportunities) for employers.
- In recent years there have been significant increases in self-employment, business start-ups and the number of small businesses. This is likely to continue.
- There will continue to be takeovers and amalgamations among the world's biggest corporations.
- More people will work from home for at least part of the time.

- Fraudsters will continue to find ingenious ways to separate businesses and citizens from their money.
- Politicians will continue to promise a business-friendly environment and a reduction in bureaucracy. Whether they will deliver these things is another matter.

5 Seven things to remember

- When preparing a cash forecast, remember that the need for cash might peak in the middle of a period.
- Allow for contingencies when preparing budgets and forecasts.
- Allow for seasonal factors when working with accounts, budgets and forecasts.
- Don't spend too much time getting the figures exactly right. Sometimes nearly right figures produced quickly are more useful than exactly right figures produced slowly.
- Thank your staff for their contribution and discuss the figures with them as appropriate.
- Don't allow fixed costs to be too high.
- Remember the consequences of inflation. Inflation may be low today, but it has been high in the past and may well be high in the future.

6 Seven great quotes

- 'When I have to read economic documents I have to have a box of matches and start moving them into position to simplify and illustrate the points to myself.' – Sir Alec Douglas-Home (1903–95), British prime minister
- 'A bank is a place that will lend you money if you can prove that you don't need it.' – Bob Hope (1903–2003), American comedian
- 'In the long run we are all dead.' – John Maynard Keynes (1883–1946), English economist
- 'Money is like a sixth sense without which you cannot make a complete use of the other five.' – W. Somerset Maugham (1874–1965) in *Of Human Bondage*

- 'Annual income twenty pounds, annual expenditure nineteen [pounds] nineteen [shillings] and six [pence], result happiness. Annual income twenty pounds, annual expenditure twenty pounds ought and six, result misery.' – Charles Dickens (1812–70) in *David Copperfield*
- 'In this world nothing can be said to be certain, except death and taxes.' – Benjamin Franklin (1706–90), American statesman, scientist and author
- 'It is well enough that people of the nation do not understand our banking and monetary system, for if they did, I believe there would be a revolution before tomorrow morning.' – Henry Ford (1863–1947), American industrialist

7 Six great sayings and a story

- 'Give a man a fish and he will eat for a day. Teach a man to fish and he will eat for a lifetime. Teach a man how to create an artificial shortage of fish and he will eat steak.' – Jay Leno
- 'The chief business of the American people is business.' – Calvin Coolidge (President of the USA, 1923–9)
- 'Choose a job that you like and you will never have to work a day in your life.' – Confucius
- 'Turnover is vanity. Profit is sanity.' – Anon.
- 'Corporation: an ingenious device for obtaining profit without individual responsibility.' – Ambrose Bierce in *The Devil's Dictionary*
- 'I have found no greater satisfaction than achieving success through honest dealing and strict adherence to the view that, for you to gain, those you deal with should gain as well.' – Alan Greenspan
- 'Two non-financial managers were walking through a wood and were suddenly confronted by an angry bear. Seeing his companion putting on running shoes, one said, "That's no use. You can't outrun the bear in those". "I don't have to," came the reply. "I just have to outrun you."'

PART 3
Your Strategy Masterclass

Introduction

For most aspiring managers, at some point in their careers, their Personal Development Plans will include the demand to have 'greater strategic thinking ability'. We have the perception that executives operating at board level have this 'strategic thinking ability' but seldom find the route to obtain it for ourselves. The purpose of this part of the book is to provide that route. Strategy, like any other discipline, can be learned and practised. This part takes you on a journey to explore what organizational strategy is, where it fits within the context of each business, and then gives an examination of internal, external, marketing, brand and competitive strategy.

To progress to an executive position, a wide range of skills and attributes are required. Aspects such as good leadership skills, strong communication skills, commercial understanding and the ability to understand other people are all needed. Equal with these vital elements is the ability to have a good grasp of strategic thinking.

Good strategic thinking is at a huge premium in business. Far too often we see elementary errors made by very highly paid executives who undoubtedly should know better. We see businesses with successful niche products try to expand beyond their niche and then realize that it was a gargantuan error. We see successful companies stumble due to an inability to see threats or opportunities. We see companies over-expanding within their market and wondering why they trip over. The business history books are littered with organizations that supposedly exhibited a degree of 'excellence' but failed; companies who were supposedly 'built to last' but clearly weren't; companies who were supposedly moving from 'good to great' but the leveller of time has consigned them to mediocrity or even collapse.

CHAPTER 15

Understand what strategy is and what it isn't

People mean different things when they use the word 'strategy'. It is easy to define linguistically – from two Greek words 'stratos' (army) and 'ago' (to lead) and as such is about 'leading armies'. However, that is not a useful definition for business – the military analogy, as we shall see later, is mostly an unhelpful analogy. Strategy has often developed a mystique of something that is achieved by highly intelligent beings in the boardroom contemplating things so difficult to imagine that those outside the boardroom simply would not understand. This, too, is unhelpful. Strategy is simple. It is about establishing where you want to be and planning to get there. This chapter unpacks some of the myths and outlines some of its various meanings. To be an effective strategic thinker, we need to avoid the myths and 'speak' each of these meanings fluently, with the ability to move between them at ease. These 'meanings' are all strategy – they are all the right answer – so do not choose between them; understand them all.

For both the myths and the meanings, I will use ideas already available. The myths will be drawn from those in my book *Strategies of the Serengeti* and the various meanings will be my adaptations of those used by Henry Mintzberg *et al.* in *Strategy Safari*. So, with an African theme to our journey (journey is 'safari' in Swahili and the Serengeti is a vast plain spanning much of Tanzania and Kenya), let us firstly consider what strategy is not.

Strategy is not military

Much of our business terminology has military roots, from the title of 'Chief Executive Officer', to taking holiday being referred to as 'going on leave'. Strategy has a military definition but a military focus to business strategy would be disastrous. The military focus is on defeating the enemy. In business, the focus is on profitably satisfying the customers' needs. Treating the customer as the enemy would not yield a business that lasts!

Any military option has an end – victory. In business, ongoing success is the aim. Strategy aims for long-term survival and longevity, not a single definitive 'victory' end point.

Military operations have a limited sphere of activity – even the world wars did not encompass the entire world. Business can choose to limit itself or can choose to be globally omnipresent. The sphere of activity is not limited to geography. There is no rule in business that prevents a timber company from making rubber boots, then rubber cables, then the wires within cables, then telecommunications, then mobile phones (US: cell phones). We know the above company now as the Finnish giant Nokia – the military analogy would have been too limiting for their success.

Some military analogies and terminology can be useful, so do not cast them aside. However, the overarching framework of strategy is that it is much bigger, longer lasting and much more widely encompassing than the military aspects often used to describe strategy.

Strategy is not only for the hyper-intelligent

Perhaps this is a myth that is too flattering for executives to seek to defuse – although some of the decisions mentioned in this book will undoubtedly question the wisdom of some executives, albeit with the benefit of hindsight. When an organizational role includes 'strategic responsibilities', it is sometimes set apart as of greater worth and requiring higher calibre than tactical or operational responsibilities. As we shall see in the next chapter, all aspects – strategic, tactical and operational – are required for success and each is equally punctuated by potential business minefields.

We all do strategy. Perhaps part of your reason for reading this book is to understand strategy and develop your strategic thinking ability – that in itself is something that is part of your personal strategy of increasing business skills, presumably with the aim of career advancement or the success of your own business. Your very reading of this book is therefore an act with strategic intent.

Strategy is equally applicable to the global giant and the sole trader. One very smart business strategist I know left school with negligible qualifications and runs a hairdressing shop in the UK Midlands. He has steered it very successfully with a strong understanding of the customers (generally older clientele), the market (they want consistency and the same stylist as they had the previous week), the competitors (who are often seeking to be fashionable or trying something new), his distinct offering to the market (a strand of consistency for his customers in an ever accelerating world) and appreciation of his competitive advantage (i.e. what he does better than competitors – recognising his customers' requirements and meeting them). He doesn't call it 'strategy', he calls it 'common business sense'.

When my son was less than two years old, he embarked on a strategy aimed at acquiring a cuddly rabbit made by one of his elder sisters at a 'build-a-bear' workshop. It took him over six months of persistent strategic implementation – but it was successful.

If you and I, someone without qualifications and a young child can formulate and implement strategies effectively, the myth is disproved – strategy is not only for the hyper-intelligent!

Strategy is not only for the top board

In *Strategies of the Serengeti* I call this 'the elephants mating myth' – the myth suggests that strategy is something that is done at very high level, with a lot of grunting and groaning and takes about two years to see any measurable results.

Far too often in business, we have middle management paralysis. They choose not to take action as they are waiting for direction and wisdom from the board. Seldom does this waiting produce the strategic direction they crave. Good management teams readily communicate sufficient vision and direction to inspire and enable the middle management to make decisions and take action. Poor management teams do not communicate and get what they deserve – middle management is afraid to take action in case it is not in accordance with the strategy they think the senior executives must be working on, but seldom are.

Strategy formulation is for all levels of the business – we each create the strategy pertinent to our role and level. For some it may be the direction of the whole company; for a retail store manager it may be about where to site the best-selling products and how to allocate shelf space to the entire range. Either and both are strategy. Strategy is for all.

Strategy is not a big document

The annual strategic planning process of some organizations is a time-consuming exercise on filling in spreadsheets, completing a SWOT analysis[1] (see also Chapter 4) and compiling a compelling narrative, often accomplished with the use of more human resource than it would take to manage a small nation. The result, after copious revisions, is a cumbersome document. This is not strategy; it is the production of a work of narrative fiction of questionable use.

Strategy is not an annual exercise, it is an ongoing evolving discipline. It constantly changes in response to initiatives and changes in the market and the business. Recently, I was talking with a senior clinician in the British National Health Service. He had generated an idea and sought to implement it but was told that he could not have the resources for it, regardless of the almost immediate benefit it would yield because 'it is not in your strategic plan'. The advice was to put it into next year's strategic plan and when that was signed off by the executive, he could enact it. This would be a delay of many months and would see many months' benefit foregone – madness. In this case the strategic plan has become a limiter, an inhibitor and a barrier to initiative and progress.

In MBAs, all students are taught about 'emergent strategies' (opportunities and the ability to take advantage of them), which were unforeseen. Innovative, fast-moving companies are much better at taking such advantages than those encumbered by a concrete business plan. They are also taught about 'unrealized strategies', which were pertinent at the time the strategic plan was developed, but became redundant between that time and the present. For example, the 2008 global banking crisis suddenly threw the market into turmoil. All banks' expansive and acquisitive strategies became instantly unrealizable and the immediate implementation of survival strategies became paramount. By 2009, none were following their beautifully created strategic plans of 2008.

It is worth completing a strategic plan, on the condition that it is as an ongoing exercise and takes no more than a few days to compile, as it sets direction and seeks to draw together disparate activities. However, a strategic plan as an inhibitive cumbersome document is not strategy, it is bureaucracy.

Strategy is and is not like a journey

The journey analogy has significant merit but it also has limitations. Following the journey template below will add value to your strategic planning and is worth doing.

Journey template

- *Where am I? – a realistic assessment of your current position*
- *Where do I want to get to? – your intended business destination*
- *What are my options for getting there?*
- *What are the various bases on which I make that choice? – for example, is time critical? Is there a geographical remit or limitation?*
- *For those options, what resources will I need?*
- *Once a choice is made, what are my staging posts? – where should I be in six months? One year? Two years?*
- *Do I have agreement and buy-in from all relevant stakeholders?*

Now start the journey.
- *Check – am I on track? Am I meeting my staging posts? Is this destination still my destination?*

This is a good and valuable exercise, which I recommend. However, the journey analogy has disadvantages in that, like all analogies, it can break down. To perpetuate the analogy, if my journey were from New York (present location) to San Francisco (intended destination), I could have options of fly or drive. Perhaps I will choose to drive and acquire the relevant resources – car, credit card, map and so on. I then start the journey. I keep on track and am meeting my staging posts.

In this simple example, San Francisco will always be west. I will not wake up one morning and find that plate tectonics has moved San Francisco into Canada. I will not wake up one morning and find that roads no longer exist and so the motor vehicle in which I am travelling is now redundant technology and requires immediate replacement. However, in business, such factors can occur. The destination can change rapidly, indeed instantaneously. The route to market or mode of travel can change equally rapidly and good strategy is able to encompass this.

An example of such change could be the impact on US company Hoover when UK entrepreneur James Dyson developed the bagless vacuum cleaner. Both the 'destination' and the 'mode' to get there changed for Hoover – the old way of doing things was no longer appropriate. Hoover was previously able to sell the vacuum cleaning machines at a low margin as it would make a large profit on the repeat purchase consumables of the vacuum cleaner bag. Dyson changed the market in one stroke. Hoover could no longer rely on a strategy of large profits and ever increasing sales from the old technology and had to readjust strategy. The lost opportunity that Hoover had to eliminate this threat will be discussed later.

So, do use the journey analogy when formulating strategy, but do also bear in mind that the route and destination is for constant consideration and may change in response to external or internal factors at any time.

Having established what strategy is not...

- military
- only for the hyper-intelligent
- only for the top board
- a big document
- totally like a journey

...let us now consider what strategy is. This is not easy as different people use the word to mean different things. If you are given the task to 'become more strategic' in your Personal Development Plan, it is quite difficult to make that SMART (Specific, Measurable, Achievable, Relevant, Timely), which is always a good challenge to those who have requested that objective for you! Part of the reason for this is the variety of uses of the term and the nebulous nature of several of these uses.

Strategy Safari by Henry Mintzberg *et al.* is a superlative journey through the various aspects of academic strategy and in my opinion should be read by all students as part of their academic study of strategy. However, for the non-academic, he adds, in Chapter 1, a summary of his five Ps of strategy based on a 1987 article[2]. I will replicate his five Ps with my own interpretation and examples.

Strategy is a plan

As such, strategy is an intended course of action that steers an organization to achieve what it has set out to achieve. It is a plan that gives us a destination, or vision – it demonstrates an intended direction and it gives us guidance on where to go and where not to go.

However, few of us ever do exactly as we planned – the market is constantly changing and the strategy adapts accordingly. Sometimes, things just do not go as planned or sometimes we make decisions that are not part of the plan.

Strategy as a plan is fine – but the plan is an intended route from which there may be considerable variation. When Nokia was felling trees, it had no plan to move into telecommunications – the plan evolved on a step-by-step basis.

Strategy is a plan, but a constantly evolving plan.

Strategy is a pattern of behaviour

The second 'P' is that of strategy as a series of behaviours that form a pattern. The organization generates a consistency of behaviour that becomes its strategy. In the vehicle industry, the Italian company Ferrari produces some of the greatest works of motorized technology on the planet. A Ferrari is all about aspiration, expensive, fast, sporty. The pattern of behaviour of this brand and company has generated an icon. If I were to suggest a budget-priced, small-engined Ferrari family car or estate (US: station wagon), you would correctly laugh – it does not fit the pattern of behaviour and so would be a wholly inappropriate choice.

Conversely, involvement in the world Formula 1 championship fits exactly into the behavioural pattern of the brand and company – which is why they do it.

Volkswagen is a highly successful German vehicle manufacturer. They have a range of brands encompassing different areas in the market:

High: Bugatti, Lamborghini, Bentley
Medium to high: Audi
Medium: Volkswagen
Medium to low: Skoda, Seat (Seat is making a market change to become a more sporty offering but emerged from this low end of the market.)

However, the introduction of the luxurious, technically superior, beautifully crafted Volkwagen Phaeton defied all of their carefully arranged multi-brand strategy. A US$ 100,000+ vehicle with a VW badge on it does not fit the pattern. VW equals mid-market; US$ 100,000+ is higher end of the market. The Phaeton did not fit with the pattern and was rightly rejected by the car-buying public. VW were manufacturing at less than 20 per cent of the capacity for this unwanted non-pattern product. It exhibited a wrong strategy by not understanding that strategy is a pattern of behaviour.

Strategy is a position in the market

My perception of the differences between the 'pattern' and the 'position' is that 'pattern' is the behaviour you choose – it is internal to the business and within your control. I perceive 'position' as an external, market-related aspect of strategy – where you are in your chosen markets. Here, you are less in control, with the potential to be buffeted by the waves of the competitive activity and the ever-shifting winds of the customer's desires.

What position in the market will you choose and why? Some companies choose to sell a product as cheaply as possible, aspiring to gain profitability through high volume, while another will choose to sell a smaller volume of more expensive premium-priced products. I may pay £5 for a bottle of the French wine Cahors, but I may pay £50 for a champagne. The companies producing both have strategies to be profitable, the former having to sell many more bottles than the champagne producer. Some companies will choose to position themselves in a distinct niche, some will position themselves as a mass-market provider. Coca-Cola is the world's number one brand and number one carbonated drink. However, in Scotland it is number two. IrnBru rules the geographical niche of Scotland. IrnBru has chosen a position of geographical niche that has proven sustainable over decades despite every effort by the global number one to become the Scottish number one.

Strategy is a perspective

Mintzberg uses the P of perspective to mean the organization's way of doing things in a similar way to how Marvin Bower defined culture as 'the way we do things around here'[3]. I would prefer to use his own example of the Egg McMuffin but in a slightly different way.

The Egg McMuffin argument 1
It is merely a minor product extension. McDonald's have taken their standard burger product, softened the bun slightly, extracted the burger and relish, substituting it with bacon and egg. The Egg McMuffin is a product change – a variety of an existing product.

The Egg McMuffin argument 2
It is a wholescale change of approach in the market. Previously, McDonald's burgers were an 11 a.m. to 11 p.m. offering. The McMuffin has allowed the business to create a breakfast market offering a new eating occasion to their menu and a new opportunity to buy at McDonald's for its customers. McDonald's can now serve the public, and make money, from 6 a.m until 11 p.m.

Whichever perspective you take will impact your strategic decision-making. If VW had the perspective that the VW brand is mid-range, they would not have launched the Phaeton. If Mercedes-Benz had the perspective that they were executive saloon specialists, they would probably still dominate that market. If McDonald's had the perspective that they were a burger chain, they would not have created a breakfast market.

Strategy is a ploy

Others will use the word 'strategy' to mean a 'ploy' or a specific action aimed at outmanoeuvring a competitor. One of my favourite ploys was Marlboro day, 2 April 1993, when cigarette manufacturer Philip Morris cut the price of their branded cigarettes in the US by 20 per cent in response to ongoing erosion of their sales by lower price alternatives. The price of Marlboro's stock fell by 26 per cent (approx US$ 10 billion) and other branded companies suffered stock falls as 'the death of the brand' was heralded. This, however, was a myopic western-centric focus. It was also a ploy. Competitor J. R. Reynolds had little option but to copy the strategy or lose ground. They therefore also suffered loss of cash, profitability and stock price. Once Philip Morris estimated that J. R. Reynolds were sufficiently cash-weakened to be unable to respond, they launched a marketing campaign in Russia and Eastern Europe, which resulted in Marlboro being a highly sought after, profitable and successful brand there. It was at the very top of that market for well over a decade until Japanese Tobacco managed to topple it – a great ploy in the US to gain success in the higher growth Eastern European market.

The Western press focused almost exclusively on the effects in the US and ignored the wider global successes, which were longlasting and highly profitable. Even in the US, Marlboro regained its lost stock price within two years and history has shown it to be a ploy that generated success sustained for a considerable time.

Summary

Understanding what strategy is and what it isn't is not easy because so many people have different opinions on the matter and use different definitions. Many also perpetuate myths that are unhelpful to understanding strategy. In this chapter, we have shown that strategy is not:

- military
- only for the hyper-intelligent
- only for the top board
- a big document.

We have also shown that strategy can be considered to be like a journey but that the analogy, like all analogies, breaks down. Strategic destination, intention and route can change more dramatically than seismic transformation can change a landscape.

We have shown that strategy can equally be some or all of the five Ps:

- plan – an intended set of actions
- pattern – a consistent behaviour
- position – a location of products in a market
- perspective – a view, opinion or stance
- ploy – a manoeuvre.

The intention of strategy is to give direction, boundaries and co-ordination of effort to seek to achieve our objectives for our organization. Without this, the organization will almost certainly fail.

'There are two types of business: those who have their strategy right and those who are going out of business.'
Stephen Berry

Fact-check (answers at the back)

1. What is the definition of the word strategy?
   a) Planning a journey ☐
   b) Creating activity ☐
   c) Achieving results ☐
   d) Leading an army ☐

2. Why is the military analogy inadequate? (note – 2 correct answers)
   a) The terminology is inappropriate in business ☐
   b) The chain of command is different in business and the military ☐
   c) It assumes an endpoint of victory when business has no end point ☐
   d) Military focus is on the enemy, strategy on the customer ☐

3. What are the dangers of a strategic plan document?
   a) It may get lost ☐
   b) It can become too static and inflexible ☐
   c) It is not seen by everyone in the company ☐
   d) It can be used to prop open fire exits ☐

4. What are the advantages of using the 'journey' analogy for strategy?
   a) It is easy to understand and communicate ☐
   b) It creates a solid unchanging plan ☐
   c) Many people use it ☐
   d) It may identify hidden resources ☐

5. What is the first step in using the journey analogy for strategy?
   a) Analysis of where we are ☐
   b) Analysis of where we want to get to ☐
   c) Consideration of obstacles on the route ☐
   d) Understand why we want to make the journey ☐

6. Why would a low-cost Ferrari family car be a bad idea?
   a) The price would be wrong ☐
   b) It does not fit the pattern of behaviour that has made the brand successful ☐
   c) As a ploy, it would be too radical ☐
   d) Americans prefer American cars ☐

7. Why have Volkswagen not manufactured the Phaeton at maximum capacity?
   a) It is a high-tech, superior vehicle and the complexities of the computer systems mean that it takes longer to manufacture ☐
   b) It has not been adequately marketed as all its attributes have not been advertised sufficiently ☐
   c) It is a high-prestige car with a medium-market badge – and does not fit the pattern of behaviour of the VW marquee and so the public have rejected it ☐
   d) As it is new technology, it is prone to breaking down ☐

CHAPTER 16

Understand what drives strategy and what strategy drives

The purpose of strategy is to take an organization from where it is to where it wants to be. As such, strategy does not exist alone, in isolation from all other aspects of the business; it is integral to everything within the business. Most organizations have the following:

- a vision
- a strategic plan
- a budget
- a culture
- a structure
- a brand
- a public relations message
- corporate and social responsibility (CSR) initiatives.

However, these are frequently disparate and unconnected. For example, the organizational structure is not about getting people's names and roles in boxes, then connecting them with lines and dotted lines. The organizational structure is not about communication, nor about reporting. Its primary purpose is to facilitate the effective implementation of the organizational strategy. If it is not doing that, it is the wrong structure. There is nothing new in that argument – Alfred Chandler stated it in 1962 – but many organizations have not listened. Many see the aspects above as distinct and not inter-related.

This chapter will show where strategy fits into the business, what drives strategy and what strategy affects. As a bonus, it will also contextualize the other factors above – where they fit into business.

Organizational vision

The primary driver of any organization is its vision. This is what it seeks to achieve – its purpose on this planet.

> *'Good business leaders create a vision, articulate the vision, passionately own the vision, and relentlessly drive it to completion.'*
> Jack Welch

> *'The very essence of leadership is that you have to have a vision.'*
> Theodore Hesburgh

> *'We think too small, like the frog at the bottom of the well. He thinks the sky is only as big as the top of the well. If he surfaced, he would have an entirely different view.'*
> Mao Tse-Tung

All other aspects of the business must be driven by this vision as they are the means by which the vision becomes a reality – and this includes the organizational strategy.

In many cases, so called 'vision statements' are mere words on paper – they are not visions. For a vision to be a vision, it must achieve certain tasks:

- Drive and direct the business
- Inspire and motivate the staff
- Determine and set the goals
- Initiate and steer the strategy
- Establish and challenge the ethics, values, modus operandi – 'the way we do things around here' (Bower).

Vision impacts everything. If it doesn't, it's not a vision. Some authors and consultants try to make different definitions of vision, mission, or purpose. I don't support such semantics and have never seen such a discussion add any value. I am happy to use those words interchangeably but prefer 'vision'. Most importantly, its job is to propel everything which the organization and the people in it seek to do.

The most important people in the success or impotence of a vision are the organizational top team. If they merely pay lip service to a theoretical set of words, the 'vision statement' simply isn't a vision for the organization. If, however, they are the most passionate drivers of the vision and 'live' the vision more strongly, consistently and fervently than anyone else, both they and the vision are doing their jobs.

How does the vision drive strategy?

The vision states the intention. This will drive a series of goals. I have seen these goals in many formats for many companies, but for the vast majority they seem to be the same five – a goal each on:

- what we do
- how we do it
- our customers
- our people
- money.

Some readers will now be wondering why they have just paid hundreds of thousands of dollars to a consultancy to help develop their goals – and yet they still have these five!

The purpose of the goals is to set out what needs to be achieved in order to make the vision a reality. Some writers use the word 'objectives' for these goals. I choose not to as 'objectives' are frequently used in personal performance management where the objectives are SMART. The 'goals' we are now discussing do not necessarily have to be SMART. They can be so – this is not a prohibitive statement, it is just not a necessary requirement. For example, if the goal is 'to have the best, the most innovative and the most satisfied staff in the industry', it is an ongoing goal – the T of 'timely' is missing.

These high-level goals, driven by the organizational vision, are not intended to be changed frequently. They should have equal longevity with the vision. Conversely, the 'objectives' of Personal Development Plans should be achieved and developed as progress in the plan proceeds. The 'goals' do not change very often, if at all; the 'objectives' can change as fast as you can achieve them.

These goals then drive the strategy. The strategy comprises the things that the business is doing in order to achieve the goals in order to make the vision a reality. Whether the 'things' are the strategy of plan, pattern, position, perspective or ploy, their task is to achieve the goals so that the vision is accomplished.

To continue our goal example of 'to have the best, the most innovative and the most satisfied staff in the industry', we would put in place strategies to achieve this goal. These would include:

- A remuneration strategy – you will not get the best people in the industry without a top quartile pay policy.
- A recruitment strategy – people are not a blank canvas – they come with experience and preconceptions. If the goal involves the best, the most innovative and the most satisfied, the recruitment strategy needs to target those who show the attributes required and therefore are more likely to be satisfied in your business. You would not recruit a conservative, risk-averse person to a company that prizes innovation – the company will not achieve its goals and the person will be dissatisfied and stressed.
- An engagement strategy – actions to ensure that the staff are emotionally engaged with the business and its vision. It is a truism that a person's physical presence at a place of work can be bought, but their emotional engagement has to be earned, coaxed and nurtured.
- A leadership strategy – the adage that people tend not to leave companies, they leave bosses, inevitably has an element of truth in it. If our goal includes 'satisfied staff', we need to have a strategy for generating the best business leaders we can.

There are many more staff related strategies, but for brevity I will pause there and ask you to derive another five or six areas of strategy to achieve this goal. Perhaps you may choose to look at:

- location strategies – office location and amount of home working
- premises – don't expect creativity in a sterile office
- the performance management process – the outputs of a good 'PM' process are direction, development and motivation
- a bonus, reward and recognition system
- technology
- staff learning, training and development
- organizational communication
- and many more.

There is nothing new in this progression of Vision – Goal – Strategy. I have seen a variety of versions, for example MOST (mission – objective – strategy – tactics), POST (purpose – objectives – strategy – tactics), VAST (vision – aims – strategy – tactics), PAST and so on. They all seek to do the same thing: to drive the vision into reality by creating goals (or objectives or aims), then generating the strategies to achieve the goals and then going further to let the strategy drive the shorter-term tactics, which then, when accumulated, realize the strategic intent (i.e. achieve what you set out to achieve).

Sometimes I observe conversations seeking to differentiate between strategy and tactics. Again, as with vision, mission and purpose, I would term these discussions non-value-adding semantics and have never seen them yield any benefit to a business. One person's tactics can be another person's strategy depending on their role and position within the business. I would advise progressing through to practical action rather than debating about which box something should sit in.

The ladder of business success

However, I would argue that stopping at 'tactics' is one step short. I would also argue that this progression does not adequately engage or position the elements such as brand, culture and structure that we mentioned at the beginning of this chapter. To alleviate these omissions, I use a 'ladder'. With the

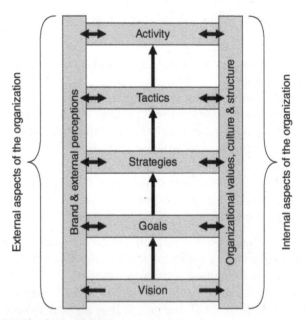

The ladder of business success

ladder analogy, we start climbing at the bottom rung and move upwards. Each rung is important and if one is missing the ladder becomes dangerous and has the potential of not achieving its purpose (in our case, business success). It should also be noted that, for a ladder to function correctly, each rung should be firmly connected to the uprights on each side and also that the uprights are parallel – that is, they are both going in the same direction.

The rungs

The progression from vision to tactics has been discussed. However, by adding the fifth rung, activity, I am seeking to ensure that what we do on a day-to-day basis is firmly driven by the organizational vision and hence each little activity from each individual is taking us one step closer to making the tactics succeed, which combined result in a successful strategy, which collated mean achieved goals, which then result in a realized vision.

For example, the UK retailer John Lewis has achieved a great progression from vision to activity in the rare instances

240

when the customer is dissatisfied and seeks to return a product. The vision is about success in its areas of activity as a high street retailer; the goals include aspects of customer satisfaction. It is easy to have satisfied customers when everything is going well and there are many strategies John Lewis instigates to enhance this. However, it takes genuine class to have exemplary customer satisfaction when things have gone badly. John Lewis therefore has strategies to enhance customer satisfaction that relate to the times when dissatisfaction is encountered. This percolates into tactics that include how they train their staff to deal with customers, their process for handling problems and, the one I want to focus on, for when the customer wishes to return a product.

So far we have a clear link between the vision and the tactics of dealing with returned goods. But what if I went into a store with a product to return, probably stressed by the situation, and then had an argument with a member of staff exhibiting poor attitude and no desire to assist the customer? The faulty product, my own stress and the poor attitude of the staff all compound to give me a wholly dissatisfied scenario and I may decide never to shop at that store again. The strategy is clear – strategies to ensure satisfied customers. The tactics are clear – an array of tactics to deal with returned goods. However, in this example the whole compilation of vision up to tactics would collapse if the activity was wrong – the staff member was unhelpful and did not enact the tactics, or strategy or goals, and negatively impacted on the vision.

In many retail stores worldwide, that is the experience customers have when returning faulty goods. Not in John Lewis. In John Lewis, a customer enters the store to return a product. The place to go is clearly marked. The staff are well trained, polite, helpful and utterly professional in ensuring that the customer walks out of the store with a superlative customer experience, a new, working product (if that is what they want) with no problem, no argument and more importantly, with an attitude that means they will return to John Lewis to shop again.

Anyone can provide good customer service for satisfied customers. Few manage it for dissatisfied customers. I use the

John Lewis example of this connectedness of the ladder when speaking at business conferences in the UK. So far dozens of people in the audiences will willingly extol the virtues of John Lewis from their experience of when things have gone wrong and they return a product. I ask them to give John Lewis a score out of 10 for their customer experience when in such a stressed and negative scenario. Most give 10. Many give 9. But I've only heard two people give low scores of 4 and 5, and in fairness, I think the 4 contributed to her own misfortune!

A more international example in the retail sector is that of the Apple shops. The vision, and everything about the company, is about innovation, superior technology, cutting-edge design, passion for the brand and high fashion electrical products. By simply walking into a store you observe activities that illustrate all of these. The rungs are fully connected and the strategies are in their rightful place – driving the tactics and daily activities in order to achieve the goals needed to make the vision a reality.

The left upright

This represents all external factors of the business – the brand and the perception of the company by all outside of it: customers, potential customers, suppliers, shareholders, the public, governments.

If this left upright exists separate from the rest of the business, the ladder in our analogy would collapse. The vision drives the goals and in due course the strategy, tactics and activities but it also drives the left upright. The business, driven by the vision, uses strategies, tactics and activities to impact and influence everything on the left upright. This is where brand strategy, advertising tactics, and public relations activity interface. They do not exist on their own; they are part of the ladder of business success seeking to make the vision a reality. If a brand strategy is in conflict with the vision, it is a wrong brand strategy.

The strategies of corporate and social responsibility exist here. Their purpose is to present the company in the best manner for achieving the perception it requires, ultimately to assist in achieving the vision. Toy manufacturer Hasbro has built a children's hospital in Rhode Island, US. It is a monumental and wholly admirable commitment to children. It is also a huge physical barrier to any criticism of the commercial and profitable New York Stock Exchange listed company as it seeks to market its products to children. This is a corporate and social responsibility strategy seeking to enable the business vision. Virgin Atlantic Airline collects passengers' spare currency and channels it, as many other airlines do, into doing good in developing world communities. The in-flight video shows VAA crew, in their uniforms, interacting with children in sub-Saharan Africa. It is part of a very convincing public relations strategy, about which the staff seem genuinely engaged. Does it help achieve the vision? Absolutely! Having seen the video in-flight, it adds positive impressions about the company, brand and staff in my mind – so I am more likely to return as a customer.

The right upright

This represents all the factors that are internal to the company and therefore within its control. Some of them are easier than others to control – structure is relatively simple to construct, culture is infinitely more complex – but they are still internal factors that the company can influence at will.

The purpose of strategy is to make the vision become a reality (via achieving the goals). The purpose of structure is to facilitate the success of the strategies, tactics and activities, which in due course (via strategies and goals) seek to make the vision a reality. The purposes of culture or values or organizational processes are all the same – to achieve the vision. In many cases, this connection does not seem to be realized; the link of rung to upright is then broken and the ladder is unsafe.

Strategy (and tactics and activity) interface with all these elements. We can have a strategy of cultural change – to help achieve the vision. We can have a strategy of embedding our company values – to help achieve the vision.

Failure to make these vital connections, either between the progression of the rungs as we climb the ladder or between rungs and either of the uprights, generates an unsafe ladder. This leads to poor co-ordination of business activity, lack of direction and purpose, and uncertainty. It is ultimately a sign of poor leadership as it is one of the core responsibilities of the top executives to make their vision a reality. Failure to make these connections means that an organization runs the risk of being dragged in one direction by its budget, another direction by its brand, a third by its values, another by its culture and yet another by its vision. Any business being dragged in so many directions by such varied competing factors is doomed.

Summary

Strategy, or any other facet of business such as culture, brand, recruitment, structure or public relations, should not exist in a separate bubble with the organization appearing as an amalgam of a vast number of these unrelated bubbles. The organizational vision drives everything – including strategy. The vision is the statement of desire – what or where the business wants to be. This will require the achievement of a number of goals. The job of strategy is to find a way or route to achieve these goals. This way or route is then broken down into lower-level, shorter-term chunks termed 'tactics', which in turn are translated into the day-to-day activity of every employee. Each person is therefore making small contributions to the achievement of the vision with each action.

All strategies fit here – driven by vision and driving action – whether they are brand strategies, advertising strategies, human resources strategies, whole-company strategies, product strategies or any other of the myriad possible strategies that a business will embark on as it seeks to turn its vision aspiration into a reality.

Fact-check (answers at the back)

1. What drives everything in a business?
   a) The vision ☐
   b) The strategy ☐
   c) The Chief Executive ☐
   d) The customer ☐

2. Why do some 'vision statements' not actually fulfil the function of a vision?
   a) They are not adventurous enough ☐
   b) The staff cannot recite them ☐
   c) They do not direct and inspire the people ☐
   d) The customer doesn't understand them ☐

3. What did Theodore Hesburgh say about vision?
   a) Organizations should have one ☐
   b) They must be well communicated ☐
   c) A lack of vision will give a lack of direction ☐
   d) Vision is the very essence of leadership ☐

4. Which of these is NOT a requirement of a vision?
   a) To determine and set the goals ☐
   b) To initiate and steer the strategy ☐
   c) To establish and challenge the ethics ☐
   d) To communicate the business to the customers ☐

5. Why does the ladder model use the term 'goals' rather than 'objectives'?
   a) To ensure a differentiation between these and performance management objectives ☐
   b) Because they are aims rather than achievable targets ☐
   c) Because they do not have to be SMART ☐
   d) Because the author prefers football terminology ☐

6. What is the purpose of an organization's structure?
   a) To show where people fit into the business ☐
   b) To help the successful implementation of the strategy ☐
   c) To demonstrate who reports to whom ☐
   d) To give staff career aspirations ☐

7. What is the purpose of an organization's culture?
   a) To keep staff motivated ☐
   b) To make the workplace an enjoyable place to be ☐
   c) To help the successful implementation of the strategy ☐
   d) To give the Human Resources department something to talk about ☐

8. Why should strategy, vision, culture, brand, budget and so on be integrated?
a) It makes them easier to manage ❏
b) Lack of integration pulls the company in many different directions ❏
c) It looks better for shareholders ❏
d) It saves duplication of effort ❏

9. What is an organization's vision?
a) A statement of what it sees as its purpose and what it seeks to achieve ❏
b) A statement that will inspire the employees to greater achievement ❏
c) A statement to draw all aspects of the business together ❏
d) A statement of how the business sees itself in the marketplace ❏

10. Who are the most important influences on whether the vision succeeds or fails?
a) The employees ❏
b) The customers ❏
c) The top team/board ❏
d) The Human Resources department ❏

CHAPTER 17

Understand internal strategy

Strategy can apply to the direction taken by the entire business; for example, whether it focuses on a small niche market such as Scottish beverage IrnBru or a ubiquitous global market such as Coca-Cola; whether it focuses on selling large numbers of low-margin products or a smaller number of higher-margin products, such as the budget airlines or the executive-focused global carriers; whether it seeks to innovate, like Gillette, or follow the leader as Wilkinson Sword does; whether it progresses one idea at a time in the market, as Apple usually does, or multiple ideas unsure of which will succeed, as drug companies do. However, these sorts of strategic decisions are likely to be beyond the reach of most readers. For most people, their first encounter with business strategy is in implementing some form of internal strategy. It is still strategy – any of the five Ps – it is still driven by the organizational vision, and is still vital in moving towards achieving the company goals.

This chapter will explore some of the areas within any business where we need success. Each of them is critical and a failure in any one can generate an inability to achieve what the company has set out to do. The chapter will focus on the internal building blocks of business and the strategies to get them right.

The building blocks of business

There are a number of key areas in business that are critical for success. We need to ensure that we have strategies in place to generate a desired outcome for each of them. The 'building blocks of business' model identifies seven areas and aims, to impress on any business the importance of strategies to manage and maximise the benefit of each of them while also identifying potential vulnerabilities and then generating internal strategies to remove these vulnerabilities.

The model can also be used at department or team level, so the aspiring manager can use this structure early in their career.

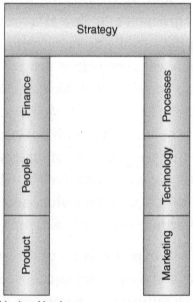

The seven building blocks of business

Most of us will have taken examinations at some point in our lives. In almost all exams, a score of six out of seven would have generated a healthy pass (over 85 per cent!). However, in this structure six out of seven is not good enough. Six out of seven will leave one vulnerable area through which failure can flow into the company, division or team. The overall internal strategy – part of the right upright of the ladder of business success – is to derive strategies for developing each of the seven areas. We will consider some aspects of each of the seven, but first pose a question: *Where is the customer?*

The seven building blocks do not include the customer, yet we have established that the aim of business is to profitably satisfy customer needs. Surely this model cannot be suggesting that we ignore the customer in strategy formulation?

Indeed, it isn't. The customer has to be paramount in each of the blocks, not a separate block on its own. Unless each block is customer focused, it is unlikely to be performing its role effectively.

Throughout this chapter I will give some examples of relevant strategy from well-known companies but also some from my own experience and career. All my career examples are true but the companies remain anonymous to protect my former work colleagues!

Product

Product strategies are about producing what people will buy. Traditionally we have expressed such strategy as meeting a customer need, but as Apple have shown with the iPhone and iPad, they can create the need – the customer didn't know they needed an iPad until the late Steve Jobs told them that they did!

Progressing this, the 'need', is equally valid whether it is a real need or a perceived need. In Japan, it is common practice to wear a facemask to prevent the transmission or receiving of cold or flu germs from other people. The germs are airborne and so are able to pass freely through the mask, which has little practical purpose. However, the need is perceived and millions are sold to Japanese citizens worldwide. Similarly in the Western world, millions of dollars, pounds and euros are spent on vitamins, supplements and herbal concoctions with no discernible scientific advantage – but the advantage is perceived and profits made as a result.

Conversely, I sometimes hear of businesses complaining that their product is extremely useful for meeting a customer need, but the customer does not seem to realize it. If the customer does not realize it, the need is not perceived, so there is no use for the product until the customer does realize it. To get a 'tick' in this product box, the product must meet a clearly defined need and the customer must be fully in agreement that it does so. The organization needs to have in place product strategies to enhance this. These would include new product development strategies.

Further aspects of product strategy will be discussed in the next three chapters on marketing, brand and competitive strategies. We will therefore save exploration of considering 'product' until then. For this chapter, we will just acknowledge that a product meets a need of a customer – a real or a perceived need.

People

We have already covered some examples of people strategies in the previous chapter (remuneration, recruitment, engagement, leadership, working environment, performance management, bonus reward and recognition). We will therefore be brief in the examples in this section.

I worked briefly in one business where the strategy was to pay the manufacturing staff the lowest pay possible. I also worked in a company where the remuneration strategy was that we would pay the highest in the industry by some considerable amount so that anyone leaving would be paid significantly less for the same job in any rival company.

For both these businesses, I would say that the remuneration strategy was right. For the former, the work was repetitive, functional and did not require significant training, skill or even intelligence. Staff turnover was high as people found better paid jobs, but we were always able to recruit from the ranks of the unemployed. The strategy resulted in keeping costs down and therefore keeping prices to the customer as low as possible. In the second company, the skill requirements were immense. Our reputation was as the premier quality provider in that market and, to my knowledge, we were never the cheapest on any of the tenders we won. Customers were buying a result, not a commodity. Our high-pay strategy meant that we were able to choose from the best and the most enthusiastic people in the industry – that strategy enhanced our brand and external perception, and was a strategy wholly in line with achieving our vision of high-quality accomplishments.

Customer-focused people strategy is about prioritizing the effectiveness of those who interface with customers. In one company, we produced the organization organogram with the customer at the top. The highest employee on the chart was the receptionist – the customer's first point of contact with the company. Customer-focused people strategy is about training people to give 'John Lewis level' service and rewarding them when they do. The same applies if the customer is an internal customer in your business.

Finance

We have considered having the right product in the market and reviewed some product strategies, but have we got the right product to profitably meet our customer needs? The inclusion of the word 'profitably' is vital as most customers would love to acquire a Rolls Royce car for £1. The customer wins and the company would fail. When car maker British Leyland made the Mini in 1959, they were selling it for £500. It is said that German manufacturer BMW, who ironically now own the Mini brand, looked at the car and concluded that they could not manufacture it for any less than £520 and so concluded that British Leyland must be making a loss on each vehicle. They were. British Leyland had made a simple error of not understanding the building block of finance. They sought to learn from their mistakes. In the 1970s, the nationalized behemoth produced the Hillman Avenger. They worked out how much the car had cost them to make, added a suitable margin and placed the car on the market at £822. The problem was that comparable cars were being sold significantly more cheaply – the Ford Escort at £635 and the Vauxhall Viva at £690. They had made another classic mistake of financial strategy – cost plus pricing.

Being successful in this building block is about getting the right product to the right customers at the right price, which means that the customer buys and the company profits. It sounds so simple, but so many mistakes are made. Here are some true examples from my finance career.

Example 1 – flexible plastic manufacture

I worked for a company that made millions of plastic bags for bread, confectionery and snacks, carrier bags and others. Company folklore was that bags made from polypropylene (a type of plastic) generated greater margins than polythene bags. So, when we were behind target on margin, we would ask the sales force to focus on polypropylene. One day I decided to investigate that folklore. It may have been true 15 years earlier when the company was formed, but my investigation showed that polypropylene had a lower margin and therefore when we were short on margin we were instructing the sales force to exacerbate the situation by selling more low-margin product! This would constitute a failure in the finance block of the 'building blocks of business'.

Example 2 – food industry

In another company, we produced a fantastic high quality product, a salmon and broccoli tart. It was an exemplary example of good factory-produced food. However, we found that the customer was only prepared to pay a small premium for this superlative product and if we raised the price higher, demand would fall. We reluctantly took the decision to cease production and use the productive capacity to increase sales of higher-margin, lower-quality and less-exciting quiche Lorraine. Profits from that manufacturing line soared. Producing the product at the price the customer feels is correct is vital for the finance block.

Example 3 – solid plastic manufacture

I had to oversee a manufacturer for a short period of time – it made plastic dustbins and watering cans. Some costs in any environment are fixed – they do not alter with the quantity produced – such as the rent and rates of the factory or office, the office and sales staff salaries, and the rental charges on the cars of the sales team. These costs are then spread or proportioned across each product so that the British Leyland Mini error is not replicated. I saw that this company was taking seven seconds to make a waste bin. Competitors were taking three seconds. The company was therefore producing less than half the quantity of product that the competitors could in the same time. This also meant that the amount of overhead apportioned to each waste bin, assuming both companies' costs to be equal, was more than twice that which the competitors apportioned. This company was therefore either settling for a lower margin or pricing their product too high.

Example 4 – hospital

This example raises the issue that the cheapest may not be the best. In two examples, a centralized procurement department made changes to items used by medical surgeons. One was cheaper paper towels on which they dried their washed hands prior to and during operations. The other was cheaper latex gloves, which they used while operating. In both cases, the procurement decision was detrimental. The paper towels were so thin that the surgeons were using four or five every time they washed their hands, compared with two paper towels previously. Use of paper towelling, at the slightly cheaper price, more than doubled and overall costs increased. The new latex gloves were thinner with a lower-quality latex – but cheaper. For many surgeons, the gloves tore when being put on and so were immediately discarded and another pair used. Again, overall usage rocketed, overtaking the cost saving and overall cost went up. Purchasing strategies need to be thought through!

Customer-focused finance is about providing the product at the right price on the market. Business-focused finance is about producing the product at the right cost to make a profit. The correct price is always what the customer is willing to pay and so the best pricing strategy is often to work backwards from there:

● How much is the customer willing to pay?
● How much can I manufacture the product for?
● Does the difference between the two give me adequate margin (or profitability)?
● If not, what strategies can I put in place to increase the value in the customer's opinion and what strategies can I put in place to drive down costs?

Processes

This is an often neglected area of strategic focus but can yield great benefit, as McDonald's and Amazon have proved. One of the slickest processes I have witnessed is how McDonald's make a burger. In my job, I often train Finance Directors. I sometimes advise them to visit McDonald's to observe the conversion of raw material into finished product, which is then packaged and rapidly sold – converting it into cash. I tell them that every process in their businesses should be that smooth – whether it is your customer's interface with you or whether it is the generation of your management accounts. Better processes decrease costs and so interface with internal finance strategies, lead to less people frustration and so interface with internal people strategies, and can have external customer consequences too, as Amazon demonstrate.

Amazon pioneered 'one-click technology' to ensure that it is as easy as possible to buy from them. They recommend potential purchases based on your previous purchase history. They will do everything they can to make the sales process as quick and as easy as can be.

The world of behavioural psychometrics (Myers Briggs, DISC, and over 100 others) has not changed significantly since the creation of these tools in the 1920s to 1940s. In most cases we complete a paper-based questionnaire, send it to an expert for analysis and some time later receive their time-intensive deliberations by post. More recently some have moved to online evaluations which, for the higher-quality more useful reports, are then subject to the same expert deliberation and a delay of only a few days before receiving a document. EvaluationStore.com has built itself as the provider of a process that does what coaches and experts take hours to produce in just a few minutes. An online evaluation is completed and before you have made a cup of tea, a full report and analysis has entered your inbox. They haven't changed the evaluation, just the process by which it is done and by which it is delivered to the customer.

Technology

The critical factor in considering internal technology strategies
is the use of the word 'appropriate'. The overarching question
is whether your strategies will yield the appropriate level of
technology for the business. It is easy to get seduced by a
desire for the latest or greatest when it is not required. One UK
discount retailer deliberately chooses the cheapest and lowest
level of technology they can get away with. This minimizes their
expenditure and the pattern of behaviour (internal) fits with the
low-cost positioning in the market (external). Conversely, it would
be ludicrous for hi-tech Apple stores to adopt that strategy –
there would be an internal/external, pattern/position mismatch.

In Europe and the US, where both labour costs and
educational levels are high, high technology levels are likely
to be more appropriate than in some other parts of the world.
One friend was visiting a hospital in a remote area of sub-
Saharan Africa. Some high technology had been generously
donated by a well-meaning American charity. However,
the hospital did not have the expertise to use it. It was
inappropriate technology and lay redundant.

A 2011 example of technology being inadequate was
the gadget website EBuyer. They saw the last Monday of
November as an opportunity to sell a range of products,
online, at very heavily discounted prices – mostly £1. Cameras,
games, laptops were offered for £1. However, the increased
demand for the products sent website use rocketing and
EBuyer had horrendously miscalculated the impact on their
server capacity – the website crashed, leaving customers
unable to buy due to inadequate planning of the technology.

Marketing

Marketing strategies will be considered more fully in Chapter 18, so we will move on.

Strategy

Every board I have ever been on and every board I have ever worked with has, at some point, degenerated to what I term its 'highest level of irrelevance'. The board comprises Directors, yet, despite our job titles, we often undertake the less strategic tasks of managing. One of the reasons for this is that it is more within our comfort zones – we are more experienced at the roles that have taken us to the board-table than we are at actually functioning as a board. Our challenge is to ensure that the board (or divisional leadership team) exercises its mandate and requirement to operate at strategic level. If we achieve this, we will be exercising our roles more correctly and undertaking those vital tasks such as considering alternative strategies, exploring whether a strategy is working or not, whether strategic aspects are on track or falling behind.

The best way I have found to do this is to implement the CIMA strategic scorecard (Chartered Institute of Management Accountants). A free-of-charge explanatory download can be obtained from their website CIMAglobal.com.

Strategic position	Strategic options
Strategic implementation	Strategic risk

*The CIMA strategic scorecard*TM

Most of us have used versions of Kaplan and Norton's 'balanced scorecard', although I rarely ever see one that is truly balanced – they are usually heavily financially biased. This is a good tool for assisting with the operational aspects of the business and as such is a management tool, not a board-level tool, where Directors should direct. My suggested way of keeping strategy on the board agenda and ensuring that the conversation is about the right things and at the right level is to have the four aspects of the scorecards as standing items in the board meeting and in the board information pack – of equal, if not greater importance than the financial report.

What the board members discuss in this strategy section will be different each meeting and they will be dependent on the compilers and providers of board information producing a workable, consistent and appropriate set of material for each meeting. Examples of what should be discussed at each point could include:

- **Position:** Here they would consider large-scale external aspects such as the five Ps or small-scale internal aspects such as those covered in this chapter.
- **Choice:** The evaluation of options, the basis of choice, parameters and requirements of that choice.
- **Risk:** What could go wrong? Are there risks in the supply chain? Risks to the customer choice with alternatives and substitute goods? What competitor activity is under way or expected? What internal risks (right side of the ladder) are evident?
- **Implementation:** Are we on track? Is a strategy working? Is it within the parameters we agreed and achieving the requirements we set?

In each case, there will be good information available and relevant discussion possible, but also the process of methodically considering strategy like this will highlight where there is an absence of good-quality information. For example, if we are unaware of competitor activity, this should set all board members' neural alarm bells ringing and the information should be sought.

Summary

Are we selling the right product, with the right people, at the right price and cost, by the right process, with the right technology and the right marketing, and is our overall strategy correct? The 'building blocks of business' mode guides us through this strategic thought process. It seeks to develop a business that actively considers all these aspects, and hopefully can in due time answer 'yes' to each of those questions.

In order to get these right, each block has to have the customer as its focus, but each aspect is internal, within our control or influence. As a template for consideration, it therefore provides us with a checklist of important aspects to contemplate in the strategic development of our business. Used critically, it can highlight weak points in our business strategy and provide the focus of how to improve.

Strategy isn't only about external factors and manoeuvring in the marketplace; it is also about getting ourselves in the right shape and the right format to be effective as a business. Strategies for success should include strategies to improve and maximise these internal factors as well as the more high-profile and arguably more exciting external strategies.

Fact-check (answers at the back)

1. What are the building blocks of business?
   a) Product, people, finance, strategy, process, technology, marketing ❏
   b) Product, research, customer, advertising, distribution, logistics ❏
   c) Product, price, plan, place, people, promotion, ❏
   d) Plan, pattern, position, perspective, ploy ❏

2. Why is 'customer' not a building block?
   a) Companies should focus on getting their business right – the customer will follow ❏
   b) There are always sufficient customers if the marketing is correct ❏
   c) Too much customer focus decreases profitability ❏
   d) The customer should be at the heart of every block in the model ❏

3. What is needed for success in the product block?
   a) Having a product available to sell ❏
   b) Having a good process of continuing product development ❏
   c) Having a product that the customer realizes meets their need ❏
   d) Having a range of alternative products for the customer to choose from ❏

4. What is the right price to charge?
   a) A price that satisfies the customer's need and makes a profit ❏
   b) A low price to gain market penetration ❏
   c) A price that makes a profit to make the company sustainable ❏
   d) The highest price the customer will pay ❏

5. What are the sections of the CIMA strategic scorecard?
   a) Customer, market, product, marketing ❏
   b) Analysis, option, choice, implementation ❏
   c) Strategic position, options, risk, implementation ❏
   d) Finance, price, cost, profit ❏

6. What would get a 'tick' in the technology block?
   a) Strategies to secure the best available technology ❏
   b) Strategies to implement new technologies more quickly ❏
   c) Strategies to ensure that your technology is better than the competitor's technology ❏
   d) Strategies to ensure the most appropriate level of technology ❏

7. What have EvaluationStore.com done to psychometric profiling tests?
   a) Changed the process by making it online and instant ❏
   b) Changed the product by making it more modern and relevant ❏
   c) Changed the marketing by having only an online offering ❏
   d) Changed the strategy by merging behavioural and personality evaluation ❏

8. When would the people remuneration strategy be appropriate to pay the lowest possible?
   a) When it is manual work, not office or clerical work ❏
   b) When the company needs to save money ❏
   c) When it is work in a developing country without a full infrastructure ❏
   d) When the work is of a low skill level, easy to train and recruit for ❏

9. When would the people remuneration strategy be appropriate to pay the highest in the market?
   a) When a country has a high standard of living ❏
   b) When the job is highly skilled and the company wants the best employees ❏
   c) When it is a fair-trade business and the payment to the producer should be enough to live on ❏
   d) When there is a labour shortage and companies are competing for employees ❏

10. What was/is wrong with the finance strategy of cost plus pricing?
    a) It could have had mistakes in cost calculation ❏
    b) It does not contain contingency in case of manufacturing price movements ❏
    c) It is purely internally focused and does not consider what the market will pay ❏
    d) It is old fashioned and more modern methods should be used ❏

CHAPTER 18

Understand marketing strategy

The Chartered Institute of Marketing defines marketing as:

> *'The management process responsible for identifying, anticipating and satisfying customer requirements profitably'*

but adds:

> *'In the fast-moving world of business, definitions rarely stay the same.'*

Marketing strategy would then be the set of processes, or the path taken, to turn that definition into a reality for your organization. However, the 'profitability' requirement and 'customer' centrality demonstrates that it is focused on the commercial sector. Not-for-profit, government and public sector organizations should equally be concerned about marketing. This definition therefore has some omissions. Conversely, many would argue that the definition is too broad – taken literally, it encompasses the majority of what a business does – from procurement and manufacturing to logistics and finance.

The American Marketing Association defines marketing as:

> *'The activity, set of institutions, and processes for creating, communicating, delivering, and exchanging offerings that have value for customers, clients, partners, and society at large'.*

And an online dictionary defines it as:

> *'The total of activities involved in the transfer of goods from the seller to the consumer'.*

The point is, again, that, like strategy, brand, culture and so on, there is no one clear, unambiguous or even widely accepted definition of marketing.

This chapter will explore what marketing and marketing strategy involve, give a funnel template for considering different strategic aims of any marketing activity and pose a few challenges to think about.

What does marketing involve?

When considering marketing strategy, Business Studies students at secondary schools (US: high schools) are usually taught about the 9Ps of marketing. Each 'P' is one aspect of marketing and each is part of the strategic mix aimed at ensuring business success. When developing our marketing strategy, we are seeking to develop a co-ordinated series of activities, using these 9Ps to facilitate the success of our overall organizational strategy. These Ps are not something to be looked at in isolation; they are the tools for the marketing part of our overall business strategy:

- **Product** – ensuring that a product meets a customer's needs and having a system in place to ensure that this is monitored as customers' needs and wants change.
- **Price** – any product or service is only successful if it is sold at a price that the customer finds acceptable. This 'P' is about getting the price right.
- **Place** – the product must be available – at the right place in the right time. Online trading has revolutionized the 'Place' of marketing as 24/7 availability is now the norm through websites.
- **Promotion** – the communication to the market and the messages that the organization is projecting.
- **Physical layout** – how products are presented to the customer, for example in a retail environment. Supermarkets and grocery stores tend to put essentials such as bread and milk towards the rear of the store to ensure that customers have to walk past many other products to obtain them – and then hopefully make a spontaneous additional purchase. Similarly, it is probably impossible to shop at Ikea and only emerge with one item – their use of layout in their stores takes the customer on a room by room journey with multiple purchasing ideas in each room.
- **Processes** – ensuring that the process enhances the customer buying experience, not hinders it. Compare the positive experience of Amazon's one-click ordering to the torturous

fight through copious numeric options and inevitable queuing to bad-taste music on many company helplines.

- **Provision of customer service** – how the positive customer experience is maximised. British retailer John Lewis, from Chapter 16, exemplifies success here.
- **People** – ensuring that anyone who comes into contact with a customer is exhibiting the desired marketing message. For example, telephone financial services call centres must have staff who are quick, polite and knowledgeable if customers are to trust them with their money.
- **Physical evidence** – seeking to give the customer evidence that the purchase will achieve what the customer required prior to purchase. For example, written testimonials of holiday hotels and exemplary cleanliness in a doctor's surgery.

Art, not a science

One of the problematic aspects of any marketing effort, with any of the 9Ps, is that it will almost certainly not achieve the anticipated result! If we initiate an advertising campaign (part of the P of promotion) aimed to increase sales by 5 per cent during the duration of the campaign, it is a judgement call, using experience and experts, of what to do, how to do it, where to do it and when to do it. There is usually no ability to spend US$ 10 million on a campaign and receive an automatic guaranteed return of US$ 50 million in additional sales. This campaign may achieve nothing, may exceed expectations, may have an impact only for the duration of the campaign or may have no immediate impact but see results in future months. In all of those examples, the campaign did not achieve what it set out to do – a 5 per cent sales increase for the duration of the campaign.

There are also very limited opportunities to develop a 'scientific or control experiment' – different marketing strategies in different areas to establish which was most effective; or a marketing initiative in one area and not in another to observe the differences. Even when it is possible, it is not guaranteed that the same result would be achieved upon repetition or, if they are different geographic regions, that the results would be the same if what was done in region A was then done in region B and vice versa.

Marketing therefore requires significant acts of judgement and opinion regarding what would be most effective and most appropriate. In many cases, the actual results are significantly different from the expected results. By 2007, the British confectionary manufacturer Cadbury (now part of Kraft, US) had suffered an erosion of customer confidence due, in part, to a contamination scare in 2006 and its associated expensive product recall and fine by the British Food Standards Agency; and also partly due to the production of Easter eggs with traces of nuts but with no warning of this for those with nut allergies – a potentially fatal condition. Cadbury needed to bring itself back to stronger customer awareness and a more positive image. A marketing campaign for its flagship brand, Cadbury Dairy Milk (CDM), with co-ordinated newspaper, billboard, cinema and television elements was launched in the UK in August 2007 featuring a gorilla drumming to Phil Collins' song 'In the air tonight'. No one could have anticipated the level of success. The YouTube version of the advertisement achieved 500,000 views in the first week, over 6 million within three months; the gorilla had 70 groups set up by fans on Facebook; and various parodies of the advert appeared as advertising homage. Sales of CDM increased by 9 per cent (worth approximately £18 million) and research by YouGov showed that 20 per cent more of the UK population viewed CDM positively after the advertisement campaign than before. The campaign was later expanded internationally.

Marketing may not be aimed at increasing sales

A common misconception is that the function of marketing is to increase sales. That can be one very important function of marketing, but not always.

Sometimes a marketing strategy aims not at achieving the aspects such as greater market share or increased sales, but at less tangible aspects or at minimising negative occurrences. The purpose of a specific piece of marketing effort could include reasons and aims such as:

- **Maintaining the present position** – few could forget brands such as McDonald's or Coca-Cola, but they continue their high advertising to remain where they are – global top ten brands. Gradual erosion of the message in the customer's mind is almost inevitable unless the message is continually reinforced. Business can be like trying to walk up the downward escalator – if you stay still, you will move backwards. Maintenance marketing seeks to prevent this downward movement.
- **Minimizing the negative impact** – such as that undertaken by Toyota after the tragically fatal consequences of vehicles accelerating unintentionally and beyond the ability of the brakes to halt the car. The *Los Angeles Times* claimed that there were 1,200 such instances (8 November 2009). In January 2010, Toyota initiated a mass recall of approximately 6.5 million cars to solve the problem. Without effective marketing communication, customers may have been reluctant to buy Toyota again. The impact has relegated Toyota to 11th most valuable brand in 2010 and 2011 from its height of 6th in 2007 and 2008, but the brand is still valued by Interbrand at just under US$ 28 billion (it peaked at US$ 34 billion in 2008).
- **Response to competitive action** – having scored such success with its gorilla advertisement, Cadbury could not rest. Mars's Galaxy chocolate launched a campaign based on targeting women in 'indulgent moments'. Galaxy increased sales by 12 per cent to £80 million and Cadbury had to respond by almost doubling its marketing spend on CDM in 2007–8.
- **Awareness marketing** – some marketing is about starting the potential customer on the route to becoming a purchaser. Efforts at increasing the customers' knowledge of the existence of the company, organization or product are the first step on the journey, but funds from purchasing may not flow in until considerably later in the journey.

- **To change perception or behaviour** – much of the activity in the not-for-profit sector fits here. Governmental advertising on alcohol awareness is not intended to increase alcohol sales!
- **Corporate social responsibility** – where a company seeks to communicate its activities to raise its profile as a responsible corporate citizen; for example, in 2011 the UK's National Westminster Bank (part of RBS) launched a national television campaign outlining elements of its community action programme – from how staff go into schools to teach finance, to fundraising for charities.

The marketing funnel

Marketing strategies to achieve any of the 9Ps should be thought through – you need to know exactly what they are intended to do. Ill thought through, vaguely defined, un-specifically targeted marketing effort is frequently wasted effort and wasted money. The strategic intent of any marketing initiative is just as vital as the intent in any other area of strategy: precisely what is any aspect of a marketing strategy seeking to achieve? To help explore this, we can use a 'marketing funnel' to segregate various targets for our marketing strategies.

Awareness

The aim of marketing targeted here is to ensure that those in the group of potential customers who are unaware of the organizational offering become aware of its existence. It is not about sales, but it is the first step towards a sale. Whichever of the 9Ps are used, the message should be consistent with the brand. No one who watches Formula 1 motor racing will fail to notice Ferrari. Few of us move on to the next step of considering purchasing a Ferrari, but the marketing has achieved its objective of alerting us to the existence of the brand.

It is an important point that, in many cases, it is not an automatic aim to progress through the funnel. Traditional, older marketing thinking would seek to drive customers through the

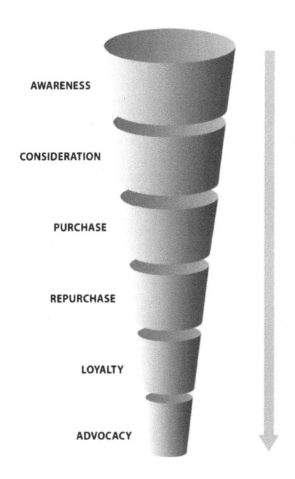

The marketing funnel

funnel and the construction of the diagram hints at a wider audience for awareness, fewer for consideration, even fewer for purchase as some are lost at each stage. Some traditional marketing approaches seek to maximise the speed with which they take customers downwards in the model and minimise the loss of customers at each stage in that movement.

However, not every business and every product wants to drive large quantities of customers all the way through the funnel into the 'advocacy' grouping. In his book *How Brands Grow*, Byron Sharp argues that with a product that ...

- has a low purchase value
- is a frequent purchase product
- has a wide choice of alternative competing products
- is a rapid or impulsive purchase decision

...a business will create greater business growth from attracting a wide number of customers to buy once than it would from a smaller number of customers buying frequently. Soft drinks, shampoo, beers, wines, many foodstuffs and snacks would be relevant examples.

Consideration

The second sector is marketing activity that is aimed at generating the possibility of purchase in the mind of the potential customer. Not purchase per se, but being conscious of the possibility of purchase. Sometimes the customer movement from 'awareness' to 'purchase' is a huge leap and needs strategies to position the product as a possibility – these are the strategies of 'consideration'. They may take a long time or a short time, but they have a distinct message from the 'buy me' message seeking purchase.

I renew my car every three years and am presently driving a Jaguar. The local Mercedes Benz dealership keeps in telephone contact about every nine months to alert me to news of their products – a marketing strategy aimed at this sector of consideration.

One frequently used tactic in this area is to aim for the product being viewed as having parity with a market leader or with a successful market player. Pepsi has produced some excellent 'anti-coke' advertisements. Coca-Cola outsells Pepsi in all areas of the world excluding the Arabic-speaking world. By attacking the number one, Pepsi seeks to put itself on parity with the number one in the consumer's mind and hence put itself into the category of being considered for purchase as an alternative to the number one.

Purchase

This is marketing effort, any of the Ps, aimed at encouraging the actual buying of the product/service for the first time. It is not unusual for inexperienced marketers to seek to start here without having paid appropriate attention to the previous stages and then wondering why their efforts do not achieve their desires.

Repurchase

These are activities that aim to generate repeat purchase, not necessarily habitual purchase at this phase, just repeat and maybe regular purchase. Budweiser is the best-selling beer in the US and they have spent millions of pounds trying to get firmly established in the British market. Their marketing uses a wide range of the Ps, but they do not appear to generate the repurchase required for firm establishment as a dominant brand. The problem is that we Brits have a different perception from our US cousins of what a beer should taste like. In conferences in the UK, I will sometimes illustrate this point by asking anyone who has ever had a Budweiser to raise their hand. About 90 per cent will normally do so. My follow up question asks those who regularly drink 'Bud' to raise their hands. Never more than 10 per cent raise their hands. My third question is then 'Tell me, where is the problem in Budweiser's strategy?'. The show of hands has made it self-evident. They have great advertising but it is aimed at the first three stages of the funnel – and has been immensely successful there. They have not, however, aimed anything at the fourth stage – repurchase – and would find that difficult for a European palate. However, despite almost saturation success at first purchase level, they have continued to pour millions of pounds/dollars into the same hole. Now that Anheuser-Busch is owned by European In-Bev, this futile waste of marketing resource has finished.

Loyalty

Here, we are seeking marketing activity that aims to generate a strong preference of the customer for our product. Marketing strategies in this segment seek to turn repurchase into regular, or habitual, purchase. An example here would be the use of loyalty cards where frequent purchase generates benefits that may or may not apply to the product. My hotel loyalty card enables me to have weekend stays as a benefit while my airline loyalty card allows a wide choice of benefits, including the product – free flights – and a vast array of non-flight related goods.

Advocacy

Strategies here seek to develop customer loyalty to the point where they actively recommend the product/service to others and marketing activity here should also facilitate their ability to do so. This is the territory of First Direct Bank – pioneers of telephone and then Internet banking. First Direct started a 24/7 telephone banking system on Sunday 1 October 1989. The first 24 hours resulted in 1,000 calls. The concept was simple – banking without branches. Everything could be achieved over the telephone. By 1997 the Internet was emerging as a safe and rapidly expanding business vehicle. The extension from telephone banking to Internet banking was a natural progression. For each of the last 25 years, polls by MORI and NOP have shown First Direct to be the most recommended bank. A whopping 36 per cent of customers join because they were given personal recommendations – that is the result of existing customers becoming advocates.

Every element of our marketing initiatives should know what it is seeking to achieve and the funnel is an exceptionally useful device to assist us in targeting our marketing strategies and activities.

Above and below the line

You are likely to hear these expressions in discussions about marketing strategies. It will be no surprise to the reader that marketers disagree on exactly what the 'line' is and that they abbreviate the expressions to ATL and BTL. The origins of the terms were from the accounting world when some types of marketing earned the marketing agency a payment of a commission (ATL) and others did not (BTL), but marketing costs have not been charged in this way since about the 1960s, so the reason for the differentiation of two types of marketing expenditure is no longer relevant. However, the terms frequently remain.

My personal preference in terms of definitions is about the line being one of overt visibility and direct customer communication through public media. So ATL would include advertising in newspapers, billboards, radio, cinemas and on televisions. BTL, by my definition, is about things that happen in the background without direct use of public media, such as flyers, email marketing, end-of-aisle promotions, and sponsorship.

My 'line' of media and direct communication is not a universally accepted definition. Some retain a form of accounting line and others a line that separates mass marketing from niche marketing. However, in real business communication with marketers, my definition is widely understood if somewhat outdated.

A more modern variant is 'through the line' (TTL), which is a sensible co-ordination of both ATL and BTL to be mutually supportive and thus amplify the marketing impact.

Measuring marketing

Marketing spend is an investment for the business and as such requires accountability, control and scrutiny like any other investment. Determining your methods of measurement and what results you are measuring is the key.

Any marketing activity will incur an investment cost. Along with this, you will set:

- distribution targets – proportion of geographical coverage
- rate of sale – for example how many units are sold in a retail store in a week
- repeat purchase rates
- penetration – proportion of the target population who have purchased your product
- redemption rates – for example, how many money-off coupons were used, or for an on-pack promotion (such as a code on a drinks can, input to a site may win the customer £1,000) how many people entered the competition
- sales uplift targets.

The essence of any monitoring of any investment is to establish what you seek to achieve by the investment and then to measure the extent to which you achieved your objectives. Investment in marketing is no different.

There are a myriad of econometric marketing packages available that can strip out different effects such as in-store promotions and pricing to simply identify the effect of the one aspect you are considering – for example, the increased rate of sales due to your advertising campaign rather than the price and promotion effects.

Summary

Marketing has no simple agreed definition, but we have considered it as the 9Ps of getting the right product to the customer in the right way at the right price. An integrated marketing strategy considers all of these Ps and uses them in harmony to achieve the business aspirations. However, marketing strategy and marketing efforts are not exact – they are not a scientific formula where X advertising + Y on-pack promotion = Z sales. Indeed, in many cases marketing activity is not specifically aiming at increasing sales. This often makes justifying it and measuring it difficult.

A useful template for considering marketing strategy is the 'funnel', which demonstrates six distinct aims of a marketing initiative, strategy or campaign. All marketing activity should be able to state precisely what it is aiming to do – whether it is one of the categories not aimed at increasing sales or which of the six elements of the funnel it is seeking to further. Vague marketing aims are likely to be poor strategy and a waste of money. Well thought through, co-ordinated targeted marketing with specific outputs is infinitely more likely to yield success.

Fact-check (answers at the back)

1. What is the definition of marketing?
   a) Persuading people to buy your product ❏
   b) Presenting your product as an attractive alternative ❏
   c) Selling products, which don't come back, to customers who do ❏
   d) There is no one agreed definition of marketing ❏

2. Which of these are not in the 9Ps?
   a) Provision of customer service ❏
   b) Performance ❏
   c) Physical layout ❏
   d) Provision of evidence ❏

3. What does the P of 'place' refer to?
   a) Making the product available to the customer ❏
   b) Where in the market you choose to sell your product ❏
   c) Whether your sales are online or physical ❏
   d) Which countries you choose to sell your product in ❏

4. Is marketing an art or a science? (Note: two answers)
   a) A science because it can be measured ❏
   b) A science because we have inputs (spend) and outputs (results) ❏
   c) An art because it involves judgement ❏
   d) An art because the results are not able to be predicted specifically ❏

5. Which of the following is NOT a reason to undertake marketing activity that will NOT increase sales?
   a) To keep position in response to a competitor marketing campaign ❏
   b) To spend to minimise the negative impact of a problem ❏
   c) To ensure that the marketing budget is fully spent ❏
   d) To initiate a campaign aimed at making potential customers aware that the product exists ❏

6. Which of the following would NOT be likely to be a marketing strategy aimed at 'awareness'?
   a) Sports sponsorship ❏
   b) 'Buy two get one free' promotions ❏
   c) Placing a product on a TV programme where it can be seen by the viewer ❏
   d) Presence at a large public event (e.g. the Bristol Balloon festival (UK)) ❏

7. Which of the following would NOT be likely to be a marketing strategy aimed at 'consideration'?

a) Initiating research with your product alongside the market leader product to communicate results in the press ❏

b) Showing how your food product compares with others in nutritional value ❏

c) Demonstrating your product's reliability compared to competitors ❏

d) Each online purchase generates a voucher code for money off the next purchase ❏

8. Which of the following would NOT be likely to be a marketing strategy aimed at 'loyalty'?

a) Introduction of a customer card that gives bonuses and discounts for ongoing purchases – such as Eurostar 'carte-blanche' programme ❏

b) Reducing the price to ensure that the customer does not go elsewhere ❏

c) Member's magazine – such as Toyota's 'Club Toyota magazine' ❏

d) Collector card – such as Nero coffee's 'stamp' per purchase, where ten purchases permits a free coffee ❏

9. Which of the following would NOT be likely to be a marketing strategy aimed at 'advocacy'?

a) Money off your next purchase when you introduce a friend ❏

b) Viral marketing via social websites – you pass on details to your friends ❏

c) Free sampling of the product in a shopping mall ❏

d) Initiating a competition where the customer can increase their chances of winning if they give you five email addresses of their friends. You then email advising them that their friend has recommended them ❏

10. Which statement about measuring marketing effects would be the wisest?

a) Marketing is more difficult to measure than other investments ❏

b) Marketing is just like any other investment – choose what you want to happen and measure it ❏

c) Marketing is too complicated to measure using conventional techniques and so requires specialist monitoring ❏

d) Marketing cannot be measured effectively and effort doing so is usually counterproductive ❏

CHAPTER 19

Understand brand strategy

Brand strategy is one subset of marketing strategy. There is a lot more to marketing than just brand strategies but the emphasis, importance and power of the brand mean that brand strategies deserve a chapter to themselves.

There is no universal definition of a brand – like vision, strategy, culture, values – we all have perceptions of what we mean by a brand, but these may differ from someone else's definition of a brand. This does not aid effective communication.

A brand can be:

- an identification mark on skin, made by burning (especially an owner's identification on an animal's body)
- a fictional character from J. R. R. Tolkien's Middle-earth
- the name of a beer produced in Wijlre, Netherlands
- a play by the Norwegian playwright Henrik Ibsen
- a verb – to accuse or condemn, openly or formally, for example to 'brand' as disgraceful
- a type of sword: a cutting or thrusting weapon with a long blade
- the name of 31 separate villages throughout Germany and Austria
- a trade name: a name given to a product or service
- the sum of all the characteristics, tangible and intangible, that make an offer unique
- the immediate image, emotion or message that people experience when they think of a company or product.

While the last three, above, are all perfectly acceptable, I will suggest a widely embracing definition:

> *'a trade name and all associated factors, attributes and messages of a product or offering'*

An organization will want to enhance, develop and protect these factors. This activity is termed 'brand strategy'.

The purpose of brands

The origin of the use of the word 'brand' in this business context is from the cattle farmer's habit of placing an identifying mark on his cattle's skin, originally by burning; these days kinder paint-based methods are common, which state that the cattle belongs to a specific farmer. The individual cow or steer then 'stands out' as belonging to this farmer. Modern business branding has the same purpose – to identify ownership and to seek to ensure that the product stands out to the customer or potential customer.

Few products are identical to every competitive offering on the market. A Mars chocolate bar is different from a KitKat, which is different from Toblerone. For many of us, we have a shortlist of chocolate bars we prefer and our shortlist may include these three. In each case, the owning company (Mars, Nestlé and Kraft respectively) want their product to stand out to us and, by doing so, enable them to be our choice of confectionery.

In this chocolate bar example, the three global giant confectionery companies are using their brands in three slightly different ways. Mars uses the brand for both purposes – standing out and identifying ownership; KitKat merely seeks to stand out from other rival products and has an additional prominent Nestlé logo to identify ownership; and Toblerone seeks purely to stand out with reference to Kraft's ownership of the brand in negligible small print.

How a brand functions

Identifying ownership and standing out are just the first step. The brand gives the product or service an identity, some would say even a personality. Customers are then buying into this identity or personality when they purchase the product. Their reasons for doing so could be wide, for example:

● Image: Someone may drive a Range Rover car to identify with the prestigious image of the car – the Range Rover is aspirational and expensive, by driving it I am demonstrating that 'I am successful' in a way in which driving a Tata would not.

- Service: Many people buy certain books from Amazon despite being charged a price premium – they are choosing the brand of Amazon because it consistently demonstrates reliable, rapid delivery and security of supply.
- Quality: Large numbers of families start the day with Kellogg's corn flakes as they believe that this brand has a higher quality of product than a cheaper store own brand (or store brand, or no brand) product.

So, the brand has the purpose of ensuring that the product stands out in the eyes of the customer, that the customer therefore identifies with this brand and that consequently this ultimately persuades the customer to choose to buy. The brand therefore directly contributes to business and financial performance by enhancing the sales potential.

A brand has value

Interbrand makes an assessment of the world's most valuable brands each year. Coca-Cola is the perennial winner of this assessment, valued in 2011 at US$ 71.9 billion. With some decline in the standing of Nokia, Toyota and Mercedes, the 2011 ten highest valued brands were all American. The brand value assessment includes:

- an analysis of the recent historic financial performance of the company which owns the brand, and the value it is deriving for its owners (usually shareholders)
- the role of the brand, or the proportion of the consumer decision to purchase that is due to the brand
- the brand strength, or the ability of the brand to derive expected future financial earnings.

While some may want to question the techniques and measures used, these three aspects are critical to the success of any business – financial performance, the customer choice and securing the future. Note that these three considerations have respective timeframes of 'past – present – future'. Any successful brand will be achieving in all three areas and all three timeframes. However, all decisions are about the future – it is the only one of the three that we can change or affect. So if we want to increase the effectiveness of the brand, to increase its value, what (according to Interbrand) should we do? What should our brand strategies be seeking to achieve?

Increasing brand value

Interbrand has ten criteria by which it measures the brand strength:

Clarity

- Internal business clarity about what the brand stands for (e.g. its values and market positioning)
- Clarity on who are target customers and what causes them to choose to buy.

Commitment

- Commitment to the brand from within the business and the strong understanding of the importance of the brand
- The time and investment support the brand receives.

Protection

- The security of the brand (e.g. legal protection of proprietary aspects, design or geography).

Responsiveness

- The ability of the brand to respond to market changes, challenges and opportunities
- The strength of business leadership plus the desire and ability to evolve and renew the brand.

Authenticity

- The extent to which the brand is based on an internal truth and capability
- It has a defined heritage and a well-grounded value set. It can achieve the expectations that customers have of it.

Relevance

- The extent to which the brand fits with customers' needs or desires.

Differentiation

- The extent to which customers perceive the brand to be distinct from the competition.

Consistency

- The degree to which a brand is experienced with stability and uniformity wherever the customer encounters it.

Presence

- The spread of the brand in the market and extent to which it is talked about positively by consumers in both traditional and social media.

Understanding

- More than mere recognition, the brand is understood by the customers for its distinctive qualities and characteristics.

(Source: Interbrand; with some author adaptations, summaries and clarifications)

Brand strategies will therefore be targeted at enhancing these ten criteria, not merely to gain in the Interbrand standings, but to derive expected future financial performance due to enhanced sales performance. It is vital to make the link that strategies to strengthen these aspects of a brand are directly linked to future business performance and therefore future shareholder value; and the Interbrand identification and consideration of the criteria for 'brand strength' are a good way to understand this.

How brand strength is enhanced

Enhancing the brand and the earning power of the brand is achieved by increasing one or more of the Interbrand criteria.

There are hundreds of possibilities for how this can be done and in the space available we will seek only to give a few examples:

Brand name: A superior brand of clothing will inform me that the article will not deteriorate after just a few cycles in the washing machine (and that wearing it will not be a fashion faux-pas); a no-frills airline brand will advise me that the flying experience will be low cost but more akin to cattle transport than any business transport to which I am accustomed. In either case, the brand name identifies and will 'tick' several of the ten Interbrand brand-strength criteria. If the clothing was inferior or if the air ticket was expensive, the brand would be damaged. If my customer experience matched, or exceeded, my expectation for that brand, the brand has delivered on its promises and strength is enhanced.

Logo: A strong identifier. I don't need to read the ingredients of my Wall's ice cream to know that it will be superior to a supermarket own brand version – the logo has already given me the identifying mark of the company, which stands for high quality and therefore has also given me the expectations of the brand. Putting a Mercedes logo on an A-class or a Volkswagen logo on a Phaeton diminish the brand by reducing Interbrand's criteria of 'differentiation', 'consistency' and 'understanding'.

Straplines: UK retailer Tesco consistently states *'Every little helps'*, John Lewis consistently states *'Never knowingly undersold'*; both state that no competitor will do better. A good strapline incorporates the sales message of the brand and sums up the reason why customers should purchase from this brand. We could easily compile an A–Z of great straplines, but here are just a few entries from 'A':

- American Express: *'Don't leave home without it'*
- Automobile Association: *'To our members, we're the fourth emergency service'*
- Army (British): *'Join the professionals'*

In each case, the strapline added to the brand is communicating the reason to 'buy'. The Army was seeking young people to join – their 'buy' was people applying to join.

Shapes: Coca-cola have patented the shape of their cola bottle. The distinctive shape is now a unique brand communicator. To protect this aspect of the brand, the shape is patented – as should all aspects of brand communication be in order to aid Interbrand's third factor, 'protection', and seventh factor, 'differentiation'.

Colours: Only BP can have a green petroleum forecourt, only Cadbury Dairy Milk can have their shade of purple packaging for chocolate, JCBs (UK) and Caterpillar (US) are yellow, CNN is red. Red and yellow are to DHL what brown and gold are to UPS. In each of these cases, the colour helps to identify the brand and hence enhances its strength of communication.

Smells: Identifying a perfume by its smell is an obvious requirement for a branding strategy, as is preventing any imitation, and the same is true of air freshener and household cleaning products. However, an entire industry is emerging that seeks to attach aromas to brands with the intention of enhancing memorability and strengthening the customer's ability to spontaneously remember a brand.

Sounds: 'Plink, plink, fizz' is instantly Alka-Seltzer. Insurance provider Direct Line has a patented musical jingle, as does Intel. The sounds enhance the brand through instant recognition by customers and potential customers.

Graphics: Pepsi has a swirl of red and a swirl of blue with a curved white line between them. This graphic serves as a logo. BP's green and yellow Helios graphic serves the same identification function. In these cases, no words are needed – the graphic comfortably identifies the brand. Other examples of graphics could include words in specific fonts – such as that of the chocolate brands Cailler and After Eight. Still others could be the five Olympic rings, KFC's cartoon-style depiction of 'Colonel' Harland Sanders, a cross or 'ichthus fish' as a graphic to denote something with a Christian emphasis.

Packaging: The toughest battles of packaging are probably fought in the perfume industry where the packaging is a major brand communicator. A walk around the perfumery section of a department store is a good education in appreciating packaging as a core pillar of branding – please do it. Chanel bottles will always be 'classic' and uncomplicated, usually in neutral colours. Givenchy will be equally uncomplicated but with bold use of strong colours. Others that want to appear less classic and more innovative will be using shape novelty and high colour innovation. Each seeks to enhance the brand by the most effective use of packaging.

Extensions: JCB earth-moving equipment is tough, rugged, durable and works in harsh environments. Their launch of a tough, rugged, durable clothing range for those working in tough environments is entirely appropriate and enhances the brand. One could never imagine soft, pink JCB-branded clothing on frail supermodels – that would destroy the brand image!

Top brands in recent years

It can be an interesting exercise in seeking to understand brand strategy to consider how brands are moving. Consider the possible causes of these movements and ask the question *'If I were responsible for that brand strategy, what would I do to enhance the brand?'* Again, this is a personal application of the learning and aims to make strategic thinking a habit for the business person.

For example, the following graph shows just a few of the highest brands over the last few years. Observe Coca-Cola as the constant number one. Ask *'What are they doing to maintain this position?'*, *'What would I do to keep that position if I were responsible for Coca-Cola?'* and also ask the negative questions *'What are the things I should NOT do? What could I do which would damage the brand value?'* An example of something NOT to do for Coca-Cola would be to change the ingredients or taste of Coca-Cola – as they foolishly sought

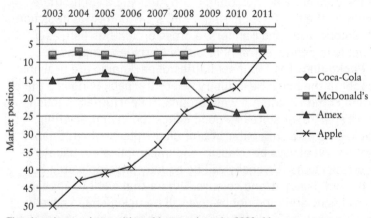

The changing market position of four top brands, 2003–11

to do in 1985 with 'new Coke'. It was a disaster and the company reverted to the original formula when customers understandably rejected it.

McDonald's has been consistent, Amex has fallen with the financial crisis that started in 2008 and Apple has soared as the iPod, iPhone and iPad have drawn it to prominence and profitability.

Below is a graph showing some tremendous brands with greater movement in value over the same time period. Citigroup, like Amex, has suffered since the 2008 financial crisis.

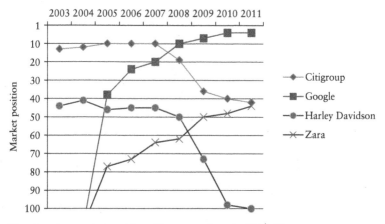

The changing market position of four more brands, 2003–11

Google, Harley Davidson and Spanish clothing retailer Zara are undergoing differing but dramatic changes. Again, as an exercise in strategic thinking, recall the three key elements of brand valuation:

● recent historic financial performance
● the role of the brand, or the proportion of the consumer decision to purchase that is due to the brand
● the brand strength, or the ability of the brand to derive expected future financial earnings.

With the aid of basic Internet-based research, identify what has happened to each, the effect you think it may have and, even more importantly, what you would do next.

Recovering from brand disaster

The graphs have shown falls for Amex, Citigroup and Harley Davidson. Decline is not necessarily disaster as good strategy can avert brand disaster and generate subsequent invigoration. A few examples:

- **Skoda:** The Czech vehicle brand was a product of the lack of competition in the formerly communist Eastern Europe and, with the collapse of communism leading to greater openness of markets, became a laughing stock and source of jokes. Volkswagen purchased a 30 per cent stake in 1991 – they had bought into what some in marketing had dubbed 'the brand from hell'. Investment, education of the workforce and taking full control in 2001 sought to rescue the brand and the first VW-influenced car was the Octavia launched in 1998. It failed. The brand had some respect in Eastern Europe but the Western European customer (especially the British) still saw the brand negatively despite the technical excellence and good reviews the Octavia received. Brand impressions are difficult to change! It had very high brand awareness, but for all the wrong reasons. The next car was the Fabia in 2000, for which the marketing parodied Skoda's poor reputation with the strapline 'you won't believe it's a Skoda'. It succeeded. The 1998 research had shown that over 60 per cent of people said that they would never buy a Skoda. By 2000 this had fallen to 40 per cent; the Fabia was selling, and as a bi-product Octavia sales picked up and the previously unthinkable happened: Skoda had a waiting list for car purchases and the brand was rescued!
- **Apple:** The US computer manufacturer was close to extinction in the 1990s with low sales levels and a low market share. The return of Steve Jobs with a new business philosophy based on cutting-edge design, simplicity of use and perpetual innovation spawned a brand resurrection and in 2011 an entry into the prestigious top ten global brands.
- **Stella Artois:** This was an iconic Belgian brand with a poor reputation in the UK due to its strength having a reported propensity for turning its consumers to violence. Its strapline

of 'reassuringly expensive' inferred quality but was tarnished by extensive price promotions. In 2007, the strapline was abandoned and a lower-strength beer was introduced, and later a cider ('cidre').

- **Johnnie Walker:** The Scottish whisky brand was in decline and perceived as a drink for old men. One excellent piece of insight reversed this decline – the insight that people drink whisky because they feel successful. Whisky says *'I've achieved'* or *'I've made it'*. The 'striding man' logo was marshalled with the strapline *'keep walking'* and the brand has recovered.
- **Guinness:** This classic Irish stout has an immense history. However, towards the end of the twentieth century it also had a reputation as an old man's drink and was in decline. Iconic advertising, use of the *'good things come to those who wait'* strapline and an association with the growing sport of rugby union have revived the brand.
- **Burberry:** This clothing brand shows the false nature of the oft-quoted adage that 'any publicity is good publicity'. Initially a high-quality, quintessentially British brand, Burberry started to be popular with English football hooligans in the 1980s. This was entirely the wrong sort of customer for the brand! The 1990s saw further brand image decline as Burberry and Burberry counterfeit products became popular with 'chavs' (typically teenagers from the lower socio-economic groups). This was compounded when celebrities endorsed the brand – but a somewhat lower level of celebrity than the higher-class image would want. Burberry embarked on a high-profile advertising-based strategy featuring the 'right kind' of celebrity endorsing the product and this symbol of the British upper class has now been rescued from the proletariat.

Summary

A brand has the purpose of making the customer offering stand out and be identified. In doing so, it aims to enhance the message to the customer to generate a sale. Each brand has a message – Rolls Royce's message includes being expensive, Ryanair's message includes being cheap – and it establishes an expectation in the customer of what the product experience will be like.

A brand is a valuable asset and methods of increasing the value of the brand, or enhancing its effectiveness in achieving its purpose, have been summarized using the criteria used by Interbrand. While there are a myriad of other ways to do this, the method is concise and a good overview.

Brand strategies are efforts that seek to maximise the benefit of the brand and hence achieve the same objective – increasing brand value and effectiveness. Such strategies must be co-ordinated, have longevity and be targeted, as should any marketing investment.

We have also observed some brands that have risen sharply in value, some that are falling and some that have fallen, only to recover.

Fact-check (answers at the back)

1. What is the purpose of a brand?
   a) To make the product 'stand out' from others ❏
   b) To increase the customer's likelihood of purchasing ❏
   c) To identify the product as belonging to a particular business ❏
   d) All of the above ❏

2. Which of the following is NOT a component of a brand value?
   a) Recent financial performance of the company that owns the brand ❏
   b) Awareness – the proportion of people who have heard of the brand ❏
   c) Proportion of the customer purchase decision that is due to the brand ❏
   d) Ability of the brand to deliver future financial benefit to the business ❏

3. What is meant by the brand strength indicator of 'commitment'?
   a) Commitment of the customer to continue buying the brand ❏
   b) Commitment of the business to the brand by time and investment ❏
   c) Commitment of the company to continuing the brand ❏
   d) Commitment of the employees to understanding the brand values ❏

4. What is meant by the brand strength indicator of 'understanding'?
   a) Understanding of the customer about the brand's distinctive features ❏
   b) Understanding of the business about the importance of the brand ❏
   c) Understanding of the company about how to leverage the brand to gain sales ❏
   d) Understanding of the employees about the nature and message of the brand ❏

5. Is clothing an appropriate brand extension for the earth-moving machine manufacturer JCB?
   a) Yes, construction workers will wear the clothes and identify with JCB ❏
   b) Yes, the brand is about being tough, outdoor and rugged – these types of clothes are appropriate ❏
   c) No, the earth-moving/ construction brand should not be diluted by entering different markets ❏
   d) No, companies should stick to what they do best – in the case of JCB, that is making construction industry equipment ❏

6. Why have Citigroup and Amex brand values fallen recently?
a) The companies have devoted less effort to supporting the brands ❏
b) In an uncertain financial future, they are investing less in brand marketing ❏
c) The aftermath of the 2008 financial crisis has reduced the short-term future earning potential of the businesses ❏
d) They have reduced their geographical coverage since the 2008 economic downturn ❏

7. What insight-led marketing strategy was the catalyst that started the recovery of the Skoda brand?
a) An increase in vehicle quality ❏
b) Advertising that parodied the previous poor reputation ❏
c) Manufacturing in Western rather than Eastern Europe ❏
d) Expansion of sales into Western Europe ❏

8. What insight led to the recovery of the Johnnie Walker whisky brand?
a) People drink whisky to celebrate their success. ❏
b) The target market for whisky is middle-aged men ❏
c) People identify with the Scottish nature of the brand ❏
d) There will always be a market for the higher-quality product ❏

9. Which of these brands has fallen in value in the last ten years?
a) Harley Davidson ❏
b) Google ❏
c) Zara ❏
d) Apple ❏

10. What tarnished the Burberry brand?
a) It was targeted as a high-class brand – this is a very small market ❏
b) It became popular with some groups of people who did not fit the brand image ❏
c) Lack of brand investment withdrew it from prominence ❏
d) Recession reduced the appeal of a high-end clothing brand ❏

CHAPTER 20

Understand competitive strategy

Business is 'red in tooth and claw' as competitive organizations fight to the death for the financial favour and patronage of their customers. Any strategy a company could initiate and implement that could give them even a minor advantage could be the factor making the difference between success and failure, between corporate life and corporate death.

In this world of cut-and-thrust, high-stakes business activity, the temptation is therefore often to focus on the actions of the competitors. However, this, as a primary focus, is almost always a mistake. In order to succeed in this battle of business, the focus must be primarily not on the other 'players' active in the marketplace but on the customer. The customer decides the winner and loser in the market and so being preferred in the eyes of the customer is the entirety of competitive strategy. In order to do this, the wise company will, of course, have a keen eye on what competitors are doing – but only to the extent to which they are seeking to keep one step ahead in the customer's opinion, one step in favour.

This chapter will give a framework by which this focus can be maintained and, therefore, competitive strategy can be constructively engaged.

Competitive mapping

A structure I have used for many years to consider the customers' view is 'competitive mapping' (CM) (see *Strategies of the Serengeti*, 2006). This has had a track record of providing customer and strategic insight in a vast variety of industries and competitive scenarios in many countries.

The first stage in developing a CM strategy is to consider the market and the buying requirements from the customers' perspective – and from their perspective only. There are many circumstances when business executives hold on to opinions, convinced that *'this is what the customers think'*, but empirical evidence states differently – who is correct? In all circumstances, the correct answer is that the customer's opinion is correct and many executives do not have the greatest of track records in discerning what customers really think.

I recall one series of discussions with a UK retailer who sold two distinct product categories – clothing and foods. At the time of these discussions, they were convinced that the two product types were purchased by the same customers. I was working for a supplier and we were convinced that the two product offerings had different customer groups with only a small Venn diagram overlap. The difference between the opinions was critical. If the retailer was correct, strategies could link the two product groupings. If we were correct, different strategies would be needed for each sector.

In another situation, also with a UK retailer, their customer research evidence showed that their perception of their customer was correct – but only in their geographic heartland. Customers outside the heartland had a different perspective, a different loyalty and a different set of priorities. Had they not realized this, they would have been treating all customers like the longstanding ones in their heartland – and in doing so misreading the majority of customers and undoubtedly then failing to recognize and meet the majority customer grouping desires.

Stage 1 – identify customer key issues

Stage 1 of CM is to consider the key issues that the potential customer or an existing customer sees as being important. These could be manifold. A non-exhaustive list would include:

- **product** – functionality, features, ease of use, performance, aesthetics
- **price/cost** – initial purchase, maintenance, operating, disaster scenario, replacement
- **availability** – distribution, convenience, location, speed, information
- **people** – relationship, ability, reputation, customer knowledge, service
- **technology** – ease of use, interface ability, flexibility, systems/processes, longevity
- **speed** – of service, delivery, use, time savings, productivity
- **accuracy** – reliability, consistency, error free, right first time, timeliness
- **image** – quality, brand, association, imputed image, perception
- **aftersales service/support** – speed, attitude, knowledge, function, problem-solving
- **additional offerings** – extra service, range, compatibility, offers, complementarity
- **environmental and ethical factors** – political, pollution, workforce, conservation, practices
- **risk** – consistency, downside, variability, security, exposure
- **flexibility** – adaptability, expandability, variability, reactivity, speed of change
- **ability** – scope, geography, skills, experience, resources.

My advice is not to simply choose from the list, but to ask the question *'What is really important to our customer?'* and only then, having compiled a list from your knowledge of the customer, to use the list as a checklist to establish whether there are any aspects you have overlooked. As a tip, once we get past 12 or 15 areas to consider, the process gets a bit unwieldy, so I would recommend halting with this maximum.

Stage 2 – ranking

Having determined what is of highest importance to the customer, the second task is to rank these key issues in order of priority to the customer. The priority of the business is, again, not relevant. In competitive mapping, we only have consideration for the customer. Getting the priority wrong can lead to poor customer targeting and missing the mark with an inferior competitive offering.

This process may demonstrate that there are actually several customer groupings – several groups of people who choose to buy your product but for different reasons. One customer who makes pet dog food has identified seven categories of dog owner, each of whom has a different purchasing reason and a different set of priorities in their purchasing. These purchasing reasons tend to flow from their core reason for owning a dog. In this case, the dog food company needs seven CM analyses to maximise their ability to create the best customer offering in the market. They can then consider a co-ordinated set of strategies in the dog food market specifically targeting each initiative to the particular customer grouping to whom it would appeal. This makes each marketing or competitive initiative in the market specific.

For example, one of the groups was 'the child substitute'. This customer owned a dog and treated it like a human child. Another group was 'the security conscious', who would have a dog as a burglar alarm with an impressive dental armoury. It would be natural to assume that the two are mutually exclusive – the 'child substitute' owner is likely to have a small, cute or 'lap' dog and the 'security conscious' is likely to have a gargantuan canine monster.

The 'child substitute' owner will have his or her dog's happiness and well-being high on their list – and so would respond to initiatives in the market that target this – the highest-quality food, food that makes the dog's fur shine, food that is a treat. The 'security conscious' owner would have strength, alertness, fitness and vitality as desirable elements and so would respond positively to initiatives enhancing those attributes in their dog. The research on 'child substitute' owners shows a predominance of single women – so any advertising, promotional activity or even the design of the packaging should be with a small dog and a woman to give the 'just like me' feeling to the customer and hence appeal more specifically. The same research shows that the 'security conscious' is more likely to be middle-aged but could be a man or a woman, so someone of appropriate age should feature in market initiatives aimed here. Another category is the 'family pet owner' – clearly the dog should be shown in a family context to appeal here.

Stage 3 – self-analysis

Having determined the prioritized order of key issues for your customer, mark, as objectively as possible where your business presently sits. If the key issues are listed on the left side and a 'poor to good' scale is placed across the top, your self-analysis may look like this:

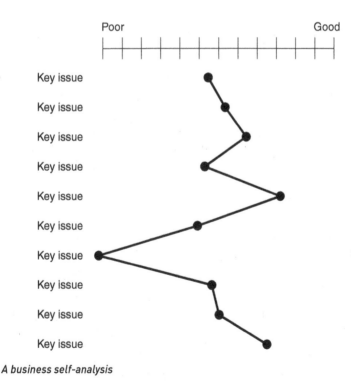

A business self-analysis

Stage 4 – analysis of competitor(s)

Having positioned your business, you may now position your competitor(s) on the same scale. Again, it is important to be as objective as possible with supporting empirical evidence.

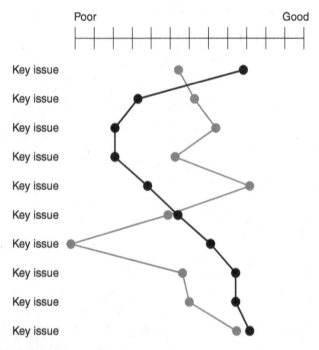

A business comparison

Stage 5 – market movements

How is your market changing? The customer may be driving a change. Many strategic analyses are static and therefore out of date as soon as they are produced. To make this more dynamic, the key issues can be marked with arrows to indicate an ongoing repositioning. For example, in the fast food market, health was previously of negligible concern. After the *Super Size Me*[4] film and the Western obesity epidemic, the fast food industry is having to respond to an increase in importance, and therefore upward prioritization on the CM, of the factor of 'healthiness'.

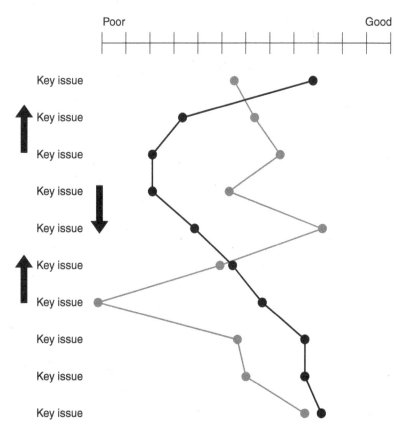

Poor   Good

Key issue

Key issue

Key issue

Key issue

Key issue

Key issue

Key issue

Key issue

Key issue

Key issue

Analysing market movement

Stage 6 – consider options

Once the competitive scenario is mapped out, a variety of options emerge:

- continue doing what we are doing
- catch up in an area where the competitor is ahead
- choose not to catch up where the competitor is ahead and seek to shift market focus away from this area
- actively seek to forge ahead – this option can be enacted where we are ahead, level or behind a competitor
- build barriers where the competitor is behind
- seek to aggressively target the competitor by dragging them backwards – this can be where they are ahead, level or behind

- choose to do nothing except keep a watchful eye on the competitor and re-evaluate if their position changes
- keep an eye on the market 'key issues', establish which ones are moving up and down. Keep an eye on your competitors and continually evaluate which 'key issues' they are directing their strategies towards.

Stage 7 – choose and implement

The CM analysis should produce decisions and actions. Analysis without resultant action is futile; action without analysis is foolish. The task of the analysis is to assist us to make informed judgements and to inspire better decision-making in our competitive arena, aiming to be the supplier who most closely matches and meets the customer's 'key issues'.

Illustrative example

To illustrate, let us consider a competitive scenario in the fast food retail market between McDonald's (M) and Subway (S) – not a definitive statement of the competitive position of these two companies, merely an estimate for the sake of example.

Issues for a potential purchaser may be: speed of service, price, freshness of product, healthiness of the food, choice of food available, location of outlet, consistency of product on different purchasing occasions, ability to personalize the purchase through options.

Rank the 'issues'

Having identified the issues of importance to the customer, the next task is to rank them. As mentioned earlier, it is important to take time to get this right as a different rank may lead to a different competitive strategy. Remember that it may be that for different customer groupings the issues are similar but the ranking is different. It would be important to recognize this and create a competitive map for each customer grouping rather than to try to oversimplify the position with a forced compression of several personas, or customer groupings, into one artificial homogenous list.

However, for illustrative simplicity, we will have only one CM analysis.

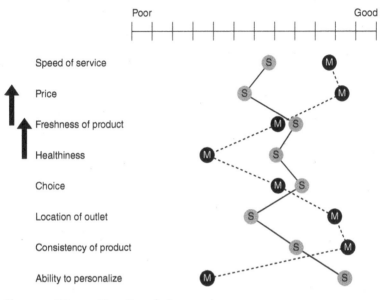

The competitive position of two rival companies

Decide what action to take

Decisions and actions

In our example, put yourself in the place of the decision-makers for McDonald's and then put yourself in the place of the decision-makers for Subway – in each case, based on this analysis, what would you choose to do?

Compare your decisions with what is actually happening in these two excellently run competitors.

For example, presently we see McDonald's taking a range of initiatives to appear more healthy and to mitigate the negative publicity of aspects such as *Super Size Me* and the UK 'McLibel'[5] legal case, in addition to seeking to assuage concerns about obesity. They are taking a range of environmental initiatives to present themselves as a responsible global business and are actively associating themselves with healthy pursuits. A non-exhaustive list of some of their initiatives includes:

- replacing polystyrene packaging with recycled cardboard packaging
- declaring the calorific content of products
- running vehicles on environmentally friendly biodiesel fuel
- restricting 'upselling' (presumptuously asking 'would that be large?' when the customer merely asks for fries without specifying a size)
- changing the internal décor from a 'plastic'-looking red to a more environmentally-sound looking green colour
- using organically grown coffee and milk plus locally-sourced products
- working with protest group Greenpeace to ensure that the soya they derive from Brazil is from sources which do not damage the environment
- sponsoring sporting initiatives.

By choosing to consider this simplified CM analysis and to draw your own conclusions, you are not merely considering strategy theoretically – you have made the first step to actually doing it! The exercise of producing a CM analysis for any market you choose to observe and then considering what actions you would take from your analysis is an excellent habit to start and the first step towards making strategic thinking an ongoing real-life consideration, not a mere academic exercise. It is this ability, which we will examine further in the next chapter as part of a route to help you be a strong strategic thinker and therefore a valuable asset in any organization for which you work.

Summary

Competitive strategy is about seeking to gain an advantage for your product or company in the eyes of the only people who matter – the customers. One simple tool for helping with this vital aspect is competitive mapping (CM) which:

- takes the factors that the customer, or potential customer, sees as important
- ranks them in order of importance
- places your business
- places competitor business(es)
- identifies market changes
- considers options for action
- drives a choice for strategic implementation.

There are many more complex analytical tools available and CM should be seen as a complement, not a substitute, for many. However, it is quick, easily understandable and also rapidly identifies knowledge gaps where we are ignorant of our consumers' opinions.

Practising completing CM analyses and then using them to drive options for consideration is quick, easy to do and a good step towards making ongoing strategic thinking a personal habit.

Fact-check (answers at the back)

1. Whose view does competitive mapping (CM) consider?
   a) The customer (and/or potential customer) only ❏
   b) A combination of various sets/categories of existing customers ❏
   c) The management of the business ❏
   d) The market in general ❏

2. How should you identify the 'key issues'?
   a) Select them from the template provided ❏
   b) Consider which your business is focused on ❏
   c) Step 'into the customers' shoes' and identify what they would think ❏
   d) Determine what the board of the business think are most important ❏

3. What factors should you consider with key issues?
   a) Balancing them between 'internal' and 'external' factors ❏
   b) Balancing them between management opinion and customer opinion ❏
   c) How important they are to the customer ❏
   d) Your ability to change them ❏

4. What would you do if your identification of key issues identified several different categories or types of customer?
   a) Blend them together to generate manageable strategies ❏
   b) Conduct a separate CM for each grouping ❏
   c) CM cannot be used in these circumstances ❏
   d) Select the most important category of customer for your analysis ❏

5. Having identified the key issues – what next?
   a) Rank the key issues in accordance with what is most important to the customer ❏
   b) Rank the issues in accordance with your ability to affect them ❏
   c) Compare the key issues with what the management team thought ❏
   d) Identify the strategies you have for targeting each one ❏

6. When positioning your company and the competitor, what is the best approach to take?
a) Use gut feel and position quickly – that is usually the most accurate ❏
b) Use objective data wherever possible, make educated guesses where not ❏
c) Use objective data where possible, identify and fill knowledge gaps where possible ❏
d) Only proceed when you have definitive undisputed data for each key issue ❏

7. What does positioning an upward arrow against a key issue indicate?
a) It is of higher importance or greater priority to the company ❏
b) The market is changing and this issue is increasing in importance ❏
c) The company is seeking strategies to raise the importance of this key issue ❏
d) Competitors are focusing their strategies in this area ❏

8. If your position is BEHIND your competitor, which of these strategies is NOT a viable option?
a) Develop strategies to forge ahead and catch up ❏
b) Develop strategies to 'drag' the competitor back ❏
c) Develop strategies to change the market, minimising this weakness ❏

d) Develop strategies to focus on your strengths and ignore this weakness ❏

9. If your position is AHEAD of your competitor, which of these strategies is NOT a viable option?
a) Forge further ahead and increase your competitive advantage ❏
b) Sit back and relax – you're winning! ❏
c) Seek to 'build a barrier' – something that prevents your competitor from catching you ❏
d) Advertise the difference, making the customer more aware of your superiority in this area ❏

10. From our illustrative fast food example – what would be the LEAST wise option for McDonald's?
a) Enable customers to personalize their burger (e.g. less or more relish) ❏
b) Keep focused on price – being the price leaders in the market ❏
c) Keep developing new strategies and processes to give even faster service ❏
d) Develop more healthy options ❏

CHAPTER 21

Keep strategy going

You have now had six chapters about differing aspects of strategy. All of them are important and it is vital to see strategy everywhere – internal, external, marketing, brand and competitive – rather than being shunted into a siding that only considers one of these. For business effectiveness, these differing elements of strategy need to work together. Having internal strategies that are not in alignment with external strategies, or, even worse, conflict with them, is madness – but unfortunately many companies have such things. Having brand strategies that do not align with your competitive strategies is futile and even destructive – we have illustrated this with a few examples and we could have used many more. Holistic strategy blends all of these aspects for success in any organization – whether profit-oriented, public sector, charity or voluntary. All should embrace a holistic strategic approach, combining all these aspects of strategy.

For this last chapter on strategy, we could consider a seventh aspect of strategy. However, all good learning requires review, consolidation and practical action points to take forward. This chapter will therefore take the points of the earlier chapters, focusing on the ongoing action that we recommend for you to develop and enhance your practice of good strategic thinking.

Chapter 15 – Understand what strategy is and what it isn't

In this chapter, we explored some myths of strategy, we considered the journey analogy, which is sometimes helpful albeit often too simplistic, and then we discussed Henry Mintzberg's five Ps of strategy.

There can be many applications from this chapter for each reader to take into their ongoing business lives. First, the myths:

- strategy is not military
- strategy is not only for the hyper-intelligent
- strategy is not only for the top board
- strategy is not a big document.

It would probably be unwise to directly lambast those who exhibit these myths in their behaviours. However, it would be wise to understand the limitations of each myth and work to eradicate these when they are observed. For example, when middle managers are gazing adoringly at the senior board expecting a strategy to fall from the sky, don't wait for it to arrive (it rarely does) – get working on the 80 per cent plus of it that you could safely already start working on as you already know much of what you should be doing and aiming for. By acting rather than waiting for what rarely arrives, you will not fall into the trap of strategic paralysis where no strategic thinking is developed due to middle managers abdicating all strategic responsibility to the board. The board do have strategic responsibility for the organization, but that should not stop each section of the organization being able to develop implementable, well thought through strategy for their areas of responsibility. Part of the responsibility of the board is to ensure that these are combining effectively and are co-ordinated – not to dictate them.

Action 1

Get on with it – start considering strategy now.

For the many organizations who consider strategy as a big document: understand the limitations of such a document – it can become a progress limiter rather than an enabler (recall the examples earlier in this book); it can make your strategy static, cast in stone, and therefore unable to act and react as the market, competition and business change.

Action 2

Be aware, identify and work to positively challenge limitations in your organization such as using a strategic plan as a limiter and static, fossilized strategy.

Often, a criteria for success in business is the ability to adapt in response to changes. The alternative is the strategy of the dinosaurs! One of the examples used in this chapter was that of Hoover's inability to respond to James Dyson's bagless vacuum cleaner, as described further in the following case study.

Case study: Dyson and Hoover

Famously fed up with his vacuum cleaner's inability to retain adequate suction, inventor James Dyson created the centrifugal action of the machine that bears his name and has made his fortune.

Dyson created 5,127 prototypes in a little over five years from his first attempt in 1978. Eventually, he had his product. He then spent the next two years seeking to find a manufacturer who would be interested. Having toured throughout Europe, he was unsuccessful. The fact that the replacement bag market was worth in excess of £100 million p.a. in the UK alone was probably a contributory factor, and as the Dyson.com website gloatingly states:

> *'... Hoover's Vice President for Europe, Mike Rutter, said on UK national TV: "I do regret that Hoover as a company did not take the product technology off Dyson; it would have lain on the shelf and not been used " ...'*

After complete rejection, James Dyson decided to press on and manufacture the product himself. Within two years, it was the UK's best-selling vacuum cleaner and has subsequently moved on to international success.

Dyson's strategy was born out of his failure to align partners to his former strategies of selling (to Hoover) or to persuade any manufacturer to make his product. His strategy was not cast in stone – it moved quickly – whether in prototype production or in the failure after failure to develop a route to get the product manufactured.

In contrast, Hoover's strategy was to focus on its profits from vacuum cleaner bags and they failed to see the threat of the new potential competitor. They failed to move fast enough and their perspective of the market was flawed. They could have undertaken a competitive mapping (CM) exercise and seen the potential, but instead they remained so set in their perspective of the market that they were unable to look beyond their own preconceptions.

Perspective was one of Henry Mintzberg's five Ps. The second application from that chapter would be to understand the five Ps:

- plan – an intended set of actions
- pattern – a consistent behaviour
- position – a location of products in a market
- perspective – a view, opinion or stance
- ploy – a manoeuvre.

Our learning here was to understand that people use the word 'strategy' to mean all five – and that they are correct in doing so. Our challenge is to be 'fluent' in being able to speak all five of these aspects of strategy. Rather than seeing them as a maze of competing definitions, consider them as equally correct but different views of strategy.

In addition, the ability to move from one to another may take strategic discussion and thought into different, challenging, more useful directions. For example, if you were at Hoover in the early 1980s and were discussing the 'plan' of the business, you could have had the ability to switch the conversation to 'perspective', challenge the established norm, consider how the domestic cleaner could be seen differently and then possibly taken the potential threat from Dyson more seriously.

Action 3

Understand all five Ps both conceptually and within your own business. Analyse your own business plan, pattern, position. Be able to move work conversation from one to another to gain a different angle and a different potential.

Chapter 16 – Understand what drives strategy and what strategy drives

In this chapter, we considered the 'ladder of business success' model as a structure for holistic strategy. It had:

- rungs that ensured a seamless flow from the organizational vision to what actually happens on a day-to-day basis
- a starting rung and starting point – for any business this is the vision, what we are here to do
- a left upright that considers 'external' strategy concerning those external to the business – competitors, customers, potential customers and even, when relevant, other interested parties such as governments, lobbying groups, pressure groups and tax officials
- a right upright that considers 'internal' strategy – aspects over which we have control and the need to ensure that they fulfil their primary purpose, that is, facilitating the successful implementation of the strategy, to achieve the goals, to make the vision a reality. These internal aspects are factors such as structure, values, culture.

Observations about ladders include that the rungs are connected to both uprights and that the uprights are pointing in the same direction. It should be so with your organization. It will almost certainly be detrimental to your business if there is any disconnect in any area of this model or if any rungs are missing. I say 'almost', but have not yet ever, in any business on any continent, found a lack of connection between rungs and uprights or a lack of alignment of both uprights or a missing rung (which means that vision fails to percolate into action) to be a positive factor.

Action 4

Construct a 'ladder of business success' for your organization. In doing so, you will be enhancing your strategic thinking ability, making connections between activities of the business and possibly identifying some areas that are not yet right and require consideration and action.

1. Start with the vision – what does your organization exist to do?

2. Move up the rungs.

- What are your goals?
- What strategies do you currently have to seek to achieve these goals?
- What areas of goals seem to have no strategy attached to them?
- Tactics – are these strategies broken down into appropriately sized and appropriate timeframe chunks?
- Actions – are these strategies being demonstrated in the day-to-day activity of the business?

3. Develop the left upright.

- Who are the relevant external stakeholders or interested parties?
- What is your message to them?

- Can you see this message being driven by your strategy or is there any element of it being evolved disconnected from the rungs?
- Is there more that should happen for the strategy to drive the external (left) upright of competitive, customer and external strategies?

4. Develop the right upright.

- Consider your structure, culture, organizational values – do they exist as separate aspects of the organization or are they integral facilitators for the successful implementation of your strategy?
- Identify where they are effective in this, their primary role, and where they are not fulfilling this function.
- Identify why this is the case. In many businesses, it is simply that executives have never previously thought that these are parts of holistic strategy and strategic facilitators.
- Consider other 'internal factors' – 'the way we do things around here' – possibly using Chapter 17's 'building blocks'.

Having developed a 'ladder of business success', it would be worth considering each aspect to determine where it is operating effectively in your company, where it is operating sub-optimally and where the connections are simply absent.

Action 5

Having identified both positive and negative aspects of the operation of your business through this tool, identify core required actions, consider who to communicate them to and how. One very wise boss I once had said, 'I can have hundreds of people who can tell me what's wrong – I want you to be the one who tells me what to do about it.'

Chapter 17 – Understand internal strategy

In this chapter, we considered the 'building blocks of business'. These are essentially a format to consider a range of the elements contained in the right (internal) side of the 'ladder of business success'. They are not an exhaustive consideration of this right upright, as aspects such as structure, culture and organizational values are not mentioned, but they are vital elements of 'right upright success'.

The 'building blocks of business' model can be used in three main ways:

- the 'benchmark'
- the 'action plan'
- the 'excellence model'.

Each of the three have value; I have seen each bear fruit in different companies and will briefly explain the thinking behind each approach.

The benchmark

For each of the seven building blocks, consider which organizations exhibit excellence in that block. Consider what they do and how they do it. Consider what you would have to do in your industry, business and situation to learn from them and increase your effectiveness in that block.

This is what I consider benchmarking should be about – looking at who is excellent at something and imitating it. Far too much business benchmarking merely compares ourselves with others who do roughly the same sort of thing and determines whether we are marginally above average! I consider this to be mostly a waste of effort when we could be considering other industries, other approaches and learning lessons in each from the best.

The action plan

This use of the blocks is an application of the 'journey analogy' from Chapter 15. As part of a strategy for developing the internal aspects of the business, consider each of the blocks in turn. This makes the analysis of the internal aspects of your business more manageable by breaking it down into relevant chunks. For each block, go through the journey analogy:

- Where are we? – a realistic assessment of our present position for each block.
- Where do we want to be? – a declaration of our intended destination for each block.
- Development of strategies to take us from present situation to intended destination.
- Staging posts – what will you do by when? Short-, medium- and long-term goals and actions.

Obviously, the journey analogy has highly adaptable questions and while these four are summaries, there may be many sub-questions you need to ask within each of them.

The excellence model

This approach takes the view of the requirements for success in your industry and your environment. Consider for each of the blocks, what is required for 'top of the class' success in your industry or position. A top tip here is not to be swayed by what already exists or what you already do – top of the class in vacuum cleaners is about problem-free operation by the customer and clean houses, not about changing bags! Focus on 'ideal' and then consider the gap between ideal and reality later – no good idea has ever been developed by someone who accepts or is satisfied with the status quo!

Chapter 18 – Understand marketing strategy

In this chapter, we acknowledged that there is no universally accepted definition for marketing, but we introduced 'the marketing funnel' as a route to understanding marketing strategy. One of the most important factors was to understand that while marketing is more of an art than a science, it is vital to have clear deliverable objectives for each marketing initiative. These must have a clear link to the 'rungs' of the 'ladder of business success' because marketing, like any other function, seeks to implement the business strategies, which seek to achieve the goals, which seek to make the vision a reality. Marketing strategies are an integral part of the left (external) upright of the ladder. Chapter 18 helps us identify these clear objectives and helps us to ensure that they are built into the ladder to seek strategic success.

Make similar considerations for marketing initiatives you see from others. Walk around 'open-eyed' – seeing marketing initiatives from other companies, particularly those in different industries to yours; and then make an assessment of their aims, intentions and where in the marketing funnel they are seeking to influence.

As stated in the previous chapter on competitive strategy, the habit of observing the actions of others, analysing them, drawing conclusions and then asking what you would have done differently were it your decision, is an excellent habit to build into your own self-development for increasing aptitude for strategic thinking. Good strategic thinking ability is at a premium in business and well worth the investment of your time and thoughts. On one occasion I was working with some 'high flyers' of a well-known global company. They were heads of departments and heads of small countries, who had the potential to move on to become heads of large departments or large countries. We were considering strategic thinking. I asked for their observations of what was happening at McDonald's, in a similar but more detailed way to our exploration of this company in the previous chapter. One individual had absolutely no idea as he never ate at McDonald's and was shocked that I expected him to be aware of a business he never frequented. In discussion, it transpired that he walked past two McDonald's outlets on the way to work and the same two on the way home, but as he had his mp3 player plugged into his ears, he had switched off from all useful thinking and was merely listening to music. One of his transformational applications from our time together was to open his eyes! He decided to walk to work observing strategy and only use the mp3 player to 'switch off his mind' on the way home when he was tired. I would recommend this approach – engaging your brain to consider strategy at every opportunity.

In this same group was a gentleman who visited the gym three times a week, again using an mp3 player to 'switch off' from the monotony of exercise. He too vowed to 'switch on' for at least one of his three weekly gym visits to mentally ponder something with strategic consequences he had observed during the previous week – another great use of time – the body and brain get exercised together!

Chapter 19 – Understand brand strategy

Again, we acknowledged that there is no undisputed definition of a brand in this chapter on brand strategies but stated that they exist to identify the ownership of a product and to make it stand out. Brand strategies are just one aspect of marketing strategies, but sufficiently important for a separate chapter to develop better understanding. As a part of marketing strategies, they too sit on the left upright of the 'ladder of business success'.

We used the framework of Interbrand's criteria for brand valuation as a basis for considering a range of actions – strategic, tactical and operational – which businesses can take to add value, or by bad actions to destroy value, in their brands. Interbrand's criteria are threefold:

- recent financial performance – a past focus
- role of the brand – the impact it has on a purchase decision – present focus
- brand strength – the ability of the brand to leverage future revenue – future focus.

As we can only affect the future, not the past, we focused on the ten future oriented factors that Interbrand measure to determine 'brand strength'.

Action 9

Make a note of the ten Interbrand criteria. Building on Action 8, when what you are observing relates to a brand, identify which of the criteria the strategy is seeking to influence. Critically appraise it and ask 'what would I have done?'.

Chapter 20 – Understand competitive strategy

In this chapter we used CM as a process and structure to understand some strategic options available in a competitive marketplace. The seven-stage process took us through a process to rapidly assess a competitive position, relative strengths and weaknesses, an analysis of the competitive threat and to identify some potential actions.

We considered a CM in theory, then a simplified CM of a fast food example. The obvious action is now to compile your own.

Action 10

Compile a CM of your business and that of your most threatening competitor. Various possibilities may emerge:

- Does the CM analysis change your perspective of how the customer thinks or even who the customer is (you may have several different customer categories)?

- Is your business best positioned to serve and target the customer?

- What are your and your competitors' relative strengths and weaknesses?

- Who is best placed to take advantage of changes you are seeing or can foresee in the market?

- What are some possible options for you to improve your competitive position?

- To which of the five Ps do these options relate?

- Are these options congruent with the rest of your 'ladder of success'?

Summary

Good strategic thinking has a good understanding and grasp of strategic issues as a prerequisite. These chapters should have given you every chance of pondering such relevant issues and a series of approaches and models to facilitate this. However, mere consideration is insufficient. Strategy is about action, not mere academic deliberation.

This final chapter has suggested ten action points, which aim to take the learning and make it an exercise in practical application. You do not have to be a Chief Executive to do them – anyone in any organization can complete these ten actions. Even public sector and not-for-profit organizations can do the competitive mapping – you still have competition, it is just of a slightly different nature (e.g. competition for central funding, charity donors, research funds, competition for gaining the desired staff).

Completing these ten action points, however, is just step one. Like the two examples of the 'high flyers' from the global business earlier in this chapter, the second challenge is to make this sort of thinking habitual. For your strategy of developing good strategic thinking to be ongoing, as all strategy should be ongoing, the challenge is to build these thoughts, processes and ideas into your daily work life. In doing so, your strategic thinking will be enhanced, your impact on your business will be enhanced, your value to your business will be enhanced and your career should consequently also be enhanced.

Endnotes

1 SWOT – a Strengths, Weaknesses, Opportunity, Threats analysis; a very popular, frequently completed but often misused analytical tool. For an exploration of how to use it more effectively, see *Strategies of the Serengeti* by Stephen Berry, 'Strategies of the zebra' chapter; also downloadable from www.StrategiesoftheSerengeti.com.

2 Mintzberg, H. 'The Strategy Concept 1: Five Ps for Strategy' *California Management Review* 30, 1, June 1997: 11–24.

3 Marvin Bower (1903–2003) c.1966.

4 *Super Size Me* – a 2004 American self-made film by Morgan Spurlock, which traced his physical and mental decline over a 30-day period, during which he ate only McDonald's food.

5 McLibel case – a British legal case, '*McDonald's Corporation v Steel & Morris* (1997)', where McDonald's sued Steel and Morris for distributing anti-McDonald's literature. The case lasted for ten years, making it the longest case in British legal history.

7 × 7

1 Seven deadly strategy sins

- Thinking that strategy is all about yourself and ignoring the market and customers.
- Making strategy development a gargantuan effort rather than a smooth, ongoing, evolving process.
- Casting strategy in stone and limiting its ability to respond and react.
- Separating strategy from the rest of the business – 'the strategy team' who then become divorced from reality.
- Having a brand strategy or marketing strategy with a life of its own rather than one that is driven by and integrated into organizational strategy.
- Driving strategy by past experience rather than future aspiration.
- Failing to understand the military mantra 'no strategy survives first contact with the enemy'.

2 Seven of the best resources

- *Strategies of the Serengeti* by Stephen Berry (Neos Publishing, 2010). Further and deeper ideas on strategy with copious real-life examples.
- www.EvaluationStore.com to assist with communication, influencing others and building great business teams.
- *The End of Leadership* by Barbara Kellerman (HarperBusiness, 2012). A challenging look at how we lead our businesses.
- https://hbr.org for online *Harvard Business Review*
- *How the Mighty Fall* by Jim Collins (Random House Business, 2009). Salutary tales of businesses that have fallen and those that have survived.

- www.businessballs.com for a wealth of free-of-charge knowledge.
- Eyes that constantly observe, ears that always listen, a mind that consistently evaluates, courage that always tries and the wisdom to sometimes say 'STOP'.

3 Seven inspiring business people

- **Asa Candler** – took Dr John Pemberton's failing cola drink product, marketed it brilliantly and grew Coca-Cola into a world-beating business.
- **Sir Richard Branson** – constantly challenged established and complacent companies with competition, and forced industries to change as a result.
- **Sir Phillip Green** – consistently innovative retail entrepreneur since he was a teenager, growing to control over 12 per cent of the UK retail clothing market.
- **Alfred Sloan** – came into the strategic mess which was General Motors and focused the business to create a multi-branded offering which had captured over 50 per cent of the US car market by the 1950s.
- **John Cadbury** – his process innovation created the solid chocolate bar and his family business went on to global success. His sons built the garden town of Bourneville for their workers – showing that they were both innovators and ethical business people.
- **Bill Gates** – took Microsoft from an idea to global dominance. Gates has become a global philanthropist combating extreme poverty and supporting healthcare.
- **Henry Ford** – transformed his market by a combination of product, process and marketing innovations, and led with drive and inspiration.

4 Seven Stephen Berry quotes

- 'There are two types of business – those who have their strategy right and those who are going out of business.'

- 'Short-termism is the enemy of success and the demand of investors.'
- 'Sometimes those at the top are the best politicians, not the best business people.'
- 'Inflexibility in strategy is as great an error as having no strategy at all.'
- 'No company journey is successful if the leaders spend more time looking at the path already travelled than the route ahead.'
- 'The primary job of Directors is to direct – there's a clue in the title. They are not controllers, not managers, not clerks – they're Directors.'
- (*In the early 1990s*) 'Bottled water? That will never catch on in the UK.' (*To prove that we all get things wrong sometimes.*)

5 Seven opportunities

- **New labour forces** – working from home is now commonplace, but there are other less well-tapped labour forces. There are hundreds of thousands of highly qualified and experienced mums (and some dads) who do not want full-time jobs but would jump at a chance to work four hours a day 10 a.m.–2 p.m. while their children are at school. How can our work patterns match those currently not working?
- **New ways of working globally** – chasing the sun is becoming more popular. A person starts some work in New York, finishes at 6 p.m. and passes it to a colleague in Tokyo (for whom it is 7 a.m.) who progresses the work. At 4 p.m. he passes it to a colleague in London – for whom it is 8 a.m. At 1 p.m. he sends the completed work to New York where it is 8 a.m. The work has had up to 14 hours of development all during the time that the New Yorker has not been at work.
- **Riding the wave** – the surfer does not generate the wave – he rides it. Always be looking for the next business wave and catch on to it before others. In *Strategies of the Serengeti* I tell the story of Corah increasing their sales x35 in 16 years by becoming a committed supplier to UK retailer Marks & Spencer – and 'riding their wave of expansion'. Stay close to the innovators.

- **Energy** – the world demand for energy is insatiable. Fossil fuels have a limited life. New ways of generating and distributing energy will always be in demand. Technology for wind, wave, water and sun power generation is well established but comparatively expensive – there must be opportunities to develop more affordable systems, processes and structures.
- **Food** – with an ever increasing world population, the demand for food increases. There is no shortage of food, just an imbalance with obesity in the West and starvation elsewhere. Food production from beef is very inefficient, from fish is more efficient and from insects is much more efficient – it will not be long before insect protein is fully accepted into our food chain – who is working on that technology now?
- **Waste** – in an ever disposable world we have overflowing landfills and a Pacific garbage patch allegedly the size of Texas. This is clearly unsustainable and so there is a demand for new technology and new solutions. Many are working in that field, many more are required.
- **Transportation** – the need to transport goods globally more cheaply will only increase; for example, vacuum packing salmon in Chile to enable it to be fresh after a long sea journey to the UK saves the cost of air transport. What other new, creative solutions can be made for foodstuffs, heavy equipment, delicate items? Delivery time by sea from China to the UK is 5–7 days – what opportunities are there to accelerate this while maintaining or reducing costs?

6 Seven things to do today

- Prepare a recession plan – strategies for the 'down' times are better prepared during the 'up' times.
- Ensure a realistic perception of your current position – not a flattering one.
- Have a clear aim of where you are seeking to go.

- Learn more about people – how to influence, persuade, inspire and communicate.
- Analyse every part of your marketing initiatives – what is each aiming to achieve? How are you measuring it?
- Visit www.evaluationstore.com/organisation_info.php to set up a motivation report – establish how inspired your team and company are.
- Do the assessment on www.StrategiesoftheSerengeti.com to see which strategies your organization is using and should use.

7 Seven trends for tomorrow

- Getting faster – the pace of change will only ever accelerate – move faster than the competition.
- Radical process simplification – it cannot take more than a couple of clicks to buy something or get the required information.
- Building communities – people like to belong, from LinkedIn groups to industry gatherings (virtual or physical) – form, belong, co-ordinate them.
- The twentieth-century answers won't work in the twenty-first century – the old models and ways of doing things have gone (no more lifecycle curves and five forces) – live in this century.
- Increased polarization – the middle ground is being squeezed by the lower end (e.g. cheaper) and the higher end (e.g. quality) – invest in the poles not the middle.
- Specialization – in a world of identical offerings (commodities) only the cheapest will win – specialize, differentiate, focus – don't slip into commoditization.
- Customer fluidity – changing to a new supplier is just a click of a mouse – so greater effort and initiative is required to generate customer loyalty.

PART 4
Your Marketing Masterclass

Introduction

Marketing is about the relationship between an organization and its marketplace, and in particular its customers and potential customers. Customers are the lifeblood of a business; without customers a business has no future. In order to succeed and make a profit, a business must therefore aim to identify and satisfy the needs of its customers. The purpose of marketing is to help the business achieve these aims. In this part of the book you will learn about the nature and techniques of successful marketing and how it can improve business performance.

Today's business world is highly competitive and changing fast, and marketing, as a body of knowledge and best practice, must respond to these changes. However, there is one fundamental fact about marketing that remains constant: it is that, to become successful and remain successful, an organization must be better at meeting customers' needs than the competition.

CHAPTER 22

What is marketing?

In this chapter we will set out to define marketing and to dispel some of the common misunderstandings regarding the meaning and nature of marketing. We will look at established UK and US definitions of marketing and some current European thinking about the definition of marketing for the twenty-first century. We will also summarize the history of marketing and how this business philosophy developed in response to increased competition.

We will consider the relationship between marketing and business performance and some of the key evidence to support the view that a 'customer/marketing orientation' can have a positive effect on profitability and performance.

We will also touch on the issue of competition and the need to consider the relationship between our customers/potential customers and our competitors in any discussion of our approach to marketing our business. We will return to this theme in more detail later in Part 4.

Finally in this chapter we will look at marketing and the business as a whole, and identify some of the key behaviours of businesses that have effectively (and profitably) made the customer/ marketing orientation the basis of their operations.

Defining marketing

In essence, marketing is a relatively simple concept but at its root lies a fundamental approach to directing a business. Its simplicity can lead to the real meaning of marketing being misunderstood or misconstrued – and this can lull us into a false sense of security. And, if we don't understand what marketing is, we had better hope that our competitors don't know either – because, if they do, they will have a competitive advantage over us.

A good way to explain marketing is to start by dispelling two common misunderstandings regarding its meaning and nature.

- **Marketing is just a posh name for selling.** WRONG! A sale is often the ultimate objective of a marketing strategy, but marketing covers a much broader range of activities than just the sale event. Selling is the exchange of a product or service for, most commonly, a monetary value. Selling can be viewed as the last step in the marketing process. If marketing has been effective, it should make selling 'easier' (although selling is never easy!) because promotional and sales effort will have been directed at those customer groups who have a perceived need for the company's offering.
- **Marketing just means advertising.** WRONG! Promotion (including advertising) is a strategic activity that focuses on transmitting informative and/or persuasive messages via a medium or range of media to defined target audiences. In simple terms promotion is, again, *part* of the marketing strategy (as we will see later). This potential misunderstanding is further compounded when news media talk about a 'marketing gimmick' when they mean a 'promotional gimmick'.

> ## Some definitions of marketing
> The UK Chartered Institute of Marketing (CIM) says that
> *'Marketing is the management process responsible for identifying, anticipating and satisfying consumers' requirements profitably.'*

The American Marketing Association (AMA) defines marketing as:

'The process of planning and executing the conception, pricing, promotion, and distribution of ideas, goods, and services to create exchanges that satisfy individual and organizational objectives.'

Both of these definitions are manifestations of the prevailing view of what constitutes marketing. However, a number of commentators are now suggesting that it is time to redefine marketing for the twenty-first century. For instance, one suggested definition, from C. Grönroos of the Swedish School of Economics, Helsinki, is:

'Marketing is to establish, develop and commercialize long-term customer relationships, so that the objectives of the parties involved are met. This is done by mutual exchange and keeping of promises.'

It is worth noting that both the AMA and Grönroos definitions refer to 'exchange'. At the heart of marketing is the process of enabling individuals and organizations to obtain what they need and want through exchanges with others.

For the purposes of this book a simple, usable definition might be:

'Marketing is the identification and anticipation of customers' needs and the profitable satisfaction of those needs.'

In essence, marketing is a business philosophy that says *it is easier to achieve your business objectives if you understand and meet customers' needs*. Customers should be the *raison d'être* of the business.

There are **four key issues** encompassed in our simple definition:

'Marketing is the identification and anticipation of customers' needs and the profitable satisfaction of those needs.'

1 **Identification** To be truly marketing oriented, a business must **identify** customer **needs**. Marketing research linked to marketing decision making is the hallmark of a marketing-oriented company.
2 **Satisfaction** Customers must feel that the **benefits** offered by the company's products or services **meet** their **needs**. If this does not happen, there is little opportunity for repeat sales.
3 **Profitable** Profit is an obvious business objective, and part of the 'consideration' (to use a term from contract law) for satisfying customer needs is to make a profit. In addition, for a business to survive and satisfy customer needs in the future, profit is essential.
4 **Anticipation** Part of what marketing needs to do is study customers' behaviour and attitudes to make it possible to **predict** how changes will affect future demand for products and services.

It is also important to stress that, when establishing and maintaining customer relationships, the seller gives a set of **promises** based on the performance of a product or service offered, i.e. the benefits inherent in the offering that the seller believes are matched to the needs of the customer. In return the buyer promises to meet his/her commitment in the exchange, generally some form of payment. Promise is a key component of marketing, not only during the first purchase but also as central to the ongoing relationship between buyers and sellers.

One way to get a better understanding is to take a brief look at the history of marketing.

A history of marketing

Some argue that marketing has been in existence whenever and wherever there have been buyers and sellers, i.e. a market. However, it is generally considered that marketing, as we understand it, developed when competition for customers intensified.

Before and during the Industrial Revolution (roughly 1750–1850 in the UK), goods were relatively scarce and producers could sell all that they could produce. The focus was therefore on production and distribution at the lowest cost. This approach to organizing a business is often referred to as a **'production orientation'**.

From the late nineteenth and early twentieth centuries, competition grew and the focus turned to selling what could be produced, by persuading buyers to choose the seller's product, regardless of whether it was the best match to the customer's needs. A clear problem with this approach is that, if the product does not meet the customer's needs, they will not purchase it again. Consequently, there will be no repeat sales and this will impact on the survival of the business. This approach to organizing a business is often referred to as a **'sales orientation'**.

From the 1950s onwards, most markets displayed intense competition for customers, and this competition drove the need to understand and satisfy customers' needs if the business was to succeed. In essence, this approach puts the customer at the centre of a firm's thinking and strategy, an approach to organizing a business that we often refer to as a **'customer or marketing orientation'**.

Marketing was once seen as the preserve of fast-moving consumer goods (FMCG) companies; now marketing and its techniques can be found in most industries. Even the public sector and charities are embracing the marketing orientation. In not-for-profit environments the main differences are that the objectives of the organization may not be expressed in terms of profitability or market share, and there is generally no real 'competitive' element.

In addition, marketing became an important academic subject – there is a reference to 'marketing' in a course syllabus at Ohio State University from 1921 – and is a central plank of management education, both undergraduate and postgraduate, across the world. I recently googled the term 'marketing MBA' and got 87.8 million results!

It is important to point out that, even now, 'production-oriented' and 'sales-oriented' organizations can still be identified in some business sectors. This situation seems to be related to:

- the nature of the particular market environments of these sectors, e.g. large purchase values, very small number of customers, complex contractual arrangements
- the attitudes/perceptions of senior management in these sectors.

Perhaps such management has been sceptical about whether marketing helps improve business performance and has therefore been reluctant to adopt the customer/marketing orientation.

Marketing and business performance

Both managers and academics have long been exercised by the 'value' of marketing to a business. In other words, if your business is marketing oriented, will you be more profitable than businesses that are not?

From a manager's perspective, the issue is straightforward: why should you invest any scarce resource (including time and money) in marketing unless there is evidence that it will make you more profitable?

Academics have also focused on this issue, not only to support managers (by seeking to distil best practice) but also to understand the fundamental relationships between independent variables (such as what we do) and dependent variables (the results of what we do).

Academic research in this area began seriously in the 1970s. Probably one of the most important studies was the Profit Impact of Market Strategies (PIMS) study from Harvard University. The basis of the study was a huge survey and a large multiple regression model. It started with hundreds of independent variables that were considered to affect the key dependent variables (i.e. profit and return on investment (ROI), often referred to as return on capital employed (ROCE) in the UK) and finished up with 37 variables that explained most (80 per cent) of the causal effect. The study identified that profit margins and ROI are strongly, and positively, related to four key variables:

1 **Business share of the target market**, relative to the share held by the top three competitors (relative market share)
2 **Customer rating of product/service performance**, relative to competitors (customer-perceived relative quality)
3 **Asset productivity**, measured in terms of value added/ capital employed
4 **Employee productivity**, measured in terms of real value added per person.

As might be expected, a range of variables influences profitability, including those associated with the relationship between the business and its marketplace (including customers and competitors) and others within the firm (such as asset productivity and employee productivity, both related to the effective management of the business).

What seems to be clear from the PIMS study is that high market share is an important predictor of business performance. This is achieved by providing customers with the products/ services that deliver benefits that they perceive match their needs best and this, fundamentally, is what marketing is all about. The second variable, customer-perceived relative quality, confirms this: to be a leader in any market you must have a better offering than that of your competitors. So marketing, as a business philosophy and as a way of organizing a business, is one important independent variable affecting the key dependent variables of profit margin and ROI.

Researchers then turned their attention to the relationship between 'customer/marketing orientation' (i.e. the implementation of the marketing concept encapsulated in our definition set out above) and business performance. During the 1990s a number of key studies were published and most indicate a positive, if sometimes weak, relationship between customer/marketing orientation and business performance.

What we can say is that the evidence shows that a customer/ marketing orientation is associated with improved business performance.

The four 'big ideas' in marketing

1 Exchange At the heart of marketing is the process of enabling individuals and organizations to obtain what they need and want through exchanges with others.

2 Promise In establishing and maintaining customer relationships, the seller gives a set of promises based on the performance of a product or service offered. In return, the buyer promises to meet his/her commitment in the exchange, generally some form of payment.

3 Matching Marketing matches the benefits in the organization's offerings with the customer's needs.

4 'Customer' or 'marketing' orientation A business that is customer (or marketing) oriented puts customer needs at the centre of their thinking and strategy.

Customers and the competition

One important aspect of the real-world situation we have not addressed yet is competition. So far, the customer/marketing orientation has placed the customer as the focus of the business. This seems intuitively acceptable – if we understand and meet customers' needs, we should win their business – but while we are focusing on customers, so are our competitors. Consequently, any effective marketing strategy must take into account our competition and the relationship between them and our customers/potential customers.

The first issue to consider is the nature of the customers' perceived needs – the customer/marketing orientation. Customers will seek to identify the best match of benefits to their perceived needs and in doing so will make judgements about the various offerings available to them.

In addition, customers will consider the price of each competitor's offering along with the benefits they perceive in each offering. In essence, customers will make a value judgement – which offering provides the most benefits at the lowest price.

We will return to these issues in more detail later.

Marketing and the business

A reasonable question to ask at this stage is this: if a customer/marketing orientation is linked to profitability, what is it we have to do to make it operational (and therefore effective) in our business?

A wide range of studies has distilled **five key behaviours** that characterize businesses which have effectively (and profitably) made customer/marketing orientation the operational basis of their businesses:

1 **Market sensing**
   This is the foundation of an effective customer/marketing orientation. We must know what our customers' needs are and, to do this, we need to use a range of sources including direct contact with our customers and tools like marketing research (which we will look at later). In addition, we know that we do not live in a static environment so therefore we need to track changes in customers' needs.

2 **Quality focus**
   The PIMS research highlighted the relationship between product/service quality and business performance, and the message is that the business must seek to improve product/service quality to maintain a competitive differential. Clearly, this must include monitoring competitive actions.

3 **Internal 'marketing'**
   It was once said that 'Marketing is too important to be left to the marketing department' and, like many humorous quotes, this has a strong basis in reality. While specialist marketing-

related functions still exist, in many modern businesses large marketing departments have been replaced by a business-wide focus on satisfying customer needs. Quite simply, all employees must know what they have to do to satisfy customers' needs, must be able to do it and must be motivated to do it.

4 **Adaptive response**

We all know that we live in a time of rapid change and it is therefore critical that businesses are flexible and able to adapt to changing market conditions and customer needs. This includes understanding how broader political, economic, social and technological factors impact on our customers and competitors.

5 **External relationships**

It is all too easy for business managers to feel they must focus all their attention on matters within the business but, as we have seen, the success of the business depends on how we interact with the outside world. Constructing effective means of two-way communication with customers is therefore paramount. This can be as simple as ensuring that customers are encouraged to tell the business about problems or any gaps in meeting their needs, or as sophisticated as using barcode/customer loyalty card data analysis and customer satisfaction research. Managers need to identify and focus on key account relationships (KAR), i.e. those accounts that are responsible for the majority of the business. Such KARs could be with your main customers or perhaps your major distributors/retailers.

Customer relationship management (CRM) programmes are designed to formalize the process of customer/ business relationships, with customer retention often a key objective. A number of software companies provide bespoke software to support the CRM function.

Summary

Developed as a strategic response to intensified competition for customers, marketing is a relatively simple concept but a fundamental approach to directing a business.

In essence, marketing is a business philosophy that says it is easier to achieve your business objectives if you understand and meet customers' needs, and research indicates that marketing improves business performance. Customers should be the *raison d'être* of the business.

Four 'big ideas' are central to marketing: exchange, promise, matching, and customer or marketing orientation. Another key aspect of strategic marketing is our competitors, who are also interacting with our customers/ potential customers.

Finally, there are five key behaviours that characterize businesses which have effectively (and profitably) made customer/marketing orientation the operational basis of their businesses: market sensing, quality focus, internal marketing, adaptive response and external relationships.

Fact-check (answers at the back)

1. Why can the meaning of marketing be misunderstood?
   a) Because it is a relatively simple concept but a fundamental approach to directing a business ❑
   b) It is not related to the real world of business ❑
   c) It is a complex academic subject ❑
   d) It is only relevant to the US market ❑

2. How can marketing be defined?
   a) As a posh word for selling ❑
   b) It is the same as advertising and promotion ❑
   c) As the identification and anticipation of customers' needs and the profitable satisfaction of those needs ❑
   d) None of the above ❑

3. What is the business philosophy of marketing?
   a) Spending the most on advertising guarantees you a profit ❑
   b) It is easier to achieve your business objectives if you understand and meet customer needs ❑
   c) Customers will buy whatever you can produce ❑
   d) You only have to convince the customer once to be successful ❑

4. Persuading buyers to choose the seller's product regardless of whether it is the best match to the customers' needs is known as what?
   a) Production orientation ❑
   b) Sales orientation ❑
   c) Customer or marketing orientation ❑
   d) Retail orientation ❑

5. Why did companies start to embrace marketing from the 1950s onwards?
   a) There were more advertising media, such as TV, available ❑
   b) Advertising agencies had been invented ❑
   c) Most markets displayed intense competition for customers ❑
   d) Mail order was a new sales method ❑

6. What does the Profit Impact of Market Strategies (PIMS) study?
   a) The relationship between strategy and profit ❑
   b) The characteristics of the best managers ❑
   c) The size of the US export market ❑
   d) The differences between capitalist and communist systems ❑

7. What are the two marketing outcomes that PIMS identified as strongly and positively related to profitability?
a) Brand logo and colour ❏
b) Relative market share and customer-perceived relative value ❏
c) Size and frequency of advertisements ❏
d) Range and content of sponsorship deals ❏

8. Why must a marketing strategy take the competition into account?
a) The rate of change in society is so fast ❏
b) They too are focusing on our customers/potential customers ❏
c) International trade is important ❏
d) The Internet is important ❏

9. What are market sensing, quality focus, internal 'marketing', adaptive response and external relationships?
a) Terms used in new product testing ❏
b) Sales management techniques ❏
c) Key behaviours of businesses that have effectively made customer/ marketing orientation an operational basis of their businesses ❏
d) None of the above ❏

10. What is a key concept of the customer/marketing orientation?
a) Exchange ❏
b) Promise ❏
c) Matching process ❏
d) All of the above ❏

CHAPTER 23

Marketing and the customer

We have learned that the customer is at the heart of the customer/marketing orientation and that it is easier to achieve our business objectives if we understand and meet customers' needs. Clearly, customers are very important to a business and to the development of marketing thought, and now we will focus on customers as individuals and as organizations.

We will begin by considering customers' motives, values and attitudes and how these influence the way they perceive their needs, and look at customer behaviour as a problem-solving process and the stages involved in that. We shall also review the differences between individual customers and organizational customers and look at the importance of decision-making units (DMUs) in the latter. We will review the importance of market segmentation and look at the ways in which markets can be segmented.

Finally, we will consider the impact of political, economic, social and technological (PEST) drivers that shape the world in which customers exist and therefore have a major influence on customers' behaviour.

Who are our customers?

A good place to start is with the question, 'Who are our customers?' At first sight this might seem a simple question. Our customers are the people who buy our products or services. Customers can be individuals, families, small and medium-sized businesses, public limited companies (PLCs), government departments, and so on. It is possible, therefore, to divide customers into two broad markets:

- **Consumer markets** – e.g. individuals and families
- **Organizational or business-to-business (B2B) markets** – e.g. businesses, not-for-profit/charitable organizations and government departments.

Customers in consumer markets

We can all relate to customers in consumer markets – a subject that is often referred to as consumer behaviour – since we are all customers: we all buy products and services as individuals.

Our definition of marketing focuses on 'customers' needs'. Some writers distinguish between a 'need' and a 'want': they say a need is something fundamental to life, such as water, food, shelter, etc., whereas a want is a desire to possess something that is less important to life. The *Concise Oxford English Dictionary* defines a 'need' as 'a want or requirement' and a 'want' as 'a desire, wish for possession, need'. For the purposes of understanding customers' needs, we can assume that a need and a want are one and the same.

When considering how customers perceive their needs, we have to embrace some concepts and knowledge developed in disciplines such as psychology and sociology. We are going to look at customers' motives, values and attitudes, and customer behaviour as a problem-solving process.

Motives

At the heart of a perceived need is a **driver**, a motive. Abraham Maslow produced a hierarchical structure of needs based on five core levels:

	Need	Motive
Lower level ↓ **Upper level**	Physiological	Water, sleep, food
	Safety	Security, shelter, protection
	Belongingness	Love, friendship, acceptance by others
	Ego	Prestige, status, accomplishment
	Self-actualization	Self-fulfilment, personal enrichment

At each level, different priorities exist in terms of the benefits a customer is seeking. The implication is that one must first satisfy basic needs before ascending to higher needs. Of course, one product or service may satisfy a number of different needs simultaneously. For example, a meal at a fashionable and expensive restaurant can meet a range of needs from physiological to ego and self-actualization.

Sex, in particular, transcends the levels of Maslow's hierarchy. A basic biological drive, sex is also a more complex motive that can involve belongingness, ego and self-actualization.

Many of the products and services we purchase in modern economic markets have a significant element of the upper-level motives at the root of our perceived needs. Examples include clothing (designer clothes and shoes) and cars (luxury saloon cars, performance cars, 'super cars').

Values

Our motives are filtered through our values. Values can be defined as our broad preferences concerning appropriate courses of action or outcomes and reflect our sense of 'good' and 'bad'. Our values develop in a number of ways but the family (socialization of children) is a major factor, along with school, religion and peer group influence.

For example, motives such as prestige and status (ego needs) would be manifested as different perceived needs in individuals with different values. We can take this example further if we consider the purchase of a prestige car: a customer whose values include a heightened sense of environmental issues is likely to have a different set of perceived needs from a customer who does not share that value. A hybrid vehicle would therefore not be equally attractive to both customers.

Attitudes

Over time, we all develop a set of attitudes. Attitudes are a predisposition or a tendency to respond positively or negatively towards a certain stimulus – an idea, a person, a situation, a product, etc. Our attitudes incorporate both our motives and our values but are also influenced by our experiences.

For instance, following the tragedy at Hillsborough football stadium in Sheffield, England, in 1989, *The Sun* newspaper published an article accusing Liverpool fans of appalling behaviour on the day. There was no truth in these claims, and the people of Liverpool responded with justifiable anger. Sales of the newspaper on Merseyside plunged from 200,000 copies a day to just a couple of thousand. *The Sun*'s customers in Liverpool changed their attitude to the newspaper in a matter of days.

Behaviour

Customer behaviour has traditionally been seen as a problem-solving process. Implicit in this is that customers act in a logical manner when selecting solutions to their needs. The steps in the process are set out below.

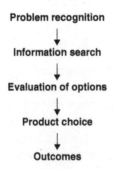

The problem-solving process

For some purchases (particularly more expensive ones) customers do actually follow such a process. However, for lower-cost (and therefore lower-risk) purchases evidence suggests that the decision process is significantly less rigorous. In addition, different customers go through more or less rigorous decision processes depending on their socio-economic and cultural situation.

Let's look at the different stages of the process in detail.

1 Problem recognition

Problem recognition is the point at which a customer articulates their 'perceived need' (see our definition of marketing in Chapter 22). In reality, customers usually have a number of perceived needs that are important to them in meeting their overall needs. Such needs tend to have different levels of importance to them – the customer's 'hierarchy of needs' – a ranked list of those needs that must be satisfied to convince the customer to buy.

For major purchases (like a home or a car) customers may have a long list of perceived needs, sometimes running into double figures. Marketers have spent considerable effort to both identify and rank customers' needs in such situations. One important finding is that, even when there is a relatively long list of perceived needs, the actual purchase decision is often based on the three or four most important perceived needs.

2 Information search

The next stage can involve a wide range of activities, including looking at manufacturers' brochures and advertisements, reviews in magazines and reports from specialist consumer advisory groups (such as Which?) and making online searches for user blogs. Personal contacts, such as family, friends and colleagues, and word-of-mouth are also important sources of information and help with forming opinions.

3 Evaluation of options

To evaluate the options, the customer compares the benefits of a number of solutions (our offering and our competitors') against their perceived needs. The customer will decide which offering has the best match of benefits to their needs, and this will normally produce a ranking of best match to least good match. One element will be price.

The customer now has to decide which offering is the best **value**, i.e. represents the most benefits at the lowest price. This can be difficult for the customer when both the number of benefits and the price vary between offerings.

> ## Second best?
> During the 1970s a leading domestic durables manufacturer (we'll call them 'the client') commissioned a research study that asked customers to rank their product and competitors' products in terms of the best match to the respondents' needs. In all the studies, the client's product topped the list. However, they achieved poor market share figures. Further research identified that the reason for this apparent contradiction (i.e. we have the best match of benefits to the customers' needs but they don't buy our product) was that the price differential between the client's product and the next best-ranked product was large enough to persuade customers to buy the second-ranked rather than the first-ranked offering.

4 Product choice

The penultimate stage in the problem-solving process, product choice, leads to the act of purchase. At this stage, buyers may experience pre-purchase anxiety, a worry about the ramifications of the act they are about to commit. Is it the right product for me? Can I afford it? Will my friends like it? In some cases this leads to the customer postponing a purchase decision. Marketers are obviously keen to minimize the effect of pre-purchase anxiety.

5 Outcomes

The final outcomes stage can be described as the 'consumption' stage, when the customer actually gets to consume the benefits carried by the offering. What we can see is that there are two stages when the customer is evaluating the product:

- the pre-purchase stage up to and including the purchase
- the post-purchase stage.

In the post-purchase stage the product must fulfil the promises made at the pre-purchase stage. Failure to do so will mean there is little likelihood of repeat purchase. This is an important business imperative: it is costly to 'create' a customer and, if we fail to satisfy them, we will provide an opportunity for our competitors.

Customers may also experience post-purchase anxiety – again experiencing the same worries that they may have had before the purchase. Marketers need to help customers deal with post-purchase anxiety by reinforcing the positive messages used at the pre-purchase stage. We will return to this later.

The customer decision is further complicated when the person who buys (i.e. pays for) the product or service is different from the person who consumes the product or service. For instance, when someone buys a present for another person, the buyer is not the consumer. In this situation the buyer is assessing whether the benefits they perceive in the offering will match the needs of the third party.

Other factors in decision making

Some of the current thinking about human decision making comes from the Nobel Prize winner Daniel Kahneman. In his book *Thinking, Fast and Slow* (2011) he presents evidence that humans are far from being 'rational agents' and are often inconsistent, emotional and biased in their decision making. Kahneman refers to two 'systems' of thinking. *System Two* is the conscious, thinking mind that considers, evaluates and reasons. *System One*, on the other hand, is responsible for the automatic and effortless mental response. *System One* works on as little or as much information as it has and is responsible for snap decisions regarding major courses of action including buying decisions. So *System One* thinking may lead a customer to select a product that they would reject if they adopted *System Two* thinking.

Neuromarketing is a further, parallel approach to looking at the brain from a marketing perspective. The term 'neuromarketing' is thought to have been coined by Ale Smidts of Erasmus University in the early 2000s and is the application of brain-scan technology, especially functional magnetic resonance imaging (fMRI), to marketing problems. One of the findings indicates that brain activity for an action begins about half a second before a person consciously decides to take an action. This suggests that we are not so much consciously 'making' a decision as becoming aware that a decision has been made. These are early days for neuromarketing and we can expect more developments soon.

Customers in organizational or B2B markets

It is generally considered that organizational markets differ from consumer markets in four key ways:

1 B2B markets have a relatively small number of customers – e.g. there are relatively few car manufacturers in Europe.
2 Demand for products and services is 'derived demand', i.e. derived from the need to meet organizational objectives rather than to be consumed for their own sake, as is the case in consumer markets – e.g. car manufacturers buy steel sheet not for its own sake but as a part of the process of producing cars for consumption by consumers.
3 Decision making concerned with specifying and procuring products and services is normally a complex interaction of individuals within and sometimes from outside the organization (including consultants) – e.g. technical staff will specify and buying professionals will procure.
4 The perceived needs of the organization will involve a complex interaction of the stated corporate needs and the personal needs of the individuals involved in the decision. The company will specify what is required but this will be interpreted by individuals and will therefore be filtered through their own motives, values and attitudes.

Like consumer buyer behaviour, organizational buyer behaviour is a problem-solving process. However, in the latter case the stages of the process are normally more rigorous. There are eight steps:

Step 1   Need recognition
Step 2   Definition of the characteristics and quantity needed
Step 3   Development of the specifications to guide procurement

Step 4   Search for and qualification of potential sources
Step 5   Acquisition and analysis of proposals
Step 6   Evaluation of proposals and selection of supplier(s)
Step 7   Selection of an order routine
Step 8   Performance feedback and evaluation

It is worth comparing this with the model of individual customer behaviour as a problem-solving process, set out above. The similarities are quite clear and, again, the real difference is in the rigour required by organizations (which is not to say that some individuals do not also adopt very rigorous processes).

The eight steps set out above are associated with a **new-task** purchase situation in which an organization is buying a product or service for the first time. It involves greater potential risk and the involvement of the largest number of decision participants.

Some organizations use decision theory models to support the buying process. The steps in the process are as follows:

1 A list of selection criteria is assembled.
2 Each criterion is given a weight in terms of its importance.
3 Each identified potential supplier is scored on each criterion.
4 Suppliers are then ranked in terms of these weighted scores.

Once a selection has been made, purchases can become more routine, even automated, and this is known as **straight rebuy**.

Between the two extremes of new-task and straight rebuy is **modified rebuy**. In this case the organization needs to modify the specification, terms, price, etc., and this requires more decision participants than straight rebuy but not as many as new-task.

When the decision participants act together, they are known as a buying centre or a **decision-making unit (DMU)**. Research has identified five key roles in the DMU:

● **Users** Those who use the purchased item, such as the production department

- **Influencers** Members of the organization who influence the purchasing decision even though they may not be centrally involved, e.g. members of the marketing department
- **Buyers** Those members of the organization who have authority to select suppliers and arrange terms of purchase
- **Deciders** Those members of the organization with formal or informal power to determine the final choice of supplier
- **Gatekeepers** Those individuals who control the flow of information into the organization and therefore indirectly influence the purchasing decision, e.g. members of the finance department through their control of budgets.

Research has also shown that the DMU usually has one member (known as the 'salient member') who has the major influence on the selection decision. This person is not always the most senior member of the group, however. The DMU can contain a number of 'champions' who favour particular solutions.

Market segmentation

Customers are different – in their values and attitudes, their incomes, age, gender, location and so on – and these differences are the reason why marketing managers seek to **segment** markets. Segmentation refers to dividing customers into segments where customers within one segment have similar characteristics and as a segment are different from customers in other segments.

> ## Examples of market segments
>
> **Geographical** – countries, regions within countries, etc.
>
> **Demographic** – based on age, gender, family size, income, occupation, education, race, religion, etc.
>
> **Behavioural** – consumer knowledge, perceptions, attitudes, uses of and responses to a product or service.

Fundamentally, segmentation of a market must be based on differences in customers' perceived needs. However, in practical terms, it is sometimes difficult to identify (and therefore to direct marketing effort at) potential customers on this basis.

While it is relatively easy to identify customers/potential customers by age or gender or where they live, such variables do not always correspond to customers' buying preferences. This has led marketers to seek to record customers' preferences through mechanisms such as loyalty programmes (store cards, air miles). An alternative approach combines a range of data sources to profile customers and create segments based on customers' buying behaviour. For example, CACI Ltd ACORN is a geodemographic tool used to identify and understand the UK population and the demand for products and services.

Other characteristics of effective segmentation

Measurable We need to be able to measure the market – usually in terms of market worth (i.e. monetary spend) or number of customers. If we can't, it is difficult to develop strategies to exploit these segments.

Accessible We need to be able to access customers in terms of the media they are exposed to and where they shop. If we lack information about these factors, it is again difficult to develop strategies to exploit these segments.

Critical mass The segment must be big enough to make it cost-effective for the company to target it.

Research in *McKinsey Quarterly* (January 2011) suggests that businesses should consider more rather than fewer segments ('think in terms of 30–50 segments, not 5 or so'). Effective segmentation is critical to successful strategic marketing and we shall return to this topic later.

The 'PEST' environment

Finally, we need to remember that all customers are subject to the influences and pressures of the broader 'environment'. In this context we are using the term 'environment' to include the political, economic, social and technological (PEST) drivers that shape the world in which customers exist and that therefore have a major influence on customers' behaviour. We can expand each element:

- **Political** includes aspects such as law making and tax policy.
- **Economic** includes the general economic climate, rate of inflation and interest rates.
- **Social** includes the prevailing attitudes in society, e.g. attitudes to smoking, recycling and energy conservation.
- **Technological** includes the increasing use of mobile communications technology and alternative (non-fossil fuel) power sources.

Some analysts have added **Legal** and rearranged the mnemonic to SLEPT; others have inserted **Environmental** (the physical environment) factors and expanded it to PESTEL or PESTLE. The model has recently been further extended to STEEPLE and STEEPLED, adding **Ethics** and **Demographics** as factors.

PEST factors have an influence not only on customers but also on all participants in the marketplace, including our organization, competitors, suppliers and distributors, and we shall return to this later.

A review ('The four global forces breaking all the trends', McKinsey & Co, April 2015) of the most dramatic changes we are facing over the next decade or so highlight four key trends:

1 **Increasing urbanization**, particularly in the emerging markets – nearly half of global GDP growth between 2010 and 2025 is forecasted to come from 440 cities in emerging markets.
2 **Accelerated technological change** – we are witnessing an exponential growth in technological developments that impact on virtually every aspect of our lives.
3 **An ageing population** – the human population is getting older and fertility is falling and this will create a smaller workforce and place a greater onus on productivity growth.
4 **Greater global connections** – there will be more movement of capital, people and information around the world.

Moreover, these factors can amplify one another, which further compounds the nature of the change we face.

Summary

Customers can be individuals or organizations. Behind every perceived consumer need is a driver or *motive*. Motives are filtered through our *values*, our broad preferences concerning appropriate and good actions or outcomes. Family, school, religion and peer group are major influences on these.

The *attitudes* we develop are our tendency to respond positively or negatively towards certain stimuli. Our attitudes incorporate our motives and values but are also affected by our experiences. Customer behaviour has traditionally been seen as a *problem-solving process*. PEST drivers in the wider environment influence this behaviour.

Organizational markets differ from consumer markets in four key ways: they are smaller, demand is derived from organizational objectives, decisions are made by groups of participants, and perceived needs contain corporate and personal elements.

Effective *market segmentation* divides customers into measurable and accessible segments of appropriate critical mass according to differences in perceived needs.

Fact-check (answers at the back)

1. What is at the heart of a perceived need?
   a) An advertisement ❏
   b) A motive ❏
   c) A film ❏
   d) A book ❏

2. What, according to Maslow, is the lowest level need?
   a) Physiological level ❏
   b) Wants level ❏
   c) Ego level ❏
   d) Self-actualization level ❏

3. What does Maslow consider motives such as self-fulfilment and personal enrichment to be?
   a) Spending to the limit on your credit cards ❏
   b) Self-actualization needs ❏
   c) Basic needs ❏
   d) Being wealthy ❏

4. What are values?
   a) Our broad preferences concerning appropriate courses of action or outcomes ❏
   b) Our ability to detect falsehoods ❏
   c) Our ability to solve puzzles ❏
   d) Our ability to recall dreams ❏

5. What are attitudes?
   a) Our ability to play sports ❏
   b) Our ability to learn a musical instrument ❏
   c) Our ability to tell jokes ❏
   d) A predisposition to respond positively or negatively towards a certain stimulus ❏

6. What has customer behaviour traditionally been seen as?
   a) A problem-solving process ❏
   b) Linked to advertising ❏
   c) Totally linked to the weather ❏
   d) Unexplainable ❏

7. Why are organizational markets different from consumer markets?
   a) There are relatively few customers in organizational markets ❏
   b) Demand is derived from the needs of the organization ❏
   c) Decision making is complex and involves both organizational needs and the personal needs of the individuals involved ❏
   d) All of the above ❏

8. In the decision-making unit (DMU), what does the 'gatekeeper' role involve?
   a) Making sure the doors are closed ❏
   b) Controlling the flow of information ❏
   c) Preventing non-DMU members from entering the room ❏
   d) Keeping the minutes to the meeting ❏

9. In addition to differences in customers' perceived needs, for market segmentation to be effective what do the segments need to be?
a) Measurable ❏
b) Accessible ❏
c) An appropriate critical mass ❏
d) All of the above ❏

10. What are the elements of the PEST 'environment'?
a) Painting, English, sociology and training ❏
b) Power, engineering, selling and transport ❏
c) Processes, experiences, solutions and testing ❏
d) Political, economic, social and technological ❏

CHAPTER 24

Marketing information and marketing research

Marketers need information to reduce risk in decision making and to improve the effectiveness of the way they allocate scarce resources.

We will consider the American Marketing Association's (AMA) definition of MR and look at the elements of this definition and at some examples of research applications.

In this chapter we will cover:

- research within the organization – types of information generated by the organization and the more formal marketing information system (MkIS) used by some companies
- marketing intelligence – its nature and some examples of sources of marketing intelligence
- secondary research – its nature and some examples of the four main sources of secondary research
- primary research – we will set out a model for the primary research process and look in some detail at each element including the sampling frame and sampling, research instruments (particularly the questionnaire), question content and type, data collection methods, analysis and reporting.

What is marketing research?

In Chapter 22 we said that marketing research (MR), linked to marketing decision making, is the hallmark of a marketing-oriented company. Identifying customers' needs is an essential element of marketing and, as we then saw in Chapter 23, understanding customers' motives and buying behaviour is complex and MR is central to how we do this.

A definition of marketing research

The American Marketing Association (AMA) defines MR as follows:

'Marketing research is the function that links the consumer, customer, and public to the marketer through information – information used to identify and define marketing opportunities and problems; generate, refine, and evaluate marketing actions; monitor marketing performance; and improve understanding of marketing as a process. Marketing research specifies the information required to address these issues, designs the method for collecting information, manages and implements the data collection process, analyses the results, and communicates the findings and their implications.'

There are three key issues encompassed in the comprehensive definition shown in the box above:

1 **MR acts as a link** between the customer and the organization and allows a two-way flow of information; the organization can use research to understand the customer and can present the customer with ideas and offerings and gauge the customers' likes and dislikes.
2 **MR captures information** about marketing opportunities and problems; the purpose of research therefore is to reduce risk in decision making and help managers make better and more successful decisions.

3 MR is a process involving research design, data collection, analysis and communication of the findings.

Marketing research is an investment for organizations: they are investing resources (normally money) to reduce the risk of wrongly allocating a scarce resource or failing to maximize an opportunity. Consequently, there is a trade-off between the cost of MR and the benefit the organization will obtain in reducing risk in decision making. Clearly, the higher the perceived risk, the more managers are likely to be prepared to invest in MR.

To understand the scope of MR, consider some examples of applications:

- market/segment size and trends – focusing on establishing the size (monetary value, unit value) of a market and/or segments of the market
- customer need analysis and attitudes to competitive offerings – to establish the perceived needs that a customer group (or segment) holds regarding a defined product/service, the ranking of these needs in their minds, and their perceptions of the benefits inherent in the various offerings (the client's and their competitors') available to them
- customer care research – to monitor customers' levels of satisfaction, etc.
- corporate identity research – to support the development or updating of a company's corporate identity
- message research – to test the effectiveness of different promotional messages
- new product development (NPD) research – assessing the appeal of a new product to a market segment.

This chapter will look at research within the organization, marketing intelligence, secondary research and primary research.

Research within the organization

It is important to place MR within the overall organizational information process. Modern information technology (IT) enables organizations to produce a wide range of information including financial and accounting, production and process. From a marketing perspective, businesses also generate a wide range of information concerning the relationship between the organization and its customers. For instance:

- sales volumes – by product range, etc.
- sales trends – tracked over time, seasonality, etc.
- sales by segment – type of customer, geographical location, etc.
- requests for product information – responses to advertisements, website 'hits', etc.
- complaints – obviously it is important that complaints are dealt with effectively, but complaints also provide a useful source of information: customers who complain may be articulating the view of a larger, silent group of customers
- reports from salespeople – particularly in B2B markets, sales reports are very important in managing the marketing/ sales effort.

Many organizations have an established formal process known as a **marketing information system (MkIS)**.

A definition of a marketing information system

An MkIS is a system in which marketing data are formally gathered, stored, analysed and distributed to managers in accordance with their informational needs on a regular basis.

The MkIS process involves four stages:

1 **Information requirements** An MkIS starts with a definition of the information requirements, i.e. the information required by managers to help them reduce risk in decision making.
2 **Data sources** The MkIS will draw on a wide range of information both from within the business (as suggested above) and from other sources outside the business. External sources include:

- marketing intelligence
- secondary research
- primary research (qualitative and quantitative).

3 **Data processing (to generate information)** There is a difference between data and information. Data are the raw facts, which may not necessarily be related to helping management reduce risk in decision making. Modern IT systems can generate significant volumes of data that can threaten to engulf managers. Information, on the other hand, is knowledge relevant to a specific requirement. The critical focus for the MkIS is that it must produce information appropriate to the decision needs of the users.

4 **Dissemination of information** For the information to be of value it must be disseminated to those who can obtain value from it. It is therefore important that the output of the MkIS is designed to meet the needs of the users, i.e. it is relevant, easily understood, clear and concise.

Marketing intelligence

There is a fairly strong link between marketing intelligence and secondary research. Marketing intelligence sources include customers, intermediaries, competitors, suppliers, new employees and the PEST environment.

A definition of marketing intelligence

Marketing intelligence is the process of gathering and analysing information relevant to reducing risk in decision making from sources that are not formal marketing research sources.

Customers

Particularly in B2B markets, companies can learn a great deal from maintaining a close dialogue with their customers, in addition to formal client relationship management (CRM) or marketing research studies.

Intermediaries

Many businesses use intermediaries such as retailers, wholesalers and distributors to take their products to market. Intermediaries are closer to the customer and often purchase from our competitors as well as from us. Intermediaries offer an excellent marketing intelligence source.

Competitors

Competitors are an excellent source of marketing intelligence. Their annual reports provide performance information, commentary on their strategy (Chairman's and CEO's statements) and information about future initiatives. Reports for all UK limited companies are available from Companies House (www.gov.uk/government/organisations/companies-house).

Also, competitors place information in the public domain to inform and persuade customers and potential customers: on their websites, in press releases (published in the business and general press), in publicity material, at exhibitions and on social networking sites, for instance. Some companies take studying their competitors to quite exhaustive lengths, including monitoring their recruitment advertising to see what type and number of employees they are seeking to hire.

Suppliers

In a similar way to intermediaries, suppliers offer a good source of marketing intelligence. They are 'upstream' from our customers but are also likely to be focusing on our customers as part of their strategic activity. In addition, they are likely to supply our competitors as well as us and so have an understanding of our competitors' strategies.

New employees

Industries and sectors can be quite 'incestuous'. Companies are often trying to attract the same type of employee, and experienced new employees are likely to have worked with one or more of our competitors. Some businesses have formal 'debriefing' sessions for new employees to obtain information from them regarding customers and competitors.

PEST

We have seen that the broader 'environment' has a marked effect on our customers and, as we will see later, on both our business and our competitors. Consequently, it is important that our marketing intelligence monitors trends and changes in our PEST environment. Businesses engage with specialist associations and trade bodies, and maintain strong links with appropriate public bodies, to help them obtain 'early warning' of opportunities or threats that may be approaching.

Secondary research

Secondary research can be described as research conducted by others, not necessarily focusing on our particular information needs. It offers the advantages of relatively low cost (compared with primary research) and is often instantly available. Moreover, some research, such as a national census, would be impossible for one organization to undertake.

However, there are drawbacks. Because secondary research does not necessarily focus on our particular information needs, care must be taken not to 'fit' the needs of the research to the information available. Also, as the research is already available, it may be too old to meet the researcher's requirements. Fundamentally, the researcher must assess the degree of accuracy of the secondary research in terms of both how and when it was gathered, analysed and interpreted.

A huge range of information can be accessed through Internet search engines but, when assessing any particular source, take care to consider both the advantages and drawbacks set out above.

There are four main sources of secondary research: government, non-departmental public bodies, trade and professional bodies, and commercial research.

Government

Governments are the main source of secondary research. They conduct research as part of the process of government and the scope of the research therefore covers virtually all aspects of life. By way of illustration, we can look at three sources.

- **UK Office for National Statistics (ONS)** (www.ons.gov.uk) collects data and conducts research on a wide range of themes including the economy, business and energy, agriculture and environment, education, health and social care, the labour market and population (including the census data). Most reports are available as free downloads and some data are available as data sets that the user can construct into tables to meet their particular needs.
- **European Commission Eurostat** (http://ec.europa.eu/eurostat) provides a very similar service for European Union (EU) countries as ONS does for the UK. Over a number of years the EU has harmonized the data collection activities of member states to allow for like-for-like comparisons.
- **US Dept of Commerce, Bureau of Economic Analysis** (www.bea.gov) follows a similar format both in terms of content and flexibility to ONS and Eurostat.

Non-departmental public bodies

Non-departmental public bodies (NDPBs) are set up to provide regulation to specific sectors. Examples in the UK include Ofwat (the Water Services Regulation Authority) and Ofcom (the independent regulator and competition authority for the communications industries). More generally, the Competition and Markets Authority (CMA) (www.gov.uk/government/organisations/competition-and-markets-authority) publishes reports on investigations into particular businesses and industries in the UK.

Trade and professional bodies

These organizations representing particular industries or professions collect data and conduct research to inform their members and to provide evidence for public relations and lobbying. For example:

- **the Society of Motor Manufacturers and Traders** (www.smmt.co.uk) publishes a wide range of reports, e.g. *Motor Industry Facts*, a profile of the UK motor industry
- **the Law Society** (www.lawsociety.org.uk) represents solicitors in the UK and their research department publishes reports such as *Trends in the Solicitors' Profession*, an annual statistical report that presents a profile of the profession.

Commercial research

A number of organizations sell research studies they have already conducted (known as multi-client research). Some organizations cover a wide range of products and services while others specialize in specific sectors. Here are three good examples:

- **Mintel** (www.mintel.com) focuses particularly on consumer markets, e.g. mobile phones and network providers in the UK.
- **Keynote** (www.keynote.co.uk) has a mainly UK focus and includes non-consumer markets, e.g. arts and media sponsorship.
- **Euromonitor** (www.euromonitor.com) carries out international research covering a wide range of products and services, e.g. Apparel in the USA.

Primary research

Primary research refers to research designed and conducted to meet specific research needs. Often it builds on secondary research, but primary research will engage directly with the defined marketplace.

1 Quantitative

This uses some form of random sampling and structured data collection (such as a questionnaire). The findings from quantitative research are representative of the population from which the sample is drawn within defined levels of representativeness, and they can be presented in quantitative form, e.g. '65 per cent of respondents think our product is very good.' Many people will be familiar with quantitative research from being asked to participate in a survey or from seeing survey findings (such as opinion poll results) referred to in the media.

2 Qualitative

Qualitative research focuses more on understanding the underlying motives and drivers for people's actions. Typically, judgement rather than random sampling is used, and sample sizes are much smaller. Consequently, the findings cannot be said to be representative in quantitative terms (as in quantitative research). Qualitative research uses tools such as depth interviews and focus groups.

3 Observation

This involves gathering data by observing relevant people, actions and situations and is selected when researchers cannot obtain the required information through direct questioning. Observation can include using trained observers (e.g. observing customers' behaviour in a supermarket) and machine-based observation (e.g. electronic counting of foot fall into a shopping mall).

4 Experimental

Control samples (two samples drawn from different populations, for instance) are used to obtain causal information about links between independent variables (e.g. socio-economic group, age, gender) and dependent variables (e.g. product preferences).

The primary research process

Primary research is a process that can be illustrated as follows:

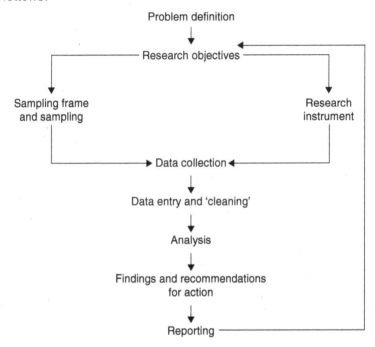

The primary research process

We can look at each part of the process in turn.

Problem definition

It is essential that the problem is clearly defined. One major issue is that the actual problem can be confused with the symptoms of the problem, and this confusion can lead to misdirected research effort. There is an old adage in consulting that says, 'A problem well defined is half solved.'

Research objectives

This stage establishes the foundation of the research study; all other stages will be based on the research objectives. Some researchers draw up a 'need-to-know' (N2K) list with the research user to ensure that all information requirements are covered by the study.

Sampling frame and sampling

The sampling frame is the 'population' of units under study, also known as the 'target population'. Units can be any group that the researcher is focusing on (e.g. individuals, households, businesses). Sampling refers to taking a representative portion of the target population. Clearly, a census (i.e. taking all units in the target population) provides the highest level of representativeness, but in most cases the cost and the time required to execute the research are prohibitive. There are two broad approaches to sampling:

- **Probability (or random) sampling** Simple random sampling means that each unit in the target population has the same chance (probability) of being sampled. There are other forms of probability sampling and one used quite extensively is stratified random sampling. In this, the sample is drawn in line with the profile of the target population under study; so if 60 per cent of a target population is over the age of 50, then the sample would reflect this by ensuring that 60 per cent of the sample is also over that age.
- **Non-probability sampling** As the name suggests, this form of sampling is not based on units having the same chance (probability) of being sampled. Non-probability sampling can be selected for a number of reasons: for instance, a B2B company may wish to discover the attitudes and perceptions of their major customers and would therefore want specific individuals to be included in the target population. Qualitative research often uses a form of non-probability sampling.

There are two other aspects of sampling we need to consider:

- **Representativeness** Researchers and users of research need to know how representative a sample is of the target population from which it is drawn. There are two elements, allowable error and level of confidence. **Allowable error** is defined as the difference between the value achieved from the sample and the true value for the population. This is normally expressed as a ±%. **Level of confidence** is defined as the probability that the true value (for the population) will fall within the interval created by adding and subtracting the allowable error.

- **Sample size** is a function of the degree of variability in the population under study and the level of accuracy of representativeness required. If all the units in a population are identical, we will need to sample only one unit, regardless of the size of the population. Where researchers do not know the degree of variability in the population (which is often the case), they take the worst-case scenario and assume that the population is equally split on any measure.

The following table shows the relationship between three examples of sample size and the associated degrees of allowable error and levels of confidence:

Sample size	Level of confidence 95%	Level of confidence 90%
500	±4.4%	±3.7%
1,000	±3.1%	±2.6%
1,500	±2.5%	±2.1%

Allowable error (±) at 95- and 90-per-cent levels of confidence associated with various sample sizes

You will note that as the sample size increases, so the allowable error decreases. The higher the level of confidence, the greater the allowable error is for the same sample size.

Research instrument

The research instrument is the means by which primary data are gathered. Some research designs use electronic or mechanical devices to gather data. Examples include website counts of 'hits', meters attached to viewers' televisions to monitor the programmes they watch, and eye cameras to study viewers' eye movements when watching advertisements. The main method of gathering primary data, however, is the **questionnaire**.

Questionnaires are a systematic way of gathering data and can broadly be divided into structured and semi-structured. A structured questionnaire is one where questions and potential answers are set up in advance (often using 'closed' questions); a semi-structured questionnaire uses a list of topics and allows the respondent to answer in their own words. Generally, structured questionnaires are used in quantitative research and semi-structured questionnaires are used in qualitative research, although there are times when formats are mixed.

Question content It is important that questions are drafted in a way that ensures that the respondents' views are recorded as accurately as possible. Questions (or statements) should aim to avoid:

- leading the respondent – e.g. 'Shopping centres are better than high streets.'
- embarrassing or pressurizing the respondent – e.g. questions about income/wealth or sexuality must be worded sensitively to ensure accurate and complete responses
- creating a status bias – e.g. 'Most intelligent shoppers compare prices. Do you?'
- ambiguous questions – questions must be unambiguous to prevent respondents interpreting the words differently, which would introduce a bias to the study.

Question types As mentioned above, there are two broad question types:

- **Open questions** allow the respondent to answer in his/ her own words. This type captures the respondents' actual words but open questions are much more difficult to analyse than closed questions.
- **Closed questions** are those where the answers are set up in advance and are therefore much easier to analyse. However, closed questions 'force' the respondent to choose an answer and care must be taken to ensure that his/her opinion is represented in the predetermined list. One approach to dealing with this problem is to include an 'open' element in a closed question, e.g. 'Other, please state.'

The following are some of the most commonly used closed question types:

- **Dichotomous questions** require a simple Yes/No answer, e.g. 'Is this your first visit?'
- **Multiple-choice questions** offer the respondent several options: the respondent may be instructed to select only one option or, alternatively, all that are appropriate to them.
- **Projective questions** use a more indirect approach and techniques like sentence completion, word association, pictorial (e.g. adding words to a picture) and storytelling.
- **Attitudinal scales** Measuring attitudes is important and researchers use a range of scales. Some of the most widely used scales are:
  - itemized – various responses are itemized to help the respondent make his/her selection, as follows:

Buy every day	Buy once a week	Buy monthly	Buy rarely	Don't buy at all
1	2	3	4	5

  - constant sum – the respondent is asked to divide up or allocate a number of points (normally 100) to indicate the relative importance of two or more attributes, e.g. 'Please divide up 100 points to reflect how important any of the following features are to you.'
  - Likert scale – this is a symmetrical agree–disagree scale where each point in the scale has a constant value relationship with the other points. In some cases the middle point is removed to create a 'forced' response, i.e. the respondent has to agree or disagree. Likert scales are complex to develop and most researchers use currently tested versions.

Strongly agree	Agree	Neither agree nor disagree	Disagree	Strongly disagree
+2	+1	0	-1	-2

  - semantic differential – this scale uses bipolar adjectives (hot–cold, reliable–unreliable, old–new, etc.) and is often constructed with seven categories between the two poles allowing the respondent to select the position that best matches their opinion.

Hot						Cold
*	*	*	*	*	*	*

Data collection

Data collection is a form of communication: the researcher poses a question and the respondent answers. There are four broad data collection approaches, two of which involve an interviewer and two of which are based on self-completion:

- **Face-to-face (f2f) interviewing** includes the 'street intercept' interviews that many of us have experienced while shopping. This is the most versatile and productive method but it is also the most expensive. The method allows for in-home interviewing, which is particularly valuable when sampling is based on the demographic distribution of a population. Trained interviewers conduct the interview, often using CAPI (computer-assisted personal interviewing) systems to aid the process.
- **Telephone interviewing** again uses a trained interviewer and can also involve computer-based systems to aid the process (CATI or computer-aided telephone interviewing). This method is the fastest and is not as expensive as f2f but it lacks the more personal contact between the interviewer and respondent provided by f2f and is therefore not so versatile.
- **Respondent panels** are based on recruiting a sample of respondents representative of the population under study. Respondents can be engaged in a number of ways including keeping diaries, completing questionnaires, etc.
- **Self-completion postal questionnaires** are posted to respondents who are asked to complete the questionnaire and return it in a pre-paid envelope. This is a less expensive method than both f2f and telephone interviewing. However, non-response rates are much higher with postal surveys and a major issue is the problem of non-response error – i.e. if those who do respond are different from those who do not, this may skew the results. In practice, researchers use a

range of techniques to maximize response rates (e.g. primer letters, reminder letters, incentives) and also test for the likely direction of non-response error.

- **Self-completion online surveys** are a new method made available to researchers by the rapid growth of the Internet. Also based on self-completion, they are less expensive. Online surveys can use questionnaires on a website or send them out by email. In addition, devices such as smartphones and tablets can be used. The Internet can be valuable for researching groups that are difficult to reach through other methods (e.g. heavy web users such as teenagers). The main drawback is again the problem of non-response error.

Focus groups

Focus groups are a standard qualitative data collection technique used to capture respondents' views and attitudes about a subject. A focus group is generally made up of a group of respondents drawn from a defined 'population'. The group meets under the guidance of a 'moderator' who introduces topics to the group for discussion.

Data entry and 'cleaning'

Data collected are generally entered into an electronic database, either directly in the case of computer-aided data collection (such as CATI and CAPI) or manually where completed questionnaires are returned as 'hard copy'. In the latter case the process of transferring the data from the questionnaire to the database can be a source of error and it is therefore important to control for such error. The researcher must be sure that what is contained in the questionnaire is identical to that entered to the database for analysis. Researchers take a random sample of entered questionnaires and compare them with the original completed questionnaires to ensure accuracy.

An alternative to manual data entry is questionnaire scanning involving a scanner and dedicated software. In addition, the researcher will be concerned that the questionnaire has been completed correctly. For instance, a particular response to a question may ask the respondent to go to another section of the questionnaire (known as 'gate' questions). Sometimes, particularly in self-completion, a respondent may complete the wrong section and this type of error needs to be 'cleaned' before analysis.

Analysis

Analysis of data has been supported by specialist software since the 1970s and became available on PCs in the 1980s. Today there is a wide range of providers of data analysis software available, e.g. SPSS and SNAP.

Primary research data in a database has two elements: the **cases** (the respondents) and the **variables** (the information captured by the questions). A question in a questionnaire can have more than one variable, such as in the case of multiple-choice questions.

The starting point in analysing the data is to run a simple count of the numbers of responses in each category for each variable, known as **frequency analysis** or one-way tabulation. Here's an example:

1 Value label	2 Value	3 Frequency	4 Percentage	5 Valid percentage	6 Cumulative percentage
Yes	1	90	32.14	32.14	32.14
No	2	180	64.29	64.29	96.43
Don't know	3	10	3.57	3.57	100.0
Total		280	100.0	100.0	

1 The value labels: the predetermined answers to the question. In this example the question would have been a dichotomous question (Yes/No answer) with a Don't know option.
2 The 'value' or coding (1 = Yes etc.) assigned to the value label and entered in the database.
3 The number of respondents by each category (Yes, No, Don't know) for this variable = the frequency of that answer. The total sample size in this example was 280.

4 The simple percentage values for each value label: here the majority of respondents (64 per cent) had answered No to this question.

5 If some respondents do not answer all the questions, the software recalculates the percentage value based on the actual total number of respondents to that question. Here all respondents have responded, so the values in columns 5 and 4 are the same.

6 The cumulative percentage count based on column 4.

The next most common level of analysis counts two variables simultaneously. This is known as **cross-tabulation**. Cross-tabulation allows a researcher to investigate relationships between dependent variables (such as respondents' attitudes and behaviour) and independent variables (such as their age, gender, socio-economic position). As we saw in Chapter 23, these relationships are important to the marketer. Here is an example of a cross-tabulation of gender and agreement/disagreement with a cited statement:

Value label	Value		Strongly agree	Agree	Disagree	Strongly disagree	Total
Male	1	Frequency	6	25	45	21	**97**
		Percentage	6.2	25.8	46.4	21.6	**100.0**
Female	2	Frequency	18	36	76	23	**153**
		Percentage	11.8	23.5	49.7	15.0	**100.0**
Total		**Frequency**	**24**	**61**	**121**	**44**	**250**
		Percentage	**9.6**	**24.4**	**48.4**	**17.6**	**100.0**

This cross-tabulation shows that there is little difference in agreement/disagreement with the cited statement between male and female respondents.

To further the researcher's understanding of the data, a wide range of statistical tests can be used.

Findings and recommendations for action

We have seen that the primary research process is a complex project management of a number of interrelated elements. This stage of the process must bring meaning and value to the research user. The starting point is to link the findings to the research objectives, assembling them in line with each element of the objectives.

Reporting

The way the findings are presented to users must be appropriate to their needs. Often this means using:

- **graphical representations** – e.g. pie charts, histograms
- **data 'reduction'** – i.e. simplifying numbers such as rounding them to make them easier to digest, e.g. 45.67 per cent 'reduced' to 46 per cent
- **summaries** – using 'executive' summaries, abstracts, etc.
- **presentations** – e.g. PowerPoint presentations.

Omnibus surveys and agencies

Omnibus surveys are multi-client surveys, so called because clients can join and leave the 'omnibus' according to their needs. The advantages to the research client include cost savings (because the sampling and screening costs are shared across multiple clients) and timeliness (because omnibus samples are large and interviewing is ongoing).

While it is feasible for organizations to conduct their own research studies, managers often choose to use **marketing research agencies** because of their experience and expertise. In addition, agencies bring emotional detachment to the problem and by providing extra resources enable client staff to concentrate on their core objectives. For more information about selecting and commissioning MR agencies, visit www.mrs.org.uk.

Summary

Marketing research (MR) acts as a link between customer and organization. It is an investment for organizations, and there is a trade-off between the cost and the benefit obtained in capturing information that reduces risk in decision making.

MR can be applied to many marketing problems including establishing segment size, and defining customers' needs or attitudes to the benefits perceived in different products. Modern IT enables organizations to produce information valuable for marketing decision making.

Secondary research is research that has been conducted by others, not necessarily focusing on our needs. The major sources are government, public bodies, trade/professional bodies and commercial research providers.

The primary research process involves defining the problem, research objectives, sampling frame and method, and research instrument and questions. When the data have been collected using an appropriate method, the findings are analysed and can be reported.

Fact-check (answers at the back)

1. What is a key issue of the AMA definition of marketing research (MR)?
   a) It's a link between customer and organization ❏
   b) It's another name for the R&D department ❏
   c) It's specific to pharmaceutical businesses ❏
   d) It's mainly an American activity ❏

2. What is a system that formally gathers, analyses and distributes information to managers known as?
   a) A talking shop ❏
   b) A marketing information system ❏
   c) An in-house website ❏
   d) A company newsletter ❏

3. What is information gathered about the general marketing environment including customers, intermediaries, competitors, suppliers and the general PEST environment known as?
   a) Office gossip ❏
   b) Marketing intelligence ❏
   c) Making contacts ❏
   d) Networking ❏

4. What is secondary research?
   a) Research conducted by others, not necessarily focusing on our particular needs ❏
   b) Research conducted after the main research ❏
   c) Research that is of less value ❏
   d) Research conducted by our customers ❏

5. How is quantitative research different from qualitative research?
   a) There is much more of it ❏
   b) The results from quantitative research can be presented in quantitative form, e.g. '65 per cent like our product.' ❏
   c) It can only be done by academics ❏
   d) It is free ❏

6. What is sampling, where each unit has the same chance of being sampled, known as?
   a) Probability or random sampling ❏
   b) Unknown sampling ❏
   c) Researcher's sampling ❏
   d) Explainable sampling ❏

7. What are the two broad question types?
a) Right and wrong ❏
b) Open and closed ❏
c) Short and long ❏
d) Difficult and easy ❏

8. What is one of the problems with self-completion data collection (including web-based)?
a) Analysing them ❏
b) Non-response bias ❏
c) Preventing fraud ❏
d) Handling complaints ❏

9. A primary research database has which two elements?
a) Time and cost ❏
b) Completed and aborted ❏
c) Right and wrong ❏
d) Cases and variables ❏

10. What is cross-tabulation?
a) An error report ❏
b) Corrupted data ❏
c) Analysis of two variables simultaneously ❏
d) Processing of incorrect cases only ❏

CHAPTER 25

Strategic marketing

In this chapter we shall consider marketing as a strategic activity – how marketers decide what they must do to meet the organization's objectives. Marketing strategy can be seen as a marketing decision process involving a series of steps to analyse, plan, implement and control a range of activities designed to achieve the organization's objectives.

We will start by considering how marketers must review the strengths and weaknesses of their own organization (business audit) and assess the opportunities and threats in the marketplace (market audit) before conducting a 'targeting' exercise that matches the strengths of the organization to opportunities presented by different market segments. We will then see how marketers develop an integrated marketing strategy (marketing mix), and implement and control the execution of the strategy to meet the organization's objectives.

Finally in this chapter we will look at three famous approaches to developing strategy: the Boston Box, the Ansoff Box and Porter's Three Generic Strategies.

Marketing planning

Marketing planning is a strategic activity; marketers have to make a range of decisions that translate into actions in the future to achieve their objectives. Marketers have to **plan** and they have to develop a **strategy**.

> ## Two definitions
>
> **Plan** – a formulated and especially detailed method by which a thing is to be done; a design or scheme
>
> **Strategy** in game theory, business theory, etc. – a plan for successful action based on the rationality and interdependence of the moves of opposing or competing participants

Planning in marketing seeks to apply a logical and objective approach to deciding how a company's capabilities will be matched to opportunities in the marketplace so that the corporate objectives can be met. Strategy takes into consideration the 'moves' of others. For marketers, the key group of 'others' is competitors, i.e. 'opposing or competing participants'. However, for marketers, a key additional participant group is customers, whom we are neither 'opposing' nor 'competing' with. On first sight, these militaristic terms may seem to contradict the basic ethos of the marketing orientation we described in Chapter 22. The reason they are used in this context is that they reflect the nature of the process of deploying the organization's resources to achieve a defined objective.

Developing a strategic marketing plan involves a series of interrelated stages of analysis, planning, implementation and control. One might say that there are two broad elements to strategic marketing planning – thinking and doing. The ancient Greek proverb 'Think slowly, act quickly' extols the virtue of taking time to weigh up the options before acting, but it stresses the need to carry out the selected strategy without delay. Thinking helps us to reduce the risk in deciding what we should do and therefore significantly improves the probability of success. This simple proverb encapsulates the value of strategic marketing planning for the marketer.

The marketing planning process

We can translate the four stages of strategic marketing planning into a marketing planning process, as shown below.

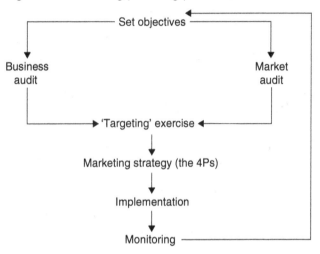

The marketing planning process

We shall consider each part of the process in turn.

Objectives

The organization will need to establish a set of objectives for the planning period (probably 12 months). It is likely that setting objectives will start with a description of a series of qualitative objectives (such as a mission statement). These will need to be 'operationalized' (made quantitative) so that performance against these objectives can be measured. Ultimately, objectives are defined in terms of, for example, percentage turnover growth on last year, improving operating profit from $y\%$ to $z\%$, achieving market leadership in a defined market/segment, and so on. There are two important points to note:

1 These objectives will be the basis for developing the strategic direction of the organization and will involve the commitment of corporate resources.

2 We must consider the objectives in the context of the market audit (i.e. the audit of the market environment within which the business operates, which we shall look at later in this chapter). Basically, we must assess how realistic the objectives are in terms of what is possible, given the market conditions. For example, it would be unrealistic for a small business with access to limited capital to set an objective to be the world market leader in building nuclear power stations within 12 months.

Business audit
The business audit is a review of the strengths and weaknesses of the business.

Examples of business strengths	Examples of business weaknesses
● Market leadership ● Some uniqueness as perceived by the customers (a differential advantage in terms of quality and/or price) ● Control of a scarce resource related to differentiating our offering from that of the competition, e.g. access to a scarce resource (such as aggregates in construction), control of patents ● A market-beating 'business process model' (i.e. how we organize our business), e.g. McDonald's, Lidl ● Profitability ● Brand loyalty	● Low market share ● No uniqueness perceived by the customers ● Poor brand appeal ● Poor business performance (lack of capital for reinvestment) ● Poor employee morale

While in no way meant to be exhaustive, the following demonstrates the types of analysis undertaken during a business audit.

Business performance (last three years)

1 Sales and contribution by type of product/service
2 Sales and contribution by type of customer
3 Sales and contribution by geographical area
4 Top ten customer segments (profile)

Marketing mix

1 Product (width and depth of product range, features and benefits, product portfolio analysis)
2 Price (cost versus price, basis for pricing decisions)
3 Channels (channel selection and positioning)
4 Promotion (including current activities and budgets/spend levels, advertising, press relations, mail, outlets, personal selling, Internet)

Management knowledge

1 Perceptions of the company's strengths and weaknesses
2 Perceptions of customers' perceived needs (e.g. of value, price benefits)
3 Perceptions of the competition (market/segment shares, high-profile accounts, capabilities in terms of strengths and weaknesses, geographical coverage, business objectives, policies, strategies, etc.)
4 Perceptions of the PEST environment in which the business operates

Market audit

This is a review of the **opportunities** and **threats** existing in the organization's business/market environment. There are two levels: the 'immediate' level and the 'general' level.

Immediate level

● **Customers** We have noted that customers/potential customers need to be segmented, i.e. placed into groups whose members share attitudes to product/service selection and differ from other segments within the same market.
● **Competitors** Perhaps surprisingly, companies embarking on a strategic marketing planning exercise often show a poor understanding of this group. We need to understand such issues as:
  – our competitors' recent 'track record' (business performance)
  – their declared corporate objectives/strategies
  – within segments, customers' perceptions of their offerings.

- Intermediaries
- Suppliers

General level
This level covers the PEST environment we have discussed previously.

- **Political** – e.g. prevailing political policies towards climate change
- **Economic** – e.g. level of growth in GNP, unemployment
- **Social** (or cultural) – e.g. society's attitudes to sustainability, energy conservation
- **Technological** – e.g. 'smartphone' technology

By combining the findings from the business audit and market audit, the marketer can assemble a **SWOT analysis** of strengths, weaknesses, opportunities and threats. This can be a powerful and very useful tool for developing the plan. One way to think about SWOT analysis is to consider it as a planning 'balance sheet': within the organization there will be strengths (+) and weaknesses (–), and in the marketplace there will be opportunities (+) and threats (–).

Within the organization	In the marketplace
Strengths + Weaknesses –	Opportunities + Threats –

The 'targeting' exercise
Targeting refers to deciding which segments the organization will select to focus on. It is the heart of the marketing planning process and decisions made at this stage have a significant effect on the overall success of the plan. The task is to match the organization's strengths to opportunities in the marketplace so that the firm can obtain the best return on effort. There are two distinct tasks:

- to rank the market segments in terms of their attractiveness to the organization
- to rank the organization against the competition in terms of attractiveness to the market segments.

These two tasks can be represented in the following matrix.

Market/segment
attractiveness to the organization

	High	Low
High	1	2
Low	3	4

Organization's
attractiveness
to the
market/
segments

The targeting matrix

- *Cell 1* This cell is the segment or segments that are highly attractive to the organization and to whose buyers the organization is highly attractive. This is the most effective matching of the organization to the segments.
- *Cell 2* Here the organization is still highly attractive to the segments but these segments are less attractive to the organization (they may be too small or offer poor creditworthiness). In this case the marketer may choose to 'sub-segment' the segments to isolate the most attractive parts that may be worth targeting.
- *Cell 3* While the segments are attractive to the organization, the segments do not perceive the organization to be attractive to them. In this case the marketer needs to assess the basis of this perception. If our offering is objectively poorer than our competition, we must do something to address this disadvantage (e.g. improve product quality). However, if we can find no objective difference between our offering and that of our competitors, the problem is one of communication.
- *Cell 4* In this case the segments are unattractive to the organization and the organization is unattractive to the segments. Marketers 'de-target' (redirect resources *away* from these segments) in such circumstances.

Marketing strategy

Establishing a successful marketing strategy involves deciding what to produce, how much to charge, where the customer will buy the product, and how to inform and persuade the customer to buy the product. Marketers have described this as the 'marketing mix' – product, price, place and promotion (i.e. the 4Ps). We will look at the 4Ps in more detail later, but we can summarize each element here:

- **Product** This term encapsulates both tangible and intangible benefits carried by products and services. The product strategy must ensure that the firm's offering carries benefits that can be matched to customer needs.
- **Price** Prices must be set to reflect the benefits customers perceive in our offering compared to offerings from our competitors; i.e. which offers the best value.
- **Place** This term generally refers to channels of distribution; i.e. where the products are sold, including web-based direct marketing channels.
- **Promotion** This is how we inform and communicate the benefits in our offering to the target market segments. It involves developing messages and selecting the most cost-effective media to carry the messages to the target market segments. This used to mean advertising on TV, on the radio, in the press and on posters, etc., and direct mail, but promotion now encompasses online marketing and public relations.

The marketer should draft separate marketing mixes (or marketing strategies) for each targeted segment, blending all the mix elements together to deliver satisfied customers and to meet the organization's stated marketing objectives.

Implementation

As we have already seen, the purpose of planning is to make our actions more effective. Planning without action is an arid academic exercise and of no real value to the organization. How the plan is implemented is therefore critical. Organizations often produce **tactical action plans** that:

1 set operational variables
2 establish time limits and deadlines
3 communicate and assign tasks
4 develop sales forecasts
5 determine action plans for individuals
6 prepare budgets.

Action plans need to be 'SMART' – specific, measurable, attainable, relevant and time bound.

Monitoring

Monitoring is a critical part of the planning process; only by using monitoring for control can we ensure that the strategy will achieve our objectives.

Not surprisingly, the first issue is monitoring the implementation of the plan in terms of achieving the stated objectives. In effect we are considering a loop that can be couched in a simple question: we have set measurable objectives but are we delivering to these objectives? We need to set appropriate timescales for monitoring and establish mechanisms to compare 'actual' to 'budget'. The purpose of this type of monitoring review is to ensure that the plan is 'on track' and, if not, to identify and make changes to ensure that we get it back on track. For some organizations, it is necessary to define the organization's objectives as 'milestones': what do we need to have achieved by the end of period 1 (to be defined by the organization) to be confident that we shall achieve our ultimate objective(s)?

In addition, the marketer needs to monitor the environment. Customers and competitors must be the main focus but general trends in the PEST environment must also be noted. We have seen that marketing research and the MkIS have an important role to play here. Where changes impact on the plan, action will be needed to respond to the changes so that they do not undermine its successful execution.

Effective marketing planning and the organization

Earlier in this Part we looked at the relationship between marketing and organizational performance and the body of evidence that suggests marketing is associated with improved profitability. However, there is also evidence that marketing planning does not always deliver improved performance, and research has been able to identify the following key requirements for the effective (and commercially successful) execution of marketing planning.

- **Ownership** It is important that those who have to implement the plan are given the opportunity to contribute to its development.
- **Rigour** The audit process (business and market) requires a significant amount of information, both from within the firm and from the marketplace. Lack of rigour in gathering, analysing and interpreting data can seriously undermine the effectiveness of the planning process. Marketers need to obtain thorough and objective information to reduce risk in decision making.

Modern IT systems and the planning process itself tend to produce a significant amount of information. Generally, 20 per cent of the information gathered accounts for 80 per cent of the information needed, so there is an additional need for selectivity.

- **Environmental sensitivity** Marketers must guard against trying to 'fit' the world outside to the plan. Change is endemic to all market situations, and planning processes must be reviewed in the light of the changing environment. Organizations must be environmentally sensitive and have the flexibility to be able to respond to changes, both opportunities and threats.
- **Company-wide appreciation** All employees need to appreciate the broad issues involved in the plan so that they can contribute to its success (i.e. share the same agendas as other staff).
- **Management belief** Senior management must believe that the process of planning will reduce risk in decision making and contribute to the success of the business. Without this belief, the process can easily lose staff enthusiasm and rigour and ultimately become a pointless bureaucratic exercise marginalized in the business.

Alternative approaches

The marketing decision process described above is used, in different formats, by a wide range of organizations, both large and small, manufacturing and services and for profit and not-for-profit. In addition, marketing consultants often use this approach when supporting clients in improving the benefits they can derive from marketing planning.

However, there are a number of other approaches to managing the strategic direction of a business. Among them are the Boston Box, the Ansoff Box and Porter's Three Generic Strategies.

The Boston Box

Larger organizations often face the problem of managing their portfolio of products (all the products they offer to the marketplace). It is important that the organization's resources support those products that offer the best return on investment. One famous approach to analysing this problem is known as the Boston Box.

Relative market share

		High	Low
Market growth rate	High	Star	Problem child
	Low	Cash cow	Dog

The Boston Box

Source: Boston Consulting Group

The Boston Box classifies products in terms of two variables: relative market share and market growth rate.

Star These products are in high-growth markets and the organization has a high relative (to the competition) market share. These products often need high investment to maintain their market position but may become 'cash cows'.

Cash cow These are low-growth, high-market-share products. They are established and successful, have low investment needs and produce a positive cash flow.

Problem child These products are in high-growth markets but have low relative market share. They require investment to maintain (let alone increase) market share and marketers have to decide whether these products will succeed or fail.

Dog These products are low growth, low market share. They may generate enough cash to maintain themselves but do not offer any medium/long-term potential for the organization.

The Ansoff Box

An alternative way to look at the organization's relationship
with its customers is to study the relationship between
products and customers. Igor Ansoff created another famous
tool, often referred to as the Ansoff Box, which looked at
an organization's product mix in terms of the relationship
between existing and new products and existing and new
customers. The Ansoff Box ranks the best return on effort in
the short term based on four product/customer relationships.

Customer

	Existing	New
Existing	1	3
New	2	4

Product

The Ansoff Box

Source: H. Igor Ansoff, *Corporate Strategy* (Harmondsworth: Penguin, 1965)

The numbers in the cells represent the ranking of each product/
customer relationship and identify that selling existing products
to existing customers offers the best return on effort in the
short term. However, selling 'new' (i.e. new to the customers)
products to existing customers offers the second-best return on
effort in the short term.

Porter's Three Generic Strategies

In his book *Competitive Strategy*, Michael Porter developed the concept of the Three Generic Strategies for outperforming other businesses in an industry.

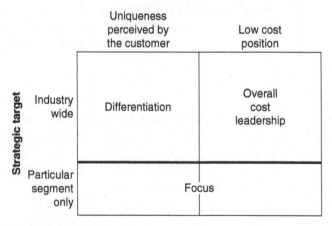

Three Generic Strategies

Source: Michael E. Porter, *Competitive Strategy* (Free Press, 1998)

Overall cost leadership Here emphasis is on cost minimization and control, so the business can still earn returns after its competitors have competed away their profits through rivalry.

Differentiation Here management seeks to differentiate the product or service by creating something that is perceived industry wide to be unique: perhaps through brand, technological advantages, patents or control of scarce resources.

Focus The management focus here is on a particular buyer group and seeks to serve that target particularly well, through either uniqueness perceived by the customer or low cost.

Porter's Three Generic Strategies are viable approaches for dealing with competitive forces. However, a business failing to develop its strategy in at least one of the three directions – a 'stuck in the middle' firm – is in an extremely poor strategic situation and is almost guaranteed low profitability.

Summary

Marketing planning is a strategic activity – marketers have to make a range of decisions that translate into actions in the future to achieve their objectives. It is a decision process that focuses on matching the strengths of the organization to market opportunities and creating detailed action plans designed to deliver the organization's objectives.

The steps involved in market planning are:

1 setting objectives
2 reviewing the strengths and weaknesses of the organization (through a business audit)
3 assessing the opportunities and threats in the marketplace (through a market audit)
4 conducting a 'targeting' exercise that matches the strengths of the organization to opportunities presented by different market segments
5 developing an integrated marketing strategy (marketing mix)
6 implementing and controlling the execution of the strategy to meet the organization's objectives.

Marketing planning is a key strategic link between the organization and its marketplace and plays a vital part in the successful management of a business.

Fact-check (answers at the back)

1. What is marketing planning?
a) A strategic activity ❏
b) A gift some businesspeople are born with ❏
c) A skill you can only learn from a business school ❏
d) A technique only management consultants use ❏

2. What does the marketing planning process start with?
a) Advertising ❏
b) Selling ❏
c) Setting objectives ❏
d) Retailing ❏

3. What does the business audit review?
a) Economic climate ❏
b) Strengths and weaknesses of the organization ❏
c) Trends in social attitudes ❏
d) Competition ❏

4. What does the market audit review?
a) Opportunities and threats in the business/market environment ❏
b) Skills in our organization ❏
c) Our sales growth over the last three financial years ❏
d) Our operating profit over the last three financial years ❏

5. What does the 'targeting' exercise help marketers do?
a) Decide which segments the organization will focus on ❏
b) Check if the plan is going to be effective ❏
c) Win prizes in business competitions ❏
d) Respond positively to journalists' requests for information ❏

6. The marketing mix involves decisions regarding what?
a) Rebates, rates, revisions and returns ❏
b) Product, price, place and promotion ❏
c) Scales, summaries, shifts and scenarios ❏
d) Training, timetables, tokens and tolls ❏

7. What is the purpose of monitoring?
a) To ensure that the plan achieves the stated objectives ❏
b) To check that employees are doing their jobs ❏
c) To decide who will receive bonuses ❏
d) None of the above ❏

8. What is the Boston Box based on?
a) Making sure that the product's packaging meets customers' needs ❏
b) Improving the in-house flow of information ❏
c) Preventing competitors discovering our strategy ❏
d) Relative market share and market growth rate ❏

9. What is the Ansoff Box based on?
a) The relationship between existing and new customers and existing and new products ❏
b) Relative market share and market growth rate ❏
c) The critical mass of markets and segments ❏
d) None of the above ❏

10. What are Porter's Three Generic Strategies?
a) Processes, solutions and testing ❏
b) Leadership, motivation and remuneration ❏
c) Production, selling and marketing ❏
d) Overall cost leadership, differentiation and focus ❏

CHAPTER 26

The marketing mix – product and price

In Chapter 25 we looked at marketing planning and introduced the idea of developing an integrated marketing strategy, the marketing mix. We saw that a successful marketing strategy involves deciding what to produce, how much to charge, where the customer will buy the product, and how to inform and persuade the customer to buy the product using the 4Ps: product, price, place and promotion.

In this and the following chapters we are going to look at each of these four elements of the marketing mix in more detail.

In this chapter we are going to look at *product* and *price*. We will consider tangible and intangible product benefits, explore the differences between products and services, and review the relationship between product features and benefits. We will then go on to discuss brands, the product life cycle, new product development and product strategy decisions.

Three forces act on pricing – the target audience's perception of value in our and competitors' offerings, our cost structure and the competition's price levels. We will look at these before considering some key issues of pricing strategy decisions.

Product

'Product' is the fundamental basis of the marketing mix. Our 'product' carries benefits that satisfy customers' needs and, while it can be a tangible, physical entity, 'product' can also be something quite intangible such as a service, an experience or an idea. In the context of the marketing mix, we can define 'product' as follows:

> *'A product is anything that is offered to the marketplace that can satisfy a customer's perceived need.'*

Our **product strategy** is the method by which we **satisfy** customers' needs. Here we are going to look at the factors affecting our product strategy: tangible and intangible benefits; the differences between products and services; features and benefits; brands; the product life cycle; new product development; and product strategy decisions.

Tangible and intangible benefits

A product can be tangible or intangible. Some writers have tried to establish a tangible–intangible continuum, with highly tangible products at one extreme (e.g. salt) and highly intangible products at the other extreme (e.g. insurance).

Tangible	**Intangible**
Salt	Insurance

The tangible–intangible continuum

It's probably accurate to say that most offerings have some element of tangible and intangible benefits as part of their appeal. Let's look at some examples:

● **Cars** The physical nature of the product has a high element of tangibility, but there are intangible benefits such as the brand and dealer service.

- **Personal computers** Again, these have a high element of physical product, but aspects such as brand and pre- and post-service support add intangible benefits.
- **Restaurants** The food is tangible but the overall benefit is made up of intangibles like the decor, the ambience, the service and the restaurant's reputation.
- **Perfumes** The core offering is intangible in terms of the benefits customers derive from the purchase but the offering is 'delivered' as a tangible product.

Differences between products and services

Given that most offerings have some element of tangible and intangible benefits as part of their appeal, it is still possible to distinguish **products** (i.e. with a high degree of tangibility) from **services** (i.e. with a high degree of intangibility). There are five key differences between products and services:

1 **Heterogeneity** Services can usually be designed around a specific requirement: a consultancy assignment can be designed to meet one client's unique needs. Products tend to be more homogeneous: for volume car producers one can only select from the specifications on offer.
2 **Intangibility** As we've seen, products with a high tangible element can be touched, tasted and taken apart to examine how they work; there is a 'trial' element. Services do not have this trial element.
3 **Inseparability** The production of a service and its consumption occur at the same time: there is a direct link between provider and customer. The production and consumption of highly tangible products, on the other hand, are separate.
4 **Perishableness** Unlike products, services cannot be stocked or held over. A hotel bedroom that is not occupied on a particular night is a revenue opportunity lost.
5 **Lack of ownership** Access to or use of a service facility does not mean the customer obtains ownership. The purchase is often time related, e.g. a hotel room reservation for three nights.

Features and benefits

Whether predominately tangible or intangible, a product must carry benefits that satisfy customers' needs. **Benefits** are those elements of the product that meet customers' needs (as discussed in Chapter 23). **Features** carry benefits.

It is important to differentiate between a benefit and a feature. Telling a customer about a feature may not enable him/her to understand how the product meets his/her perceived needs. Features are the product's capabilities; benefits are the outcomes customers 'consume' by way of meeting their perceived needs.

Features carry benefits

Let's consider an example. Many cars today have antilock braking systems (ABS) as standard. ABS is not a benefit per se but a feature that carries a benefit that fulfils a need.

- Feature: ABS
- Benefit: safer braking
- Need: safety

Customers don't care about features unless they're experienced in buying the specific type of product we are offering. For example, when personal computers (PCs) were first marketed to individuals and Small Office Home Office (SoHo) users, the promotional emphasis was on technical performance features, such as RAM, hard disk size and CPU speed. Many potential customers were put off by the 'jargon' because they could not see what benefits these features would offer to them. In essence, they asked, 'What's in it for me?' Most people now understand these terms and can judge the benefits in an offering from a list of features. In effect, the features list can become a type of shorthand between the experienced customer and the producer.

TIP *When presenting a customer with a benefit, the marketer can use a feature as evidence that the benefit exists. Our ABS example demonstrates this point well.*

Brands

An important form of intangible benefit is the **brand**. A brand is a name, term, sign, symbol, association, trademark or design which is intended to identify the products or services of one provider or group of providers, and to differentiate them from those of competitors (see also Chapter 19).

Customers develop loyalty to a brand, based on previous experience if they have purchased the product before and found that it has met their perceived needs. Alternatively, a brand can be associated with a lifestyle or particular condition that is important to the customer and that they aspire to.

In addition, brands can add value to a product: for instance, many customers would perceive a bottle of Chanel perfume as a high-quality, exclusive and expensive product. But the same fragrance in an unmarked bottle would probably be viewed as lower quality even if the two fragrances were identical. Some commentators have cited this as an example of marketers taking advantage of customers, but the intangible benefits the customer obtains from the brand meet important needs such as self-actualization and the esteem of others.

Brand extension

Although the Chanel brand started as a French fashion house, the product range now includes fragrances, fine jewellery and watches, leather goods and shoes, and even eyewear and sporting goods. This is known as brand extension – the application of a brand beyond its initial range of products or outside its category. This becomes possible when the brand image has contributed to a perception with the consumer/user, where brand and not product is the decision driver.

From the marketer's perspective, brand management seeks to make the product or services relevant to the target segments. Brands should be seen as more than the difference between the actual cost of a product and its selling price: brands represent the sum of all valuable qualities of a product to the customer. It follows that marketers must be careful not to allow anything to damage the brand's reputation. For example, when the presence of the chemical benzene was found in a small sample of bottles of Perrier water in the USA in 1990, Perrier voluntarily recalled its entire inventory of Perrier from store shelves throughout the United States. This action demonstrated to the market the importance Perrier placed on the quality of their product and their commitment to deal with any problem quickly and thoroughly – to do whatever was necessary to protect the integrity of the brand.

The product life cycle

Most products display similar characteristics to living organisms – they are 'born', grow to maturity, decline and 'die'. They have a product life cycle (PLC). For example, the stand-alone facsimile (fax) machine was launched in the 1970s and was adopted by a wide range of organizations and individuals during the 1980s. However, the spread of Internet access, email and scanning had a major negative impact on the sales of fax machines.

While the life expectancy of products varies greatly, most products go through four stages: introduction, growth, maturity and decline, as shown graphically below.

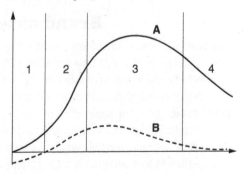

The product life cycle

The horizontal axis of the graph represents time and the vertical axis represents sales (depicted by graph line A) and profit (depicted by graph line B). We can consider some of the properties of the four stages:

1 **Introduction**

   At this stage the product has been introduced to the market, sales growth is slow and profits are negative due to the costs of launch. A particular group of buyers is adopting the new product. These are known as 'innovators' and are characterized by their desire for new experiences and a relatively high degree of risk taking. As a marketing rule of thumb, this group accounts for around 10 per cent of the market.

2 **Growth**

   If the product is perceived to have benefits matched to customers' needs, it will become more widely adopted. Sales will grow quickly and profits will follow suit. The growth stage is driven by a group of buyers known as 'early adopters' who have an appetite for new (and better) solutions to their needs but who lack the risk taking of the innovators. This group generally accounts for around 20 per cent of the market.

3 **Maturity**

   At some point the product's sales growth will slow and it will enter its mature stage. Commonly the longest period, sales and profits peak during the maturity stage. This stage is characterized by the adoption of the product by the majority of the market, known as the 'late adopters'. This group accounts for around 60 per cent of the market.

4 **Decline**

   Eventually, the product's sales are likely to decline. This can be due to new products being seen as a better match to customers' needs, changing customers' attitudes or increased competition. Even during this stage, new customers are adopting the product. These 'laggards' can be characterized by a generally conservative outlook and a low threshold to risk. This group accounts for around 10 per cent of the market.

The marketer will obviously face different strategic issues for each stage of the PLC and may have a portfolio of products at different stages. It is worth noting the relationship between the PLC concept and the Boston Box we looked at in Chapter 25. In simple terms we can align the two as shown below.

PLC	Boston Box
Introduction	Problem child
Growth	Star
Maturity	Cash cow
Decline	Dog

New product development

Customers change and the PEST factors change and exert an influence on customers. Consequently, the marketer must be alert to the need for new solutions to customers' needs. **New product development (NPD)** is therefore an important element of the organization's product strategy. New products cost an organization until they reach growth stage and some products do not achieve this stage and fail, with the resultant impact on the organization's profitability. The marketer needs to maximize the chances of a new product becoming established (i.e. reaching maturity in PLC terms or becoming a 'cash cow' in Boston Box terms). NPD success is linked to the **diffusion of innovation**, i.e. the way new ideas or products are communicated through certain channels over time to a marketplace. Several factors determine whether and how quickly an innovation will be adopted:

- **Relative advantage** Potential adopters must perceive that the innovation is an improvement over the previous solution to their needs. In some NPD situations, the customer has a poorly defined need because there had been no solution to their needs up to that point. This is the 'anticipation' element of our definition of marketing.
- **Compatibility** Potential adopters must perceive the innovation as being consistent with their existing values, past experiences and needs. An idea that is incompatible with their values and norms will either not be adopted at all or not be adopted as rapidly as an innovation that is compatible.

- **Relative complexity/simplicity** If the innovation is too difficult to understand or use, it is less likely to be adopted.
- **Trialability** If the potential adopter may try or experiment with the innovation, this will increase the chances of it being adopted.
- **Observability** The more easily an innovation is visible to others, the more this will drive communication among peers and personal networks. In turn, this will create more positive or negative reactions (i.e. the effect of 'innovators' on 'early adopters').

Product strategy decisions

Marketers have to make a series of decisions regarding the product offering. We can summarize these decisions under four headings:

1 **Core benefit** As we have seen, the product must carry benefits to meet the customers' perceived needs. In general terms the marketer needs to understand the hierarchy of needs (the relative importance of customers' perceived needs) and ensure that the product carries benefits (tangible and intangible) matched to these needs.
2 **Actual product** Decisions in this area include product design, styling, quality, colours, branding and packaging. In effect, this is the manifestation of the core benefits.
3 **Augmented product** Decisions in this area involve anything that can add value to the customer (and differentiate our offering from that of the competition) and could include installation, warranty, credit facilities and after-sales service.
4 **Product range (depth and width)** Decisions in this area involve the 'width' of the product range (e.g. small family hatchback, family saloon car, executive saloon car) and the 'depth' (e.g. range of engines on offer, trim levels, equipment levels).

For companies to ensure continued evolution, they must define their industries broadly to take advantage of growth opportunities. They must ascertain and act on their customers' needs and desires, not bank on the presumed longevity of their products. An organization must learn to think of itself not as producing goods or services but as doing the things that will make people want to do business with it.

Price

This is the second part of the marketing mix and, while all parts of the mix are inextricably linked, there is a particularly strong link between product and price. At its basic level, price is the amount a customer must pay to obtain the benefit(s) from a product or service – the **exchange** we referred to in Chapter 22.

In considering price strategy, we are going to look at the three interrelated forces acting on any organization's decisions regarding pricing (the **'pricing triangle'**) and pricing strategy decisions:

- the target audience's perception of value in our and the competition's offerings
- our cost structure
- the competition's price levels.

We can represent this interrelationship as the pricing triangle.

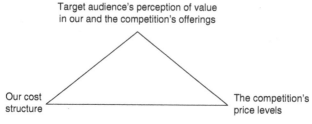

Target audience's perception of value
in our and the competition's offerings

Our cost
structure

The competition's
price levels

The pricing triangle

The target audience's perception of value

Value is the customer's perception of the match of benefits in
an offering to their needs and is measured by the customer's
willingness to pay for it. We can illustrate this with a simple
example: a customer sees three products (A, B and C) as
having *exactly the same* benefits matched to his/her needs.
However, the products have different prices.

Product	Price
A	225.00
B	264.00
C	210.00

In this situation the product with the lowest price (i.e. product
C) offers the best value, i.e. the most benefits at the lowest
cost. We can present this as a simple equation:

$$Value = \frac{Benefits}{Price}$$

Many of us will be familiar with the process of deciding on a
particular make and model of a product and searching for the
lowest price supplier.

However, if the three products are perceived to have *different*
bundles of benefits, the job of assessing the value in each product
is made more difficult for the customer. Customers adopt a range
of strategies to deal with this situation. Some do a thorough
analysis of the benefits offered by the competing products and
calculate the best value on this basis. Others will focus on just
one or two of their most important perceived needs and decide

on that basis. Others will rely on their experiences of particular brands, while some will always choose the lowest price option, regardless of the benefits on offer.

Consumer durables (products such as cars and washing machines) and many products purchased by organizations have an added value component of **cost over time**. For instance, an airline company will be interested not only in the purchase price of an aeroplane but the running cost over time. It may include issues such as taxes on carbon emissions.

Price can also be inextricably linked to the customers' perception of quality and hence value. With a luxury brand such as Chanel, if the product were 'too cheap', it would be difficult for the customer to accept that the benefits they perceive in the product can be obtained for such a 'low' price. This phenomenon is known as '**customer dissonance**' and further illustrates the link between product and pricing strategies.

Our cost structure

Price and cost are not the same. Price is ultimately controlled by customers' value perceptions; cost is the monetary value of producing and delivering the product, including profit. We need to define costs, which fall into two broad groups:

- **Variable costs** are so called because they vary directly with the level of production – the more we produce, the more variable costs we incur. Examples are raw materials, labour and operating expenses directly related to production.
- **Fixed costs,** also known as overheads, do not vary with the level of production. Whether we make anything or not, we will still incur these costs. Examples are office/factory rent, business rates and salaries of sales staff and management.

At a certain level of units of production (and hence revenue), the total cost (fixed and variable) matches the revenue value. This is known as the **breakeven point**: as production increases from this point, the organization will make profits.

From the marketer's perspective, cost sets the limit to the low end of pricing. The following table considers six scenarios (A–F) of differing relationships of the key variables of units of production, which are number of units, unit price, revenue (units of production x unit price), variable cost (VC) per unit, VC per unit x units of production, fixed cost (FC) and profit/loss.

	Scenario					
	A	B	C	D	E	F
Units number	5,000	5,000	5,000	15,000	5,000	20,000
Unit price £	10	20	10	10	10	10
Revenue (units × unit price) £	50,000	100,000	50,000	150,000	50,000	200,000
VC per unit £	4	4	8	8	10.5	10.5
VC per unit × units £	20,000	20,000	40,000	120,000	52,500	210,000
FC £	30,000	30,000	30,000	30,000	30,000	30,000
Profit/loss £	0	50,000	−20,000	0	−32,500	−40,000

A This is an example of the simple breakeven position. In this scenario 5,000 units at a selling price of £10.00, a variable cost (VC) per unit of £4.00 and fixed costs (FC) of £30,000 will yield breakeven.

B In this scenario the price is double that of scenario A while all other factors remain the same. In this case the organization would deliver a profit of £50,000. This example demonstrates the effect on the 'bottom line' of increasing price levels.

C This scenario is the same as A apart from increased variable costs (up from £4.00 per unit to £8.00) and this yields a loss of £20,000.

D This is the breakeven position based on the costs in scenario C. The units of output need to triple (from 5,000 to 15,000). This demonstrates that, when the difference (known as the 'contribution') between the selling price and the variable cost is relatively low (£2.00 in this case), units of output have to increase significantly to achieve breakeven.

E This scenario is the same as A but with increased variable costs (up from £4.00 per unit to £10.50), £0.50 *more* than selling price. This scenario yields a loss of £32,500.

F In this scenario units of output have quadrupled but losses have increased (from £32,500 to £40,000). This demonstrates that increasing output will only worsen the organization's losses when variable costs are *above* selling price.

The competition's price levels

This is the third point of our pricing triangle. We can do everything we can to understand our customers' needs, match benefits to needs and try to give the customer the best value proposition, but we mustn't forget that our competitors will be doing the same.

TIP

Some products are difficult to differentiate from one another – such as nails and screws (fixings) and petrol – and with these the lowest price strategy will win.

Different approaches

Organizations adopt different approaches to pricing. For instance, the US retailer Walmart (Asda in the UK) bases its strategic positioning on being the lowest price provider in a broad industry sector. BMW, on the other hand, seeks to differentiate its offering across a range of market segments and it bases its product pricing on customers' perceptions of the value they see in the BMW brand. Chanel adopts the focus approach, targeting particular market segments and differentiating its offering through its exclusivity.

In many organizations pricing offers the marketer the most immediate and flexible tool in the marketing mix because it is relatively easy to change prices. Consequently, many organizations rely on price cuts to generate sales or to meet a competitive threat. But this may be a 'double-edged sword': although a price cut may generate sales in the short term, it may undermine the customers' perceptions of the value of the product.

Price-cut sales promotions seem to promise two important benefits:

- they generate increased sales volume
- they induce non-buyers to trial and then perhaps become regular customers.

We can consider each in turn:

- It is true that temporary price promotions do generate a sales 'spike'. However, research by Ehrenberg, Hammond & Goodhardt (1994) suggests that around 80 per cent of the people who buy a brand on a price promotion deal already use the brand anyway and the company has a reduced margin on these sales. Sales volume is one thing but profitability is quite another.
- Ehrenberg *et al.* demonstrated that there is no long-term effect on loyalty/repeat buying rates from price-related sales promotions. Where customers 'brand switch' in line with the promotion, they return to their original brand when the price promotion is lifted.

To be effective, the marketer must remain vigilant and aware of not only what competitors are doing but, equally importantly, what customers are thinking and doing with regard to their offering and that of their competitors. This underlines the importance of marketing information and research.

Pricing strategy decisions

Pricing decisions must take into account the three forces described in the pricing triangle above. However, price is also part of the overall marketing mix and interrelated with the other parts of the mix. If we choose to operate in an undifferentiated market (e.g. petrol retailing), our pricing strategy will reflect the fact that it is difficult to differentiate our offering from that of the competition in terms of additional benefits matched to customers' needs. On the other hand, if we operate in the luxury goods market (e.g. fragrances, fine jewellery, watches), we can expect to be able to use our benefits (including intangibles such as brand) to differentiate our offering from that of the competition. Products and services must therefore be 'price positioned' so that:

- the customer perceives the value in the offering
- the customer perceives our offering to be better value than that of the competition
- we are able to make a profit (defined here as the surplus after subtracting total costs from total revenue) in the medium term.

Time and pricing

Time is an additional variable to consider. The product life cycle demonstrates the link between units purchased (revenue) and time. When a new product is launched, some organizations choose to set a high price. This is called **market-skimming pricing**. As the product moves into the mature stage, prices can be reduced to stimulate increased adoption. This is known as **market-penetration pricing**.

Summary

In this chapter we focused on two parts of the marketing mix: product and price.

Product is anything that satisfies a customer's perceived needs, and involves both tangible and intangible elements. Services tend to be more intangible than products. Features are a product's capabilities and carry benefits, which may be tangible (such as safer braking) or intangible (such as brand).

The product life cycle is introduction–growth–maturity–decline. Although new product development is expensive, finding new solutions to changing customer needs is vital.

Three forces influence pricing: audience perception of value, cost structure and competitors' prices. A key concept is value – benefits against price. When all offerings carry the same benefits, the lowest price offering represents the best value.

Cost is not the same as price but is the monetary value of profitable production/ delivery and includes fixed and variable elements.

Fact-check (answers at the back)

1. What is a product ?
a) The outcome of customers' spending ❏
b) The motive driving customers' needs ❏
c) The end result of a purchase ❏
d) The fundamental basis of the marketing mix ❏

2. Do products have either intangible or tangible benefits, but not both?
a) Yes, that's correct ❏
b) Only for services ❏
c) No, products can have both intangible and tangible benefits ❏
d) Only for luxury food products ❏

3. What is a product feature?
a) The basis for an advertising campaign ❏
b) The product's capabilities that carry benefits to customers' needs ❏
c) The best aspect of a product ❏
d) An article in a magazine about a new product ❏

4. What is a brand?
a) The packaging ❏
b) The theme for an advertising campaign ❏
c) A new product idea ❏
d) An important form of intangible benefit ❏

5. What is the growth and subsequent decline in a product's revenue over time known as?
a) Product life cycle ❏
b) Product trajectory ❏
c) Product roller coaster ❏
d) Product big dipper ❏

6. What is new product development (NPD) success linked to?
a) The diffusion of innovation ❏
b) The advertising budget ❏
c) The product's time in development ❏
d) The time of year it is launched ❏

7. What does Levitt's concept of 'marketing myopia' say?
a) Customers do not see all the products available to them ❏
b) Customers do not see all advertisements ❏
c) Marketers cannot see all the potential customers in the market ❏
d) Organizations must be customer oriented rather than product oriented ❏

8. What is price?
a) What it costs to make a product ❏
b) The printed price before you start haggling ❏
c) The amount a customer must pay to obtain the benefits from a product or service ❏
d) Always set to be 10 per cent lower than the competition ❏

9. What is the value equation?
a) Needs/benefits ❏
b) Tangible benefits/intangible benefits ❏
c) Price/cost ❏
d) Benefits/price ❏

10. What are total costs made up of?
a) Prices and costs ❏
b) Variable and fixed costs ❏
c) New and existing costs ❏
d) None of the above ❏

CHAPTER 27

The marketing mix – place

In Chapter 26 we focused on the first two parts of the marketing mix – product and price. Now we are going to focus on the *place* part of the mix, the third of the 4Ps.

In its simplest terms and probably original sense, place is where the 'exchange' (of product or service for the price) takes place. The term marketplace can conjure up images of stalls in open market squares, bazaars and souks and, as we said at the beginning of this Part, marketing began with this fundamental relationship between buyers and sellers. In the modern context, however, place focuses on how products and services are distributed to customers.

In this chapter we will look at channels of distribution, types of channel, channel characteristics and some of the key issues in decisions related to distribution channel strategy.

Place and distribution

In the modern context the 'place' part of the marketing mix focuses on how products and services are distributed to customers. This **distribution** may refer to the physical distribution of products or the channels of distribution:

- **Physical distribution** is the *planning, monitoring and control of the distribution and delivery of manufactured goods* and forms an important part of ensuring that the product is available to customers in the quantities required at the time they want to buy.
- **Channels of distribution** are the third parties that make the product or service available for use or consumption by the customer.

We can imagine a simple channel of distribution as follows:

In our example, if a manufacturer uses a retailer, then the retailer must add a cost to the manufacturer's price. For this to make business sense, the retailer must **add value** to the marketing process. Retailers, or intermediaries in general, can add value in a number of ways:

- Dealing with a small number of retailers is more **economical** for the manufacturer than dealing directly with a large number of end customers.
- Retailers will take much **larger volumes** of products than end customers and this offers cost savings to the manufacturer in terms of physical delivery.
- The **location** of retail premises meets customers' buying behaviour, e.g. in out-of-town shopping centres.
- For some goods, the **reputation** of the retailer, e.g. Harrods, can enhance the product's perceived value.

It is probably easier to think of channels of distribution in the context of products than of services because, as we have seen, 'inseparability' is a characteristic of services (its production and consumption occur at the same time). However, services can be delivered through intermediaries too. Examples are travel agents and mortgage brokers.

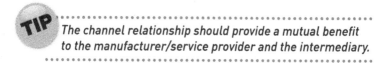

TIP *The channel relationship should provide a mutual benefit to the manufacturer/service provider and the intermediary.*

Channel types

There are two broad types of distribution channel available to the marketer: intermediaries and direct.

Intermediaries

Intermediaries are independent organizations that carry out a number of activities associated with adding value to the marketing process. The two main groups are retailers and wholesalers.

Retailers include organizations such as:

- supermarkets (Tesco, Sainsbury's)
- department stores (House of Fraser, John Lewis Partnership)
- high street chains (Topshop, Next)
- convenience store groups (Martin McColl, Spar)
- independent retailers, including speciality stores
- franchises (McDonald's, IKEA, Subway).

Franchises

Strictly speaking, a franchise is not just a channel but a business format model. The franchiser engages with a number of franchisees, providing them with a business format (brand, product sourcing, training, publicity, etc.) to extend the franchiser's business coverage and to provide the franchisee with a proven business model. Franchises include many famous names.

Wholesalers primarily sell goods and services to those buying for resale and/or business use. They include:

- wholesale merchants – sell primarily to retailers and can be general (i.e. sell a range of products, e.g. Booker Wholesale) or specialist (i.e. fish wholesalers, e.g. M&J Seafood, part of the Brakes Group)
- cash-and-carry wholesalers – sell from fixed premises and do not normally deliver; buyers come to them for their requirements (e.g. Selco Builders' Warehouse)
- industrial distributors – sell to manufacturers rather than retailers and can carry a range of stock to meet customers' needs (e.g. Nationwide Fuels who supply a range of industrial lubricants to industry in the UK)
- producers' co-operatives – are prevalent in the agricultural market; members assemble groups of products to be sold to customers and share the profits.

Direct channels

Organizations often choose to trade directly with customers because of cost issues but also because of the potential for building customer relations. Direct channels can be broadly divided into two groups: traditional and new media.

Traditional channels

These are 'traditional' in the sense that they have been used for some time. The following are some of the best-known examples:

- Direct mail – involves posting promotional material direct to the potential customer's home or office and encouraging customers to buy direct (e.g. *Reader's Digest*).
- Catalogue-based home shopping – is a variant of direct mail, where a catalogue is forwarded to the customer and they are encouraged to purchase products represented in the catalogue (e.g. Littlewoods catalogue).
- Inserts – are promotional material placed in selected magazines with instructions for buying direct.
- Telemarketing – uses the telephone to sell directly to customers in both consumer and B2B markets.

- Direct selling – includes door-to-door selling and party plan (e.g. Party Plan UK) in consumer markets.
- Personal selling – can include own salaried staff and/or sales agents. Sales forces are common in B2B markets where there is a strong benefit from personal relationships between the salesperson and the buyer.
- TV shopping – is more accurately known as direct response television marketing (DRTV). DRTV is common in the US and now more widespread in other markets such as the UK following the proliferation of satellite and free-to-air channels. DRTV involves the direct promotion of a product to the audience and typically a freephone number for them to make their purchase.

New media
The explosion of digital-based technology has opened up a wide range of new channels for marketers. Of major use in promotion (which we will discuss in the next chapter), new media also offer additional channels of distribution.

- Websites – are widely used by all sorts of organizations and individuals and have been described as 'online shop windows'. Clearly, with the addition of e-commerce (the transactional element), organizations can trade directly with their customers, opening a new channel. Many organizations have traditional retail channels but also trade direct from their websites.
- Specialist sites – e.g. eBay have a seller development team committed to helping sellers grow their business within the eBay channel.
- E-direct mail – is used in the same way as traditional direct mail but using email to communicate a particular message or to direct the recipient to a website.
- Mobile phone marketing – has been made possible by the growth in ownership of smartphones and 3G/4G networks and associated software so customers can purchase through their mobile phone.
- Podcasts and vodcasts – are audio and video (respectively) files that can be downloaded to a mobile device. Marketers are experimenting with different approaches to using these technologies as effective channels.

Changing channels

One important component of distribution channels is **change**. As with the influence of change on the marketing process, decisions related to distribution channels are no different. Channels are subject to similar PEST and market forces as products, and over time different channels grow and then decline in a way that resembles the product life cycle.

Traditional channels are making way for new media channels, and one major change has been the Internet share of retailing. The chart below shows the Internet share in percentage terms of the average weekly value of all retailing in the UK in the period 2006–17.

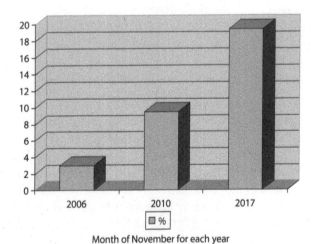

Month of November for each year

Internet share (%) of average weekly value for all retailing in UK
Source: Retail sales: Office for National Statistics, UK, April 2018

These data show the significant growth (up from 3 per cent in 2006 to 19.7 per cent in 2017) in market share obtained by Internet-based retailing out of all UK retailing. Perhaps one of the best-known Internet retailers is Amazon.com. The business was incorporated in 1994 and trades in the USA and a number of other countries in Europe and Asia. Net sales in the year to 31 December 2017 were $177.87 billion, up from $10.7 billion in 2006, and a 31 per cent increase from $136 billion in 2016.

Channel characteristics

The type and nature of channel relationships are based on an agreement between the parties involved and can be quite diverse. To take a simple manufacturer/retailer example, this could be a medium-term contractual relationship or a more informal, flexible relationship.

Some producers establish exclusive channels; car manufacturers, for example, have 'dealer networks'. In this case there is a much stronger 'partnering' theme to the relationship than there would be in a less formal manufacturer/retailer relationship. Dealers agree to invest in their business in support of the investment of their manufacturer partner, and manufacturers commit to supporting their dealers through promotions and so on.

The relative 'power' of the players in a distribution channel can vary quite significantly. For instance, in our example of the car manufacturer and dealer, one might say there is a 'symbiotic' (mutually advantageous) relationship. However, in different markets different members of the channel can have significantly more 'power' than the other members. Two extreme examples of this **channel captaincy** are:

- **UK supermarkets** Kantar Worldpanel estimates that Tesco, ASDA, Sainsbury's, Morrisons, Aldi, Waitrose and Lidl accounted for 87 per cent of retail food sales in the UK in 2017. This places the large supermarkets in an extremely strong bargaining position with their suppliers.
- **Luxury goods** With luxury goods the manufacturer selects the retailer and gives that retailer an exclusive territory, agreeing not to sell to any other retailer in a designated area. Rolex, the luxury watch manufacturer, operates in this way. Its 'dealer locator' page on their website enables customers to identify where they can buy Rolex watches in a particular area. The strength of the brand gives the manufacturer the power to select retailers and negotiate terms.

While channel members depend on one another, they often act alone in their own short-term best interests. Maintaining a mutually beneficial relationship can therefore be difficult.

Clearly, the greater the investment and the longer the contractual relationship, the more likely it is that channel members can operate in a mutually beneficial way.

Distribution channel strategy decisions

As with all aspects of marketing, the starting point must be the organization's target customer segments. They must ask two key questions:

- does the channel put the product in the right place: where the target customer wants to buy it?
- does the channel add value?

Marketers often consider the channels their competition utilizes and may choose to be in the same channel so that customers see their product at the same time as they see their competitors'. For example, a proprietary food brand might want to be in the same supermarkets as their direct competitors. Alternatively, marketers may wish (or be forced) to adopt different channels from their competitors. A good example is smaller specialist food producers using online and other channels (such as farmers' markets) to 'bypass' the supermarkets to reach their target customers.

The marketer must be alert to channels changing over time. The growth in online channels is part of the reason for the recent decline in revenue experienced by UK high-street retailers.

Summary

In this chapter you learned that 'place' in the marketing mix is largely about channels of distribution – how a product/service is made available to the customer. Marketers can use intermediaries – retailers, wholesalers – if they add value to the marketing process, or they can trade directly with customers to reduce costs and increase the potential for building customer relations.

Direct channels can be broadly divided into traditional and new media. The recent significant growth of the Internet in terms of percentage share of the value of all UK retailing is one example of how different channels grow and decline over time.

Channels can have different characteristics. Some are exclusive relationships, like the dealer networks in the automotive market. Sometimes the intermediary can be the most powerful member of the distribution channel, as is the case with leading UK supermarkets.

Some organizations choose to be in the same channels as their competitors; others select channels offering a different route to their customers, such as direct marketing rather than retailers.

Fact-check (answers at the back)

1. What is a channel of distribution?
   a) Selling to Europe ❏
   b) Those third parties that make the product or service available for use or consumption by the customer ❏
   c) The spread of sales in different markets ❏
   d) None of the above ❏

2. Why must an intermediary like a retailer add value?
   a) Because of the common law of contract ❏
   b) They are only a service provider ❏
   c) They add cost so, if they do not add value, there is no reason for a producer to use them ❏
   d) They are overrated ❏

3. Why are wholesalers different from retailers?
   a) They do not advertise ❏
   b) They sell to those buying for resale or business use ❏
   c) They have the highest sales volumes ❏
   d) All of the above ❏

4. What are two aspects of direct marketing?
   a) Traditional and new media ❏
   b) Profitable and non-profitable ❏
   c) Bulk based and individual units ❏
   d) Products and services ❏

5. Why is change over time important when considering channels?
   a) Because of seasonality ❏
   b) Because of the increasing cost of travelling ❏
   c) Over time different channels grow and then decline ❏
   d) Because of the lack of opportunities for out-of-town developments ❏

6. What does channel captaincy refer to?
   a) Taking the lead in developing a marketing campaign ❏
   b) Having control of shipping lines to Europe ❏
   c) The best retailers to use for products targeted at the leisure sailing market ❏
   d) Those members of the channel that have the most power ❏

7. Although channel members depend on one another, what do they often do?
   a) Act alone in their own short-term best interests ❏
   b) Misunderstand their roles ❏
   c) Fail to communicate with one other ❏
   d) Have different views about marketing ❏

8. What is the starting point for deciding a distribution strategy?
a) Who is available ❏
b) The production department ❏
c) Whether the channel puts the product where the customer wants to buy it ❏
d) Falling sales volumes ❏

9. Why do organizations often want to be in the same channel as their competitors?
a) They may be missing something ❏
b) Customers see their product at the same time as they see their competitors' product ❏
c) They don't want to be left out ❏
d) It is what they have always done ❏

10. What dramatic increase in sales illustrates the growth of the Internet as a channel?
a) The BBC ❏
b) The Charities Commission ❏
c) Amazon.com ❏
d) Marmite ❏

CHAPTER 28

The marketing mix – promotion

In this final chapter we will look at the last of the 4Ps of the marketing mix – *promotion*. This is the part of the mix that involves the organization in advancing and furthering its product or service in the minds of customers.

Promotion is also the most visible part of the marketing mix and can be seen alongside general entertainment on TV, radio and in the cinema and now, increasingly, on the Internet. It is understandable, therefore, that a large proportion of the general public perceives promotion to be synonymous with marketing. However, we know that promotion is only a *part* of marketing.

We will consider promotion in terms of marketing communications, the communication process, and the seven key decision areas of the promotional strategy. We will also discuss briefly ethics and regulation in this area.

Promotion and marketing communications

Promotion is the fourth part of the marketing mix and it can be thought of as the advancement or furtherance of a product or service in the mind of the customer. It is really about marketing communications and is concerned with **informing** and **persuading** customers.

Marketing communications involves developing and delivering co-ordinated messages designed to create a desired effect in a target audience. Ideally, marketing communications should manage the customer relationship over time, from the pre-purchase and purchase stages through to post-purchase and the brand's ongoing relationship with customers.

Communication is a process as depicted in the following model:

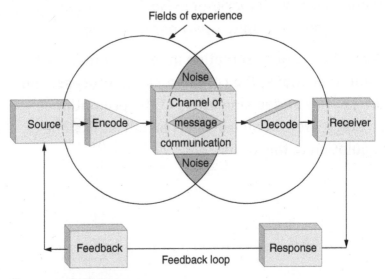

The communication process

The communication process involves ten elements:

1 **Source** – the organization sending the message to another party
2 **Encode** – the process of putting the intended message or thought into symbolic form, i.e. words and images

3 **Message** – the set of words, pictures or symbols that the source transmits
4 **Channel of communication** – the medium or media used by the source to carry the message to the receiver
5 **Decode** – the process by which the receiver assigns meaning to the message sent by the source
6 **Receiver** – the party receiving the message, normally the customer or potential customer but also including groups that may influence their opinions and behaviour
7 **Response** – the reactions of the receiver exposed to the message; this may be either a move from a state of unawareness of an offering to awareness or a move to a more committed position that will lead to a purchase
8 **Feedback** – the part of the receiver's response that is communicated back to the source, e.g. marketing research results
9 **Noise** – the unplanned 'static' or distortion during the communication process, which results in the receiver getting a different message from the one sent by the source. 'Static' could include competitors' messages, articles in magazines, blogs, etc.
10 **Fields of experience** – the more the source's and the receiver's fields of experience overlap, the more effective the message is likely to be.

Promotional strategy decisions

There are seven key decision areas involved in developing a promotional strategy:

1 Defining the target audience

In Chapter 25 we discussed the strategic process of defining which market segments the organization will target (the 'targeting' exercise). This exercise will have enabled us to define and profile the target customers in terms of both their perceived needs and their exposure to media. The organization may have multiple target segments and many of the following decision areas will be affected by their characteristics.

For example, younger target audiences can be difficult to reach using traditional media and the marketer would need to use social media (Internet and mobile-based).

2 Setting promotional objectives

While the ultimate objective is likely to be a purchase, promotional objectives will need to be drafted in terms of 'moving' the target audience towards this ultimate aim. Customers may move through a series of attitudinal stages – starting with **unawareness**, moving to **awareness**, developing an **understanding** of the benefits in the offering, and then becoming **convinced** that the offering meets their needs before taking **action** (purchasing). For instance, if the target audience is unaware of the organization's offering, the promotional objective is likely to be creating awareness. The marketer could therefore set an objective of 40 per cent of the target audience to be aware of the offering following the first stage of the campaign.

3 Creating the message(s)

The starting point for creating a message is an understanding of the task in hand. What are our promotional objectives? The message can be informative or persuasive, or both. A simple informative message may be 'Our new store opens on Monday at 8 a.m.' Persuasive messages form much of the media we all see and hear every day, in print, on television and radio, and on the Internet and mobile phones. These messages are developed by matching benefits to customers' perceived needs. Often marketers will seek to focus on the most important needs (from the hierarchy of needs discussed in Chapter 23) as the basis for their messages.

To communicate this we need to 'encode' our message so that the customer will 'decode' it with maximum fidelity. It follows that the more we know about our target audience, the more effective our messages will be – marketing research at pre-campaign stage offers a valuable resource in this context. Message design can also be influenced by the nature of the medium. For instance, an advertisement in a magazine that could be reread would be able to carry a more detailed message than a TV advertisement, but a TV advert would be able to use a range of moving images and sounds including music and dialogue.

4 Selecting the media

Media carry the message(s) to the target audiences and there are many media available to marketers:

- Advertising in print – includes national and regional newspapers, free press, special interest magazines (e.g. music, gardening), age-group targeted (e.g. *Saga Magazine*), lifestyle (e.g. *Tatler*)
- TV (terrestrial, cable, satellite and online) – carries sophisticated multimedia promotional messages
- Cinema – can run longer versions of TV adverts and can be targeted at audiences based on the nature of the film being shown
- Commercial radio – audio advertisements which, like cinema, can be targeted at particular groups based on the content of the programmes on air
- Personal selling – a very effective promotional medium because trained and experienced salespeople can interact with the customer; often a key part of B2B promotion and high-cost domestic durables, e.g. cars
- Direct marketing – postal, leaflet drop, telephone (including auto-dialling)
- Outdoor poster – includes large fixed billboards, bus stop, motorway, airport, Underground (subway), mobile (vehicle-based), inflatables
- Public relations – is the discipline which looks after reputation, with the aim of earning understanding and support and influencing opinion and behaviour. It is the planned and sustained effort to establish and maintain goodwill and mutual understanding between an organization and its public. Key to its success is the ability of the PR practitioner to place press releases in appropriate media
- Sponsorship – cash or in-kind support of anything from small regional events to major international events such as the Olympics and Football World Cup

- Online – from the proliferation of websites to sponsored links on search engines to specially designed adverts running on host sites including social networking sites such as Twitter, Instagram and Facebook
- Mobile – the growth in ownership of smartphones and 3G/4G networks has given advertisers a new medium to deliver promotional messages to people's phones based on platforms including mobile browsers, apps (software applications) and SMS (short message service)

The marketer must select carefully. The first thing to consider is which media best 'reach' the target audience. By this, we mean the number of people who will be exposed to the message carried by the medium. Clearly, the more of our target audience covered by the medium the better.

Secondly, the marketer must assess the relative cost of reaching an audience. Different media have different costs and reach, and marketers seek to create a reasonable comparison by dividing the cost of an advertisement in a particular medium by the reach (or coverage) of that medium, often expressed as a cost per 1,000 audience.

Thirdly, he/she will be interested in what the medium can 'do' for the message. Some media, such as exclusive magazines, can enhance the message by adding credibility to a product's advertisement.

5 Creating the promotional programme

The promotional programme has two components: the mix of media to be used and the schedule of activities over the time of the campaign. The following is an example of a simple programme:

Medium	Activity	Month 1	Month 2	Month 3	Month 4
TV	4 × 60 seconds	×		×	
Radio	6 × 20 seconds		×		×
Press	4 × ¼ page	×		×	
Twitter	Weekly feed	×	×	×	×
Public relations	News releases	×		×	

The key thing for the marketer is to ensure an **integrated** programme of promotional activity that enables messages to build on earlier work and for themes to be **reinforced** as the campaign progresses. All too often, messages emanate from different parts of the organization with the result that the customer receives a mixed set, at worst contradictory, that can seriously reduce the effectiveness of the campaign.

6 Setting the budget

Setting the budget is often difficult. Some organizations base their decision on what they can afford. However, this method fails to link what needs to be done (the promotional objectives) with the resources to do it. Others use a percentage of sales approach, perhaps 10 per cent of last year's total sales made available for this year's promotional budget. Again, this method fails to link resources to objectives. Probably the best approach is the objective-and-task method – assessing what has to be achieved, the tasks involved and the estimated cost of performing these tasks.

7 Evaluating the results

Promotional spend is a business investment and therefore must be measured to assess its effectiveness. Unfortunately, it is difficult to measure the return on promotional spend (in sales and profit) because so many factors influence such measures. Effectiveness must therefore be measured in terms of meeting the promotional objectives through post-campaign research.

Ethics and regulation

In promoting a product or service it is particularly important that marketers maintain an ethical approach – that they do not use the promotional process to mislead customers. It may be tempting to make unsubstantiated claims to attract attention but, in addition to the fact that such action is immoral, it is bad for business and also illegal.

1 **Making unsubstantiated claims is bad for business**
Although an organization might obtain a short-term advantage by misleading customers, if the product or service does not satisfy customers' needs, they will not buy the product again. In addition, customers who feel badly treated by a supplier will tell their relations, friends and colleagues and this form of word-of-mouth communication is very powerful.

2 **Making unsubstantiated claims is illegal**
Most developed economies legislate against bad promotional practice. In the UK the **Trade Descriptions Act 1968** prevents manufacturers, retailers and the service sector from misleading customers about what they are spending their money on. The Act empowers the courts to punish companies or individuals who make false claims.

Each product sold must be '**as described**', of '**satisfactory quality**' and '**fit for purpose**'. 'As described' refers to any advertisement or verbal description made by the trader. 'Satisfactory quality' covers minor and cosmetic defects as well as substantial deficiencies and means that products must last a reasonable time. 'Fit for purpose' covers not only the obvious purpose of an item but also any purpose determined at the point of sale by the trader.

Independent regulators

The **Advertising Standards Authority (ASA)** is the UK's independent regulator of advertising, working to ensure that advertisements are **legal, decent, honest and truthful**. The US equivalent is the **Federal Trade Commission**. Their mission is to uphold standards in all media on behalf of consumers, business and society at large.

Summary

In this chapter you learned that promotion is about marketing communications and is concerned with informing and persuading your target market. It is the most visible part of the marketing mix, appearing alongside entertainment on TV and radio, in the cinema and on the Internet.

Ideally, marketing communications should manage the customer relationship with the brand. At its root, communication involves encoding a message to be decoded by the receiver.

The seven key decision areas involved in developing a promotional strategy are: defining the audience; setting objectives; creating the message(s); selecting the media; creating the programme; setting the budget; and evaluating the results.

When promoting a product/service, marketers must not use the promotional process to mislead customers. Legislation and regulation exist to protect customers, but it is the responsibility of professional marketers to act ethically and not to make unsubstantiated claims.

Fact-check (answers at the back)

1. What is the promotion part of the marketing mix?
   a) Marketing communications ❏
   b) The 'glossy' part ❏
   c) All about TV ❏
   d) Not important to the success of the business ❏

2. Why does a large proportion of the general public perceive promotion to be synonymous with marketing?
   a) Advertising *is* marketing ❏
   b) Promotion is the most visible part of the marketing mix ❏
   c) It's part of the entertainment business ❏
   d) All of the above ❏

3. What does the heart of the communication process involve?
   a) Closing the sale ❏
   b) Getting the best price for printed materials ❏
   c) The source encoding a message to be decoded by the receiver ❏
   d) Subliminal messages ❏

4. How must promotional objectives be set?
   a) In terms of moving the audience through a series of attitudinal stages to the purchase stage ❏
   b) In terms of sales ❏
   c) According to the time of year ❏
   d) According to the number of specialist sales staff available ❏

5. What can messages be?
   a) Read or heard ❏
   b) Seen or viewed ❏
   c) Informative and/or persuasive ❏
   d) None of the above ❏

6. What is media reach?
   a) The number of people in an audience that will be exposed to the message carried by the medium ❏
   b) The reputation of a newspaper or TV channel ❏
   c) The amount a customer must pay to access a medium ❏
   d) Always much higher than the medium claims ❏

7. What are the two components of creating a promotional programme?
   a) The mix of media to be used and the schedule of activities over the time of the campaign ❏
   b) Sales staff and marketing staff ❏
   c) Time of year and product type ❏
   d) Retailer and competitor activity ❏

8. Why is it difficult to measure the financial return, such as sales or profit, on promotional spend?
   a) Because of the way costs are accounted for ❏
   b) Seasonal factors need to be taken into account ❏
   c) So many factors additional to the promotional activities influence such measures ❏
   d) Because of differences in retailers' sales systems ❏

9. Why may it be tempting to make an unsubstantiated claim?
a) To attract attention ☐
b) To mislead the competition ☐
c) To get the campaign under way quickly ☐
d) To make the shareholders happy ☐

10. In addition to regulation, for what reason must the professional marketer guard against making unsubstantiated claims?
a) It's bad for business ☐
b) Because of competitors' reactions ☐
c) Because of retailers' reactions ☐
d) None of the above ☐

7 × 7

1 Seven key ideas

- **Competitiveness is key** – we all live in a competitive environment; our very evolution as a species was shaped by competition. Success in marketing is about competing with your rivals for the hearts and minds of customers.

- **Maintain a clear understanding of the market** – markets are complex, changing environments, much like an organism. Sometimes the change is gradual; sometimes it can be dramatic.

- **Have a clear market focus** – spend real effort (time and money) on understanding the segments within your market.

- **Create (and maintain) a marketing-oriented corporate culture** – a business that is truly marketing oriented will be marketing oriented throughout the organization.

- **Master the basics (of marketing) and don't lose sight of them** – marketing isn't difficult: keep the focus on the customer, have an awareness of the competition and understand how to construct a marketing strategy.

- **Embrace new insights** – this idea may seem to run counter to the previous point, but I suggest it's actually the other side of the same coin. The 4Ps were once a new paradigm and, in the same way, new insights will emerge that warrant our attention.

- **Be outward looking** – businesses that are inward looking will miss both the opportunities and, more worryingly, the threats of change. Embrace the future, monitor trends and assess opportunities and threats that may emerge for your business.

2 Seven Cs of marketing planning

- **Customer** – everything starts with the customer – understanding and matching benefits to their perceived needs is the bedrock of an effective marketing plan.

- **Competitors** – we are not alone! While we are busy trying to meet customer needs, so are our competitors. Know who they are and understand their strengths and weaknesses.
- **Company** – have a realistic and honest understanding of your strengths and weaknesses. Knowing yourself can help you avoid making bad decisions.
- **Consideration** (transaction) – a major part of the marketing process is the transaction – i.e. goods and/or services for money. For business, marketing is not an academic exercise; it's about making money.
- **Creativity** (of compelling offerings, of strategies, of communications, etc.) – there is more and more science in marketing these days but we must remember the value of creativity, not just in the promotional department, but throughout our marketing effort.
- **Concentration** (of effort) – spend time understanding how your market is segmented and how the segments are different, and target those segments that offer the best match of your company's strengths to their perceived needs.
- **Customer care** – too many companies forget that their customers are people, and not just a number on a list. If you want a long-term business relationship with your customers, treat them as you would want to be treated.

3 Seven essentials to create power through knowledge

- **Get the maximum value from your in-house data** – businesses inevitably capture a huge amount of information on their customers. Often, such information is not gathered necessarily for marketing purposes; make sure that you 'mine' your data to obtain valuable customer insights.
- **Take advantage of data that are in the public domain** – there is a bewildering amount of information in the public domain, often of high quality (e.g. national statistics). Spend some time reviewing what's available and ensure that you have regular access to those sources of most value to you.

- **Study your competitors** – keep a close eye on your competitors and know their strengths and weaknesses – invaluable in developing your strategies.
- **Talk to your suppliers and your distribution chain** – businesses in other parts of the supply chain can offer an additional view of your market; keep a dialogue open with key executives within these businesses.
- **Use multi-client research** – obtaining primary research is fairly expensive; use multi-client sources (such as Mintel and Keynote) to enhance your market intelligence.
- **Use omnibus surveys** – a more focused version of the previous point, omnibus surveys (such as run by Ipsos, etc.) can, for a small number of questions, provide relatively large sample sizes at a very modest cost.
- **Conduct original research** – ultimately, commission your own research to focus on those issues that are most important to your strategy development. Obtain an advantage through privileged insight.

4 Seven marketing myths

- **Marketing is a pretentious word for selling** – marketing is concerned, broadly, with the identification and satisfaction of customers' needs; selling is a transaction and may be considered as the last step in the marketing process.
- **Advertising is synonymous with marketing** – advertising is a promotional tool and promotion is part of the marketing mix.
- **There is a direct link between advertising spend and sales** – the link between advertising and sales is too tenuous, complicated and long-term to permit measuring the direct impact. Enlightened advertisers monitor audience awareness and attitudinal movement as a more realistic measurement.
- **Brands just allow firms to charge more for their products** – branding helps buyers identify products that might benefit them and tells them something about product quality and consistency.

- **Special offers encourage people to brand switch** – research demonstrates that there are no long-term effects on loyalty/repeat buying rates from price-related sales promotions. Where customers brand switch in line with the promotion, they return to their original brand when the price promotion is lifted.

- **It's a 'marketing' scam** – an oxymoron often used by the media –marketing is about customer satisfaction and has no need for a 'scam'. There may be promotional 'scams' or selling 'scams' but not marketing scams.

- **Success in marketing is all about luck** – all human activities carry some risk and luck therefore must play some part in success. But you can stack the odds in your favour by using best-practice marketing techniques and sound marketing information.

5 Seven Ps

- **People** – customers are people. We have to understand their perceived needs and to keep our customers we must establish an ongoing relationship by keeping our promises and responding to the way their needs change.

- **Product** – a 'product' is anything that carries benefits matched to customers' perceived needs. The product is the key bridge between you and your customers and needs to be monitored to ensure that it remains relevant to their needs.

- **Price** – price is inextricably linked to product; the benefits carried by the product at a given price define the 'value' of the offering.

- **Place** – we need to ensure that our offerings are available to our customers and potential customers wherever they choose to shop – online or in the high street.

- **Promotion** – to effectively promote your product, you need a message that matches benefits to your customers' perceived needs and you must display that message in those media that reach your customers.

- **Profit** – profit is not a dirty word; it is, for most private-sector organizations, often the primary objective of the marketing effort. In addition, without creating a profit, businesses cannot survive to meet their customers' needs in the future.
- **People (again)** – but this time I'm referring to people within your organization and any partners you engage with to meet your customers' needs. They must know what they need to do to meet customer needs, and they must be capable and skilled enough as well as motivated to do this.

6 Seven marketing breakthroughs

- **The 4Ps** – Jerome McCarthy, in 1960, was one of the first to popularize the 4Ps (Product, Price, Place and Promotion) as a way of thinking about marketing strategy.
- **'Marketing Myopia'** – the title of Theodore Levitt's 1960 paper published in the *Harvard Business Review*, where he fully illustrated the need for marketing executives to focus on customers' needs and not on their products' features.
- **The 4Ps (again)** – Philip Kotler made the 4Ps the leading-edge basis for the development of marketing strategy in his 1967 book, *Principles of Marketing*.
- **Buyer behaviour models** – many consider J. A. Howard and J. N. Sheth's *Theory of Buyer Behaviour* (Wiley, 1969) to be the earliest attempt to model all the variables involved in how buyers select and buy products.
- **PIMS** (Profit Impact of Marketing Strategy) – this study, led by Sidney Schoeffler and started in the 1970s, examined the link (both causal and associated) between marketing strategy and business performance and gave us an insight into those links.
- ***Industrial, Marketing Strategy*** – the title of F. E. Webster Jr's book (Wiley, 1979); he was one of the first academics to concentrate on the business-to-business (B2B) sector (called 'industrial' then).

- *Thinking, Fast and Slow* – the title of Daniel Kahneman's book (Penguin, 2011), in which he presents evidence that humans are far from being 'rational beings' and are often inconsistent, emotional and biased in their decision making.

7 Seven websites to bookmark

- **Office for National Statistics** (ONS) – the home of the UK's statistical service, providing everything from census data to UK manufacturers' sales by product (Prodcom): http://www.ons.gov.uk/ons/index.html
- **Eurostat** - the statistical office of the European Union provides statistics at a European level that enable comparisons between countries and regions: http://ec.europa.eu/eurostat
- **US Department of Commerce, Bureau of Economic Analysis** – follows a similar format both in terms of content and flexibility to ONS and Eurostat: www.bea.gov
- **Companies House** – the WebCHeck service offers a searchable database of company names and company numbers, which enables you to search for information on more than 2 million companies: https://www.gov.uk/government/organisations/companies-house
- **Mintel** – a leading worldwide multi-client market research provider with an additional range of related products and services: http://www.mintel.com/
- **The Chartered Institute of Marketing (UK)** – includes qualifications, courses, insight (research, etc.) and opinion: http://www.cim.co.uk/
- **McKinsey & Company** – the site of this world-leading strategic management consultancy includes a range of services and excellent management insights and publications: http://www.mckinsey.com/

Answers

Part 1: Your MBA Masterclass

Chapter 1: 1d; 2d; 3c; 4d; 5a; 6c; 7c; 8c; 9c; 10d

Chapter 2: 1a; 2d; 3d; 4a; 5b; 6c; 7c; 8a; 9a; 10b

Chapter 3: 1b; 2c; 3c; 4a; 5c; 6b; 7a; 8c; 9c; 10c

Chapter 4: 1a; 2c; 3b; 4c; 5b; 6d; 7c; 8c; 9b; 10c

Chapter 5: 1b; 2d; 3c; 4a; 5c; 6a; 7b; 8c; 9c; 10c

Chapter 6: 1c; 2b; 3d; 4d; 5a; 6b; 7c; 8c; 9b; 10b

Chapter 7: 1b; 2b; 3c; 4b; 5c; 6b; 7b; 8d; 9c; 10a

Part 2: Your Finance for Non-Financial Managers Masterclass

Chapter 8: 1b; 2a; 3d; 4a; 5b; 6c; 7b; 8d; 9c; 10a.

Chapter 9: 1c; 2b; 3d; 4a; 5c; 6a; 7c; 8b; 9d; 10a.

Chapter 10: 1c; 2d; 3a; 4a; 5c; 6b; 7b; 8a; 9d; 10a.

Chapter 11: 1c; 2c; 3b; 4c; 5d; 6b; 7a; 8b; 9b; 10d.

Chapter 12: 1a; 2b; 3d; 4c; 5d; 6c; 7d; 8a and d; 9a and c; 10c.

Chapter 13: 1b; 2b; 3d; 4a; 5c; 6a; 7b; 8c; 9a; 10b.

Chapter 14: 1c; 2d; 3a; 4d; 5d; 6c; 7a; 8d; 9d; 10d.

Part 3: Your Strategy Masterclass

Chapter 15: 1d; 2c,d; 3b; 4a; 5a; 6b; 7c

Chapter 16: 1a; 2c; 3d; 4d; 5a; 6b; 7c; 8b; 9a; 10c

Chapter 17: 1a; 2d; 3c; 4a; 5c; 6d; 7a; 8d; 9b; 10c

Chapter 18: 1d; 2b; 3a; 4c,d; 5c; 6b; 7d; 8b; 9c; 10b

Chapter 19: 1d; 2b; 3b; 4a; 5b; 6c; 7b; 8a; 9a; 10b

Chapter 20: 1a; 2c; 3c; 4b; 5a; 6c; 7b; 8d; 9b; 10a

Part 4: Your Marketing Masterclass

Chapter 22: 1a; 2c; 3b; 4b; 5c; 6a; 7b; 8b; 9c; 10d.

Chapter 23: 1b; 2a; 3b; 4a; 5d; 6a; 7d; 8b; 9d; 10d.

Chapter 24: 1a; 2b; 3b; 4a; 5b; 6a; 7b; 8b; 9d; 10c.

Chapter 25: 1a; 2c; 3b; 4a; 5a; 6b; 7a; 8d; 9a; 10d.

Chapter 26: 1d; 2c; 3b; 4d; 5a; 6a; 7d; 8c; 9d; 10b.

Chapter 27: 1b; 2c; 3b; 4a; 5c; 6d; 7a; 8c; 9b; 10c.

Chapter 28: 1a; 2b; 3c; 4a; 5c; 6a; 7a; 8c; 9a; 10a.

Notes